# SITE FIGHTS

# SITE FIGHTS

## DIVISIVE FACILITIES AND CIVIL SOCIETY IN JAPAN AND THE WEST

### DANIEL P. ALDRICH

CORNELL UNIVERSITY PRESS
ITHACA AND LONDON

Cornell University Press gratefully acknowledges receipt of a grant from the Program on U.S.–Japan Relations and the Reischauer Institute of Harvard University, which aided in the publication of this book.

First published 2008 by Cornell University Press
Printed in the United States of America

**Library of Congress Cataloging-in-Publication Data**

Aldrich, Daniel P.
   Site fights : divisive facilities and civil society in Japan and the West / Daniel P. Aldrich.
      p. cm.
   Includes bibliographical references and index.
   ISBN 978-0-8014-4619-1 (cloth : alk. paper)
   1. Industrial location—Japan.   2. Industrial location—France.   3. Industrial policy—Japan.   4. Industrial policy—France.   I. Title.

   HC465.D5A73 2008
   338.6'0420952—dc22          2007031127

Cornell University Press strives to use environmentally responsible suppliers and materials to the fullest extent possible in the publishing of its books. Such materials include vegetable-based, low-VOC inks and acid-free papers that are recycled, totally chlorine-free, or partly composed of nonwood fibers. For further information, visit our website at www.cornellpress.cornell.edu.

Cloth printing    10 9 8 7 6 5 4 3 2 1

# CONTENTS

# Tables and Figures

## Tables

## Figures

# PREFACE

STATES OFTEN FACE VEXING PROBLEMS as they try to construct facilities that serve the needs of citizens as a whole but potentially bring unfavorable consequences into their host communities. Plans to site incinerators, waste treatment facilities, nuclear power plants, and airports regularly create backlash in communities around the world. A half-century ago the problem was less acute. A world with abundant land, cheap energy, and uncongested airports had far less need for such projects. Furthermore—and even more importantly—the citizens who were adversely affected were far more likely to accept such projects in the name of advancing the public good.

Times have changed. As energy consumption, garbage output, and airport use have increased, the demand for such facilities has soared, and the land available for large-scale projects has shrunk. Meanwhile, rising educational levels, increased environmental consciousness, declining confidence in government in the industrial countries, and greater access to information—all mean that citizen opposition to such projects is rising, and host communities are harder to find. State authorities thus face fundamental challenges: how to choose locations for controversial facilities and how to respond to local citizen opposition to such projects when it arises.

Social scientists and policymakers have demonstrated a growing interest in siting issues, as evidenced by several books on the subject (Lesbirel and Shaw 2005; Quah and Tan 2002; Weingart 2001; McAvoy 1999; Lesbirel 1998); meanwhile the acronym NIMBY (Not In My Back Yard) has become commonplace in referring to siting dilemmas. Simultaneously, the many prominent works on civil society and social capital by scholars such as Robert Putnam (1993, 1995, 2000), Theda Skocpol (1999), Jonah Levy (1999), Susan Pharr (2003), Jennifer Chan-Tiberghien (2004), and Robert Pekkanen (2006) reflect the growing recognition that studies of governance and political economy must take civil society seriously.

This book contributes to both these literatures in showing how democratic states meet the challenges of constructing controversial projects. Focusing on

Japan and adding selective comparisons with France and the United States, I frame siting as an interaction between state and civil society. Previous research has suggested that for governments countering potential resistance, the main story is about developing elaborate strategies to appease targeted communities (see Smith and Kunreuther 2001). This is far from the whole picture, however. Citizen consciousness worldwide has increased, but in all countries there are wide variations in potential for organized opposition. The basic first-order bureaucratic approach to constructing what I call "public bads" is to identify potential sites in communities that have less sturdy civil society and thus less potential for protest.

This book demonstrates that bureaucrats seek to avoid costly resistance and choose weak civil societies for sites. Literature on environmental racism argues that state agencies target local communities on the basis of race and ethnicity. Political economists contend that local support for or opposition to ruling parties best determines the outcome of siting decisions. Not surprisingly, bureaucrats themselves tend to claim that they site solely on the basis of technocratic, politically neutral criteria. Others believe that economic conditions determine siting location. But these explanations, though illuminating facets of the process, do not capture the full variation in site selection. Rather, the choice of sites turns on bureaucratic estimates of the potential for civic conflict. In all three national settings, the typical site is likely to be relatively unpopulated and rural and to have low or diminishing community solidarity and diffuse civil society, compared with the situation in alternative potential sites.

Given rising civic consciousness, though, these initial siting strategies often fail to prevent opposition from arising, and thus it is important to look at how states and citizens interact beyond original siting decisions. Once sites are picked, states have at their disposal a range of strategies (coercion, methods of social control, and incentives) for addressing whatever organized civic opposition may arise. Much of the recent NIMBY literature focuses on the success or failure of the incentive packages offered to local communities and assumes that states use only a single strategy to handle all contestation. This book explores in far more depth the strategic behavior of states to show that when civil society is weak and unorganized, states typically rely on coercive strategies to bring the project to fruition. Indeed, one of the many surprises in this account is the degree to which coercive tools such as land expropriation and police force remain the preferred and quite common strategy for locating public bads. A data set of close to 500 observations in Japan shows that more than half the siting attempts for controversial facilities involved the use of coercive policy instruments. Coercion has been the primary tool of choice for locating airports in Japan, nuclear power plants in France, and dams in the United States, to cite several examples, and in each case, weak opposition is the best explanation for the choice of strategy. Only when policymakers face organized opposition from communities with strong civil societies and their allies are they prepared to roll out a full range of incentives or resort to such social control techniques as persuasion and side payments to win compliance.

In a global context in which civic opposition to public bads siting is rising, coercion is clearly not an optimal strategy; formulas that include "soft" social control and incentives are preferable for dealing with future siting dilemmas. And indeed, nuclear power siting in Japan displays the skills of the country's bureaucrats in generating precisely these kinds of noncoercive solutions. But civil servants in all three nations adopt soft solutions only when forced to do so; not until they encounter stiff civic resistance do state decision makers set aside coercive strategies. In a way that has been claimed but rarely demonstrated by previous scholars, active and organized civil societies bring about better state solutions to thorny policy problems.

My research has profound implications for further research on both states and civil society. This book complements earlier work by Robert Putnam to show how the nature of civil society conditions a state's strategies for addressing policy problems. The location of facilities and the toolkit that states develop to handle anti-facility resistance are deeply related to the strength of civil society. Like Jonah Levy's work on civil society in France (1999), this book offers new perspectives on the role and importance of horizontal associations. Without a strong civil society, Levy demonstrates, states find it increasingly difficult to carry out a range of tasks, such as fostering long-term economic growth and providing social welfare. Similarly, I find that state authorities deviate from standard coercive policy instruments such as land expropriation and police force only under intense pressure from organized civil society. Strong civil society pushes states to develop less force-based—and hence more sustainable—strategies for handling divisive problems. Weak civil society allows state authorities to continue using standard operating procedures that rely heavily on expropriation, police suppression and surveillance, and hard social control techniques.

Drawing on two years of fieldwork in Japan and France, I use a new data set of close to 500 localities across Japan alongside case studies of nuclear power plant, dam, and airport siting in Japan and France. To gather the materials for this book, in addition to archival work, I conducted eighty interviews of at least an hour with government officials, legislators, activists, lawyers, local citizens, and academics over twenty months of fieldwork in Japan from June to September 2001 and from June 2002 to September 2003. I visited ten dam, nuclear power plant, and airport host communities in Japan to spend time with local legislators, bureaucrats, citizens, and activists. During that same period, I sent 250 surveys to Japanese local governments that hosted or were targeted for hosting a controversial facility; my response rate was more than 95 percent perhaps as a result of both repeated phone calls and faxes to initial nonresponders and the support of the Institute of Social Science at the University of Tokyo. I surveyed local authorities on several issues, including compensation, the political parties of mayors and local councils, and the involvement of fishing cooperatives.

I also sent surveys to Japan's nine major power companies about their siting of nuclear power plants, focusing on issues of timing (how much time it took to plan and complete the plan) and citizen reaction (absence or presence of local anti-facility groups, demonstrations, and lawsuits); I followed up with direct interviews whenever possible. Finally, I sent 100 surveys focusing on compensation and siting times to prefectural and local offices of the Ministry of Land, Infrastructure, and Transport, which currently handles dam and airport siting; with assistance from the head bureaucratic office in Tokyo, I achieved a response rate of 98 percent, and these surveys provided much of my collection of raw data for my data set.

To provide a basis for comparison, I conducted four months of fieldwork in France in the summer of 2004, interviewing more than twenty French officials, employees of the French utility company Électricité de France (EDF), anti-nuclear group members, and local representatives. Through one visit to a French nuclear power plant site, I was able to "soak and poke" in local civil society. For references to siting cases from the United States, I relied on archival reports, newspaper articles, and secondary sources.

In analyzing these data I have employed a combination of quantitative analysis and comparative case studies. This book integrates positive political analyses with deep-process tracing to provide a richer understanding of statistically significant inferences about the phenomena under investigation. My large data set of cases from Japan, covering the period from 1955 until 1995, enabled me to make more accurate inferences about the effects of factors that influence the selection of host communities for dams, airports, and nuclear power plants. In conducting case studies of bureaucracies in Japan and France, I could multiply my number of observations by investigating many interactions between state agencies and citizens over time. Rather than seeing each case study as a single data point, I increased my analytical leverage by analyzing multiple exchanges between the state and civil society since the end of World

War II. Finally, I carried out frequency analyses of newspaper articles from major papers in these nations to survey media coverage and issue salience.

This book has been made possible by an enormous network of support and assistance. First, I am *makir tov* to the *Ribono shel Olam* for all that I have received. The Institute of International Education Fulbright provided funding for fifteen months of extended fieldwork in Japan, which was greatly facilitated by the staff of the Japan United States Education Committee and by the Institute of Social Science at the University of Tokyo. The National Science Foundation and the Reischauer Institute of Harvard University jointly supplied summer travel money that allowed me to carry out initial fieldwork in the summer of 2001, and the Reischauer Institute provided a grant for writing in 2003–2004. Three Harvard entities—the Weatherhead Center for International Affairs, the Harvard Center for European Studies, and the Reischauer Institute—jointly funded four months of research in Paris. The Program on U.S.–Japan Relations at Harvard University provided generous support for publication.

In alphabetical order, the following individuals went out of their way to assist me: Allison Aldrich, Howard and Penny Aldrich, Reiko Amano, Kenshi Baba, Regis Babinet, Bertrand Barre, Pierre Bollinger, Brian Brox, Serine Consolino, Bill Grimes, Nobuhiro Hiwatari, Mizuho Iwata, Yuko Kageyama-Hunt, Kumao Kaneko, Donna Koepp, Ayumi Koso, Reagan Kuhn, Aaron Lasry, David Leheny, S. Hayden Lesbirel, Teruaki Masumoto, Sue-Jin McCoy, Eric Nguyen, Chana Odem, Junji Oshima, Steve Reed, Ross Schaap, Helen Snively, Tatsujiro Suzuki, Yuriko Takahashi, Yoshimi Tamura, Yves Tiberghien, Mark Vail, Steven Vogel, Masami Watanabe, and Robert Weiner. I owe each of them a debt of gratitude. Two anonymous reviewers read the entire manuscript and helped me improve it. The library of the Citizens' Nuclear Information Center (CNIC) in Tokyo provided an excellent base of information for my nuclear power chapter, and staff members at the University of Tokyo's Institute of Social Science were incredibly responsive to a myriad of requests. Thanks as well to staff at the Japan Atomic Industrial Forum, the Japan Dam Federation, and the Japan Aeronautical Association. In Paris the Centre Américain, Institut d'Etudes Politiques de Paris (Sciences Po) hosted me during my research. The archives and librarians at WISE-Paris and the French Ministry of Industry were especially helpful. The Abitbols, Gronsteins, Lasrys, Toledanos, and Yazdis were warm hosts during my time in the City of Lights.

I had the opportunity to present sections of my research in Japan at the Institute for Social Science at the University of Tokyo, the Asian Studies

Conference Japan, and the German Institute for Japanese Studies. In the United States, panels at conferences of the American Political Science Association and the Association for Asian Studies provided invaluable feedback, as did the Harvard University Positive Political Economy Workshop, the Graduate Student Associate Workshop of the Weatherhead Center, and the Society for Comparative Research Graduate Student Retreat. Susan Pharr, Jeff Frieden, Paul Pierson, and Jas Sekhon exemplified constructive direction for my professional development; Susan Pharr deserves special accolades. The Reischauer Institute at Harvard University sponsored an author's conference at which Thomas Berger, Shin Fujihira, Jonah Levy, Frances Rosenbluth, and Susan Pharr provided excellent feedback on an earlier draft of the manuscript. Christian Brunelli went far beyond the call of friendship by providing advice, books to read, and repeated suggestions for major rewrites. Roger Haydon of Cornell University Press supplied guidance and support throughout the publication process. Additionally, I owe an enormous debt to the nearly 400 respondents to my surveys and the 100 or so with whom I conducted formal interviews; in many cases I cannot reveal their identity but have sought to balance transparency with privacy.

Finally, my indomitable wife, Yael, has lived a life paradigmatic of an *eishes chayil,* bringing into the world and raising well our three children—Gavriel Tzvi, Yaakov, and Yehudis—while sustaining our household with grace and dignity through ten moves in fewer years. For more than half my life, she has kept me focused on what truly matters and shown how "a house is built on wisdom." It is to her that I dedicate this work.

DANIEL P. ALDRICH

*Cambridge, Massachusetts*

# Abbreviations

| | |
|---|---|
| AP | Associated Press |
| *AS* | *Asahi Shinbun* (Asahi Newspaper) |
| ANRE | Agency for Natural Resources and Energy (*Shigen enerugi chō, within METI*) |
| CNIC | Citizens' Nuclear Information Center (*Genshiryoku shiryōjōhō shitsu*) |
| CRS | Compagnies Républicaines de Sécurité (French anti-riot police) |
| DUP | *Déclaration d'utilité publique* (statement of public interest) |
| EDF | Électricité de France (France's electric utility company) |
| *GDN* | *Gekkan Damu Nihon* (Dam Digest Monthly) |
| JAERO | Japan Atomic Energy Relations Organization (*Nihon genshiryoku bunka shinkō dantai*) |
| LDP | Liberal Democratic Party (*Jiyūminshutō*) |
| METI | (Japanese) Ministry of Economy, Trade, and Industry (*Keizai sangyōshō*) |
| MITI | (Japanese) Ministry of International Trade and Industry (*Tsūshō sangyōshō*) |
| MLIT | (Japanese) Ministry of Land, Infrastructure, and Transport (*Kokudokōtsūshō*) |
| MOC | (Japanese) Ministry of Construction (*Kensetsushō*) |
| MOT | (Japanese) Ministry of Transportation (*Unyushō*) |
| NAA | Narita Airport Authority |
| NGSK | Nihon Genshiryoku Sangyō Kaigi (Japan Atomic Industrial Forum) |
| NDK | Nihon Damu Kyōkai (Japan Dam Federation) |
| WARDEC | Water Resources Development Corporation (*Suishigen Kaihatsu Kōdan*) |
| *WSJ* | *Wall Street Journal* |

# SITE FIGHTS

# Introduction

## Site Fights and Policy Tools

BY SOME ACCOUNTS, the location of our nation's capital was decided at a secret dinner party that Thomas Jefferson held in 1790 at his New York City residence. There, through the age-old practice of logrolling, James Madison and Alexander Hamilton hatched a plan to build the nation's capital in Virginia. "Madison agreed to permit the core provision of Hamilton's fiscal program to pass; and in return, Hamilton agreed to use his influence to assure that the permanent residence of the national capital would be on the Potomac River" (Ellis 2001, 49).

Alas, siting decisions are rarely made that smoothly. In modern democracies, governments face formidable challenges in locating essential facilities. Everyone wants cheap gasoline and lower heating bills, but no one wants to live near an oil refinery or a fuel storage facility. Huge segments of the population desire the convenience of a major airport, but no one likes to be awakened by the roar of a landing red-eye. The public needs clean water and flood control, but what families want to see their homes destroyed to make way for a new dam? Faced with strong local opposition, governments must decide where to place these facilities. While the empty Nevada desert around Yucca Mountain is clearly preferable to New York's Central Park as a storage location for long-term radioactive waste, most siting decisions involve multiple technically feasible alternatives. And, unlike those at Jefferson's fete, modern politicians rarely hammer out these decisions over a dinner party.

No existing theories can neatly capture the factors that influence the selection and construction of controversial facilities. Instances of environmental racism and political maneuvering are common, of course, but cannot consistently explain larger patterns. Consider nuclear power plant and airport siting, for example. The Indian Point reactor lies 30 miles (48 km) from Manhattan; Japan's Fukushima reactor complex is 200 kilometers from Tokyo. Haneda Airport is located near an affluent neighborhood of Tokyo, and the Lambert–St. Louis Airport expansion required the destruction of 2,300 nearby homes, six churches, and four schools in suburban Bridgeton, Missouri. But the new

1

Denver Airport, finished in 1995, sits 25 miles (40 km) from downtown Denver. Neither bureaucratic nor economic logics seem to account adequately for the spatial placement of such facilities.

In selecting sites for controversial facilities, states must choose from among a myriad of possible host communities, all of which meet certain necessary technical criteria, such as having strong bedrock or being near water sources. Scholars and citizens have intensely debated why one town but not another is selected as a host community. Some have accused developers and authorities of environmental racism, when unwanted projects are placed in localities with high concentrations of ethnic and racial minorities. Bureaucrats regularly counter such claims by arguing that they select sites solely on the basis of neutral technical criteria such as geology and seismology. Political scientists contend that political parties place nuclear power plants and other facilities in particular areas to punish their opponents, while others focus on local socioeconomic conditions. Screening villages and towns as potential host communities is the first stage in siting a controversial facility; managing a community's often contentious response is the second. That is, in addition to the question of *where,* there is an equally complex question of *how* governments interact with affected citizens in building these facilities. Modern democratic governments cannot simply choose a location by fiat and expect clear sailing afterward.

Except for the decision to go to war, no other decision by democratic governments raises more controversy and public opposition than the location of the projects that I label as "public bads." Decisions to site dams and nuclear waste storage facilities have set off hunger strikes, sit-ins, rioting, and looting; plans to expropriate land for airports have roused legions of activists throwing Molotov cocktails. States choose among a variety of policy tools to handle conflict, ranging from strong-arm tactics of coercion and eminent domain to more subtle incentives and inducements. Because inherent inequalities accompany controversial facilities, siting such projects requires modern democracies to pursue what they believe to be the common, public good in the face of popular opposition.

How state agencies handle conflict with civil society over divisive issues is a critical but poorly understood problem. This book focuses on the ways that advanced democracies manage the siting of controversial facilities. I analyze how states such as Japan and France gauge the potential for conflict by taking the measure of their local civil society and then interacting with anti-facility social and environmental movements that often envision state-initiated projects as harmful and unnecessary. Although nuclear power plants, dams, and airports provide energy, water resources, and easier transportation, all of which make modern life possible, they impose substantial costs on the communities that host them. These public works projects pit a diffuse public interest represented by the state against concentrated local (and sometimes extra-local) interests. The asymmetric distribution of costs and benefits from these "public bads" presents unique challenges for democratic governments.

If a local community selected as a host responds negatively to the proposed project—a situation that has become more common around the world in recent decades—government agencies can respond to the problem of rebellious civil society in different ways.[1] Some, such as Japan's Ministry of Transportation, the Tennessee Valley Authority, the U.S. Army Corps of Engineers, and the French Ministries of Energy and Interior, relied on coercive practices such as expropriation and even police suppression to achieve their goals of siting airports, dams, and nuclear power plants. Others, such as Japan's Agency for Natural Resources and Energy (ANRE), eschewed coercive strategies and created new tools and tactics to manage challenges in dealing with contentious civil society. Why some state agencies innovate while others remain wedded to a "standard operating procedure" (Halperin et al. 1976) raises important questions about state-society relationships and public policy choices.

## What Are Public Bads?

The projects under study here fall into the general category commonly called public goods: their operating costs cannot be fully recovered from all beneficiaries and must be either wholly sponsored or partially subsidized by the state (Brion 1991, 37). What distinguishes them from typical public goods is that they involve "entrepreneurial politics," as they "will confer general (though perhaps small) benefits at a cost to be borne chiefly by a small segment of society" (Wilson 1980, 370). While nuclear plants, for example, provide electricity to the public, those communities closest to the facilities suffer most from the disruptions involved in construction—and any accidents or catastrophes.[2] Thus, from the perspective of their impact, such projects are more accurately viewed as *public bads*. That is, they "increase overall welfare but impose net

---

1. See Aldrich (2005b) for an overview of literature on how different states handle controversial facilities.

2. Even if an accident has not yet occurred, simply living "in the shadow" of a nuclear power plant can lead to psychic costs, and many believe that real estate in such communities loses value as a result. For a discussion of psychic costs and mobility, see Deaten, Morgan, and Anschel (1982). With airports, noise pollution is the primary problem, and dams hurt local residents by forcing relocation.

costs on the individuals living in the host community" (Frey, Oberholzer-Gee, and Eichenberger 1996, 1298 n. 1).[3]

Public bads, of course, can be provided by any level of government. The facilities I focus on here, however, originate in *national* policies that provide benefits for the majority of citizens but negatively affect certain areas more harshly than others. Such projects bring with them *diffuse benefits but highly focused costs.* Cases of controversial facility siting provide an excellent window into state-citizen interaction because they are spatially bounded, generate high levels of media and secondary literature coverage, and bring out participants even in a time of declining citizen involvement in politics. Struggles in Japan over the Matsubara and Shimouke Dams, the Narita Airport, and the Tōkaimura nuclear plants dramatically raised the number of newspaper articles on these types of facilities. At the height of the short-lived anti-nuclear-power ecologist movement in France in the 1970s, thousands of citizens joined in rallies against planned reactors. Citizens feel deeply about their homes and their neighborhoods and often mobilize to make their opinions heard.

I examine siting cases involving facilities in which the government was either an initiator, as in the Narita Airport case, or an active partner with a semipublic or private utility, as in the Kaminoseki nuclear power plant complex. Businesses working alone can rarely construct these facilities because of uncertain local reactions, long time frames, and high capital costs (see Altshuler and Luberoff 2003, 4). As a result, governments often must act as entrepreneurs for these projects or become involved through intensive regulation, which, as one author has argued, "is not simply [designed] to control and limit. It is also to allow" (Brion 1991, xii). In the modern era, states may encounter internal deadlock because politicians, unwilling to face blame and reprisals, avoid such projects (Weaver 1984). The nature of these facilities creates a geographically dictated reality in which local citizens face a battery of problems. Confronting such concentrated costs, small groups have an incentive to overcome barriers to group coordination and typical problems of collective action.[4] In many cases, citizen resistance—through mass demonstrations, letter-writing campaigns, citizen referenda, and ballot questions—delays or even kills such proposals. For example, the Seabrook Nuclear Power Plant, located 16 km south of Portsmouth, New Hampshire, was first proposed in

---

3. Aranson and Ordeshook (1985, 93–94) define such problems similarly. The category of public bads includes phenomena as diverse as civil wars and terrorism (Reuter and Truman 2004).

4. James Q. Wilson argues that "when a specific, easily identifiable group bears the cost of a program conferring distributed benefits, the group is likely to feel its burden keenly and thus to have a strong incentive to organize" to decrease the potential threats (1974, 334). See also Olson 1965.

1969 with an expected start-up date of 1974. Regular marches by thousands of members of the Clamshell Alliance, combined with legal challenges and the refusal of local towns to participate in creating an evacuation plan, delayed the opening of the plant by sixteen years—to 1990.

Not all public bads generate intense, widespread opposition in civil society, of course. Different facilities bring with them varying levels of perceived risks and externalities. Analysts distinguish between *dread risks,* which are catastrophic, fatal, and uncontrollable, and *unknown risks,* which are unobservable, have delayed effects, and may be unrecognized by science (Slovic, Fischoff, and Lichtenstein 1980). Numerous studies suggest that citizens in advanced industrial countries view nuclear power plants with the most severe dread, followed by dams, and then airports (Vari, Reagan-Cirincione, and Mumpower 1994; Cha 1997; Slovic, Flynn, Mertz, Pomadere, and Mays 2000).[5]

Opposition even to the same category of facilities has not been constant across nations though. Citizens in Japan, France, and the United States may all view nuclear power plants in terms of their dread risks, but levels of response from civil society differ among cases because of such exogenous factors as political opportunities, resource availability, and government structure (Flam 1994a). Hence, opposition to nuclear power siting has been high in both the United States and Japan. In the United States, groups within civil society resisted siting plans, while the government, with its more open federal institutions, offered little support for nuclear power. In Japan, historical experience heightened the nation's concern over atomic energy and created a public sympathetic to anti-nuclear resistance. In France, on the other hand, resistance to nuclear power from citizen groups has been weaker and of shorter duration because of strong government backing for the program, connections to feelings of nationalism and national purpose, and closed opportunity structures. As a result, it would be misleading to argue that opposition to the same types of facilities does not vary across nations (see Kitschelt 1986). Political institutions and historical background mediate between individual citizen concerns over projects and expressed levels of opposition.

Within Japan, because of the dread aroused by radioactivity and the more widespread hazards connected with atomic energy, nuclear power plants face the stiffest and longest-term resistance from citizens. Dams, on average

5. Citizens in France, Japan, Korea, and the United States all rank nuclear power among their most dreaded fears and commercial aviation as the least feared, with dams in middle. Citizens in Hong Kong and Norway also rank nuclear power among the most dreaded phenomena. Because of Japan's World War II experience, most Japanese view nuclear power as a highly dreaded but *known* risk, whereas Americans, Koreans, the French, and others see it as highly dreaded but *unknown.*

submerging the homes of several hundred local residents, face less severe but still sizable resistance from anti-facility groups. Airports generate the least opposition because their externalities are so focused (primarily high noise levels affecting houses near the ends of runways). These levels of resistance can be confirmed through the success rate of siting attempts of different facilities. Developers in Japan failed to site nuclear power plants in almost one out of two attempts, but bureaucrats have achieved a success rate of close to 80 percent for dam proposals and more than 95 percent for airports. Although resistance to a project may occasionally be extreme, a better measure of the overall level of civil society's opposition is found by examining multiple siting attempts of the same type of facility over time in a given country. For example, the Narita Airport case is well known but not representative of the overall level of resistance to airports in Japan.

## The Public Bads Squeeze: Rising Need, Growing Resistance

Authorities around the world must balance rising needs for energy and infrastructure facilities against increasing resistance from civil society. Economic development and population growth create demands for energy, national defense, waste removal, transportation, and correctional facilities. Although these projects are core components of modern life, siting and constructing them often prove to be difficult, if not impossible, for many governments.[6] Polls over time and across nations have shown that public consciousness of these issues has become greater and trepidation about their effects has become more severe. A number of critical events, such as Earth Day, the publication of Rachel Carson's *Silent Spring,* and the accidents at Three Mile Island, Chernobyl, and Tōkaimura turned public opinion against nuclear power plants, waste dumps, and other projects that can have negative environmental consequences on those nearby.[7] Undergirding this shift, a rights-based, postmaterialist con-

---

6. Opponents regularly argue that any *need* is in fact inflated by project proponents, and that alternatives—such as reducing trash and waste production, engaging in substitute "green" energy sources, and reducing power usage—would make such facilities unnecessary (see Laponche 2004). This book does not debate the necessity of such projects but investigates the patterns by which they are sited and the policy instruments used to handle resistance.

7. Rachel Carson's *Silent Spring,* published in 1962, raised the alarm about pesticides such as DDT and their effect on ecosystems. Earth Day, initiated by Senator Gaylord Nelson on 22 April 1970, brought out 20 million North Americans to discuss and protest oil spills, pesticides, and other factors that affect the environment. The partial meltdown at the Three Mile Island nuclear plant in Pennsylvania on 28 March 1979 raised concerns among Americans about the consequences of serious nuclear accidents. The world's worst nuclear accident to date occurred with the meltdown of

sciousness (Mazmanian and Morell 1994; Inglehart 1998) has evolved, driven by rising incomes and increasing citizen mobilization. Transnational advocacy coalitions have repeatedly intervened in domestic siting attempts as new global norms about public bads such as dams have cascaded across national boundaries (Khagram 2004).

While some have characterized the issue of siting disputes as "unexciting and secondary" (Morone and Woodhouse 1989, x), resistance to projects such as nuclear power plants and airports has increased to the point where it has been labeled a "disease," a "syndrome," and a "dragon to be slain" (Ehrman 1990; Inhaber 1998). For example, despite a dire need, the United States, Germany, and Canada have not opened new hazardous-waste treatment plants since the mid-1980s (Rabe 1994; Seeliger 1996). In Japan, the amount of time necessary to site a fossil-fuel reactor has more than doubled since the 1960s (Munton 1996). In the United States, no nuclear plants have been sited since 1978, despite President George W. Bush's stated interest in increasing their number (*New York Times,* 2 September 2001). The time required to construct a nuclear power plant in Japan has tripled since the mid-1970s (Aldrich 2005a). And despite a widely perceived need for liquefied natural gas (LNG) terminals to transfer natural gas from tankers to conventional pipelines, none have been constructed in the United States in three decades. The pressure for new terminals is so great that in June 2005, because of fears that local involvement would hamstring and delay construction, the Senate rejected a proposal that would have allowed states to block LNG terminal siting. When authorities fail to build the dams, research laboratories, energy plants, waste incinerators, and landfills that the state perceives as necessary, they must deal with ever swelling populations that require such facilities for daily life.

Along with increasing the pressure on future generations to complete much-needed facilities, local resistance to planned projects costs developers and the government—and therefore taxpayers—money. Sabotage and violent protest from anti–Narita Airport protesters cost ten lives, delayed the opening of the facility for seven years, and created dangerous overcrowding at Haneda Airport, forcing the Japanese government to spend millions of taxpayers' dollars in wages for additional security forces. Compensation packages for Japanese

---

the Chernobyl reactor in the former Soviet Union on 25 April 1986; at least 30 people were killed, and more than 100,000 citizens had to be evacuated. Thereafter, overall thyroid cancer rates among Ukrainian youth in the area rose more than tenfold, and the long-term health effects of that accident on both Russia and Europe are still being investigated. The accident at the Tōkaimura nuclear fuel factory in Japan on 30 September 1999 resulted in the deaths of two workers and a release of radioactive gases into the nearby area.

fishing cooperatives and other anti-project associations located near controversial facilities now run into the tens of millions of dollars. Rather than
dismissing interaction with locals as "interminable dialogue over parochial
issues," as Deputy Defense Secretary Richard Lawless did when faced with
Japanese resistance to U.S. military base siting (*Economist,* 29 October 2005,
44), forward-thinking states and developers understand that facility siting is a
crucial issue.

## The Argument in Brief

The variation in patterns both of site selection and government response to organized opposition represents an important puzzle for social scientists. I argue
that *civil society, whether anticipated or encountered by the state, deeply conditions both
the selection of sites for public bads and the state's response to opposition to such projects*
(although political interference from powerful legislators occasionally plays a
role as well), and I advance two core arguments. First, state agencies initially
manage potential conflict over controversial facilities by avoiding contestation wherever possible. Despite public pronouncements, state bureaucracies
hardly pick sites for nuclear power plants, dams, and airports using only neutral technical criteria, nor is their selection of host communities based on
the concentration of minorities, economic conditions, or support for certain
political parties. Instead, authorities place facilities in technically feasible locations where organized resistance from groups within civil society is judged to
be lowest. By selecting the geologically suitable villages seen as most likely to
be cooperative, given their weak or weakening local civil society, state agencies
seek to avoid costly delays, demonstrations, and stalemate. Hence authorities
place "projects at some distance from groups with the potential to block
them" (Altshuler and Luberoff 2003, 229). Politicians can intervene in the
siting process to deflect projects from or draw them into their constituencies,
but not all have the political power and will to do so.

Despite the care involved in selecting locations, in recent decades conflict
has become all but inevitable. My second argument is that in handling resistance from contentious civil society, state agencies are more likely to rely on
coercive techniques and tools of hard social control, such as land expropriation and police force, when long-term opposition from civil society is weak.
Agencies siting controversial facilities interact with multiple localities and their
allies over time and evaluate the strength of relevant civil society on the basis
not of a single village or town but rather of numerous exchanges with citizen
groups as a whole. States continue to rely on the oldest, most reliable, and

least costly strategies in their toolkits when they can.[8] And hard social-control tools—such as blocking access points for citizens and limiting information dispersal—bring almost guaranteed results to the state; softer strategies of social control and financial incentives do not.[9] Only when authorities encounter intense opposition of long duration do they move from tactics like land expropriation and police suppression to soft social-control strategies and incentives. Even against fierce resistance, state planners rarely back away from their nationwide energy and infrastructure goals. Instead, bureaucrats facing opposition seek to change the hearts and minds of local citizens through tactics tailored toward subgroups within potential host communities.

Studies of anti-nuclear and ecology movements within civil society in industrial democracies argue that such groups have rarely altered national public policy (Giugni 2004), but I conclude that states are in fact Machiavellian.[10] In the teeth of strong civic resistance, policymakers do adopt softer and thus more costly responses to opposition. Many controversial facilities foist externalities onto segments of local communities that have difficulty building larger coalitions of opposition groups and mobilizing additional support. Dams and airports, for example, impose costs primarily on abutters: small numbers of citizens who live close to these facilities, whether in areas flooded by a new reservoir or in the noisy but narrow flight path of airplanes. In such cases, anti-facility groups find it difficult to mobilize allies willing to invest time, energy, and financial resources. Local, disaggregated groups within civil

8. Costly here refers to the expenditure of political, financial, and administrative resources, not necessarily the short-term reputational costs. The state's toolkit consists of the policy tools, instruments, and strategies it uses to meet its goals. Using coercive tools against subgroups within civil society costs states less than using softer tools, for three main reasons: first, authorities need not go to the expense of creating new tools, such as redistribution, which entail new responsibilities, time, and expenditures for state bureaucrats, since coercive tools already exist in their toolkits; second, such tools have proved effective at reducing future protest in the majority of cases (Lichbach 1995; Rule 1988), whereas softer tools have more uncertain outcomes (see footnotes below); and third, coercion may need be applied only once to reduce future protest levels (Boyle 1998), whereas softer tools require more frequent use. As others have explained, applying the softer tools to larger targets, such as entire ethnic groups, would dramatically raise the cost to the state (Bermeo 2002).

9. Much research has shown that public relations and public acceptance campaigns often produce only minimal changes in attitudes toward controversial facilities (Slovic et al. 2000, 98). Offering money to communities in exchange for hosting facilities has often had a perverse effect, driving out voluntarism and lowering support for the projects (Frey, Oberholzer-Gee, and Eichenberger 1996; Frey and Oberholzer-Gee 1997). One scholar argues that "economic strategies, including those that emphasize generous compensation packages as the ultimate balm of siting tensions, almost invariably fail" (Rabe 1994, xiv). For example, one town in Illinois that was offered $25 million to allow a landfill expansion rejected the offer (Piller 1991, 192).

10. "Machiavellian" here refers to the well-known, pragmatic, and perhaps ruthless advice that Niccolò Machiavelli gives to an authoritarian ruler in The Prince, which departs from the more republican approach he adopts in The Discourses.

society rarely affect state policy (Pekkanen 2004, 244). Accordingly, although many local communities oppose plans for dams and airports, *sustained, intense* competition between broader civil society and the state over the siting of these projects is somewhat rare.

When local and extra-local groups within civil society can keep up broad, acute opposition to state plans for facilities over an extended period of a decade or more, however, bureaucrats display remarkable flexibility in altering institutions and policies to dampen current and future resistance. For example, given the Japanese experience of nuclear weapons, the siting of nuclear power plants in Japan has been a contentious process since the earliest attempts in the 1950s. By precisely tailoring strategies aimed at those who might veto the project, while maintaining their initial goals, state authorities hope to contain current resistance and reduce the likelihood of future contestation. Because toolkits are a function of civil society, there is a strong correlation between sustained, intense opposition and the use of preference-altering policy instruments that seek to capture the hearts of local citizens.

A growing body of research has revealed the dangers of a weak civil society. Those regions with weaker horizontal ties suffer from poorer governance, weaker institutions, and even higher levels of homicide (Lee and Bartkowski 2004). Areas with fewer active members in civic, sport, and religious groups have lower levels of economic development and, in nondemocratic nations, less likelihood of transition toward stable democracy (Alagappa 2004). But this book demonstrates another important corollary to studies of networks, communities, and volunteerism: states interacting solely with weak civil society hold fewer soft policy instruments for handling contestation. Strong civil society serves as a Galbraithian "countervailing force" (Hasegawa 2004) that deepens and broadens the toolkits held by state decision makers.

## Site Selection

Bureaucrats and planners seek to avoid conflict to minimize costs—in terms of time, money, political power, and reputation—when selecting technically feasible sites for airports, dams, and nuclear power plants. I make the case that civil society strongly affects the placement of these controversial large-scale projects (cf. Hamilton 1993; Wolverton 2002). Site developers select localities based on estimates of net potential opposition to the project. Existing social networks in potential host communities, such as preexisting voluntary associations, can best mobilize and overcome barriers to collective action to stall or deflect proposed facilities (Olson 1965). In Japan and France, for example, farmers' and fishermen's cooperatives regularly play an active and vital role in the siting process and often oppose nuclear power plants because of concerns about health risks and contamination of foodstuffs. Mexican anti-nuclear movements as well have been spearheaded by local fishing and farming groups (Garcia-Gorena 1999). In the United States, residents with interests in fishing and recreation have often mobilized to block dam siting. Communities do not always speak with one voice, however; sometimes local actors, such as pro-development business associations or political representatives, may lobby in favor of hosting a controversial facility.

Villages and towns with weak civil society—such as "boomtown" communities that cannot maintain community solidarity because of rapid population increases, or rural areas facing depopulation and a loss of connectedness—are less effective in unifying to resist siting plans. In the United States, for example, private developers of nuclear power plants regularly targeted rural, depopulating areas that seemed least likely to mount campaigns against the projects. In Japan, communities selected for nuclear power plants are similarly rural, with lower population densities, higher rates of depopulation, and weakening local organizations. In one case, government planners explicitly searched for "cooperative villages" where civil society would not impede siting plans, or at least "thinly populated" ones where any resistance would be on a small scale (NGSK 6/2 [1962]: 9). In such villages and towns, any opponents of proposed facilities find it difficult to muster the political pressure—whether in the form of votes, marchers in demonstrations, or petition writers—necessary to signal to state authorities that siting in their area will prove difficult.

Another factor occasionally plays a role in highly contested siting processes: powerful politicians may intervene either to draw in or to block facilities. Although some argue that politicians seek solely to deflect nuclear power plants from their constituencies (Ramseyer and Rosenbluth 1993), I uncovered evidence that long-serving Liberal Democratic Party (LDP) members in Japan have actually drawn these facilities into their districts. The best known was Kakuei Tanaka, the former prime minister from Niigata prefecture, who openly discussed his successful drive to bring nuclear projects to his electoral district (Tanaka 1972, 102–104; Samuels 1987, 246; Schlesinger 1997, 72, 103). Incumbent LDP legislators actively promote nuclear reactors by visiting hesitant local communities slated for new power plants; to encourage community cooperation, the politicians give pep talks focused on potential financial gains. Overriding bureaucratic decisions, Japanese politicians are most likely to act as magnets for nuclear power plants but rarely intervene in less charged siting cases, such as those of dams and airports. In France, on the other hand, political intervention has primarily come in the form of cancellation; President

François Mitterrand terminated the highly contested state-sponsored plan to site a nuclear plant in the village of Plogoff (Dorget 1984).

Areas that have previously shown themselves susceptible—or amenable—to the siting of public bads display less likelihood of opposing future ones. A community that already hosts one nuclear power plant is more likely to be selected for future reactors, just as communities with exposure to a single corrections facility are likely to host future ones (Hoyman 2001). The initial acceptance of a public bad can create a deleterious cycle: the host community that becomes dependent upon the taxes and side payments provided by initial facilities, once it has spent its newly acquired funds, is forced to take on additional facilities to remain financially solvent in what anti-project activists call a "cycle of addiction" (Hasegawa 2004, 26). Alternatively, communities that already have one public bad may be habituated to controversial facilities so that additional projects bring with them no new fears—or they may have become dispirited by their initial failure to stop a siting. The communities of Kashiwazaki-Kariwa on the western coast of Japan, for example, currently host seven nuclear reactors; the town of Convent in rural Louisiana is nicknamed "Cancer Alley," thanks to the toxic emissions of thirteen nearby petrochemical plants.

Similar findings in France and the United States confirm that estimates of civil society's strength and occasional political intervention are the primary factors that determine the placement of controversial facilities. Michele Hoyman (2001), for example, has demonstrated that politicians occasionally intervene in sitings to draw prisons into their constituencies, whereas Dan Sherman (2006) underscores the role played by authorities' surveys of potential for local opposition. Given that national governments pay attention to civil society when they select hosts for facilities, they must then decide how to respond, if at all, to the almost inevitable resistance that accompanies even the best-sited of projects.[11]

## Responding to Contentious Civil Society: State Tools and Strategies

My second argument, building on the first, considers how state agencies handle civil society's resistance to planned facilities, once it develops. Some might assume that "responses" from the government to anti-facility challenges are

---

11. In many cases, despite widespread local support for a planned facility, small groups of vocal advocates wield enough power to stall or even cancel "wanted" projects (Weingart 2001). For example, the town of Midland, Michigan, campaigned actively to bring in a nuclear power plant, but "a small group of Midland residents and outside environmental groups" managed to block the siting (*New York Times,* 3 December 1971).

simply a matter of cutting down the number of planned future projects, and this has happened in several countries, including Italy and Germany, where pressures from anti-nuclear social movements and Green Party politicians forced states to end their nuclear power plant goals and to reduce siting attempts. The United States government similarly backed away from the strong financial and administrative support in the 1950s and 1960s for initial large-scale commercial nuclear plans as public opposition grew in the early 1970s. Japan and France, however, aggressively pursued initial ambitions for nuclear energy production, despite challenges from society.

Although some observers argue that the tools and institutions that states use in handling civil society are functions of their organizational structure or bureaucratic culture,[12] statutory environment,[13] or historical era,[14] I contend that the choice of dominant strategies is a function of the characteristics of potential and actual opposition from civil society. State authorities have in their toolkits a wide spectrum of policy instruments for solving sociopolitical problems. Tools that involve *coercion* derive from the state's monopoly over force; strategies involving side payments and subsidies—that is, *incentives*—seek to compensate local communities. Policy instruments can be further divided into two types of *social control:* hard and soft. Those policies that set the agenda and control the venue and thereby undercut the opposition are forms of *hard social control;* tactics intended to capture hearts and minds through persuasive rhetoric and public relations campaigns are *soft social control.* This approach does not presuppose the ethical superiority of soft over hard strategies (Grant 2006) but instead categorizes state tactics on the basis of their modes of power and goals (see chapter 2).

12. Zysman (1983) and Ōtake and Nonaka (2000) argue that strong states like France and Japan engage in strategies different from those of their weaker counterparts, England and the United States. Campbell (1988) similarly posits that the American state has fewer tools for promoting nuclear power. Garon (1997) argues that the Japanese state, far more than its Western counterparts, relies on moral suasion to mold Japanese thought and behavior in its programs for "social management."

13. Boyle (1998) and Upham (1976, 1987) argue that legal constraints and juridical environments strongly affect policy decisions and civil society-state interaction. Hence the regulations and policy environments in place may affect the choices available to state authorities, so that expropriating land from private citizens, for example, may become harder or easier depending on interpretations of legal precedent.

14. Calder (1988a) postulates that certain historical periods, often those involving public unrest, generated specific responses from the state. Similarly, normative arguments about state tool use posit a correlation between increasing citizen consciousness and higher expectations in recent decades, with more transparency and democracy in state tactics. Noakes (2001), for example, argues that over the past four decades police departments in the United States have moved from aggressive handling of protest toward a more hands-off, "managerial" style. Ekiert and Kubik (1999, 136) postulate that democratization increases the cost of coercive responses to protest, so that as democracies consolidate, they rely less on police suppression.

Table 1 provides predictions about dominant strategies for tool use. States regularly encountering communities with weak civil societies and few allies continue to rely primarily on tried-and-true coercive, hard social control techniques. If anti-project associations and networks have fewer members than competing interests—or diminishing numbers of participants—they cannot sustain long-term, high-intensity resistance to bureaucratic initiatives. Hence, policy arenas involving small-scale opposition that mobilizes citizens for fewer than five years, such as nuclear plant siting in France, are likely to involve land expropriation, police coercion against demonstrators, and limited information dispersal. When state agencies interact with communities that demonstrate moderate levels of interconnectedness and social capital, they more often use softer social control tools, such as the streamlining of siting procedures and small-scale incentives to the host communities of dams in Japan and of airports in France. Only after states struggle with strong, sustained opposition from civil society do they develop new tools that seek to alter local citizens' preferences, as in Japanese nuclear power plant siting. Under those circumstances authorities must consider the long-term consequences of purely coercive strategies. When pressed by civil society, agencies depart from the use of standard coercive tools such as expropriation and suppression, which have short-term, guaranteed outcomes, and move toward "submerged" policy instruments, which seek to change how citizens view controversial facilities over the long haul (Howard 1997; Hacker 2000).

Table 1. Dominant state strategies as a factor of civil society

|  | State tools |
| --- | --- |
| Weak civil society | *Coercion and hard social control* Examples: expropriation and state violence in French nuclear power plant and Japanese airport siting, cutting of grants in Japanese dam siting |
| Moderate levels of civil society | *Soft social control and minor incentives* Examples: closing of access points and small-scale grants in Japanese dam siting, French airport and dam siting |
| Strong civil society | *Incentives and soft social control* Examples: grants, educational programs, award ceremonies in Japanese nuclear power plant siting |

State tool use has not remained static, however. As civil societies mobilized and organized against projects, state agencies that had long relied on coercive or hard social control techniques were pushed toward adding softer, less coercive methods to their toolkits. Over time, on issues such as Japanese dam siting, dominant strategies of expropriation and closing of access points were complemented by public relations, education, and other softer policy instruments. Even the Tennessee Valley Authority, known for its uncompromising approach to siting, was eventually forced to move its public relations arm into high gear as opposition to proposed dam siting grew in the 1970s (Wheeler and McDonald 1986, 138). Agencies such as Japan's Agency for Natural Resources and Energy (ANRE) had already used softer social controls and incentives but deepened these programs in response to well-organized civil society resistance (Aldrich 2005a).

### Civil Society and the State

Analysts define the term "civil society" in a multiplicity of ways, some of which have been so expansive as to include local governments (Levy 1999) among voluntary associations. I adopt the definition of civil society as "sustained, organized social activity that occurs in groups that are formed outside the state, the market, and the family" (Pharr 2003, 316; see Ekiert and Kubik 1999, 83). Rather than being defined at the national level, the strength of civil society varies from locality to locality. In opposition to the neoliberal view of civil society as comprising groups that necessarily assist the state or at least facilitate its goals, I envision local civil societies as composed of relatively autonomous groups that can support or contest state initiatives, making it less or more difficult for states to enact policies. Further, civil society is not synonymous with protest; rather, protest is one of a variety of strategies that civil society uses (see Alagappa 2004, 5). In choosing locations for public bads, the state may not encounter actual protest but will still avoid siting in a locality with stronger horizontal associations and deeper civic ties. State authorities recognize that denser connections among citizens help them overcome barriers to collective action and engage in such tactics as mass rallies, petitions, sit-ins, and hunger strikes.

Civil society includes farmers' and fishermen's cooperatives, parent-teacher associations (PTAs), and karaoke clubs. These groups engage in voluntary activities that often have no direct relationship to political processes or policies; relatively few are formed for the purpose of pressing legislators and local leaders on political issues. Nevertheless, existing apolitical social networks can be transformed into powerful forces to work on issues of interest to members. Black churchgoers and college students, for example, were easily mobilized to join the nascent civil rights movement (McAdam 1982); Japanese birding groups transformed themselves into anti–golf course groups when their interests were threatened (Sugitani 1998); farmers and fishermen in Mexico agitated against nuclear power plants that could damage their livelihood (Garcia-Gorena 1999). Local civil society can even be enhanced and broadened by connections with transnational nongovernmental organizations (Khagram 2004), but such interventions are primarily a recent phenomenon and can backfire when domestic authorities view protest as coming from outside rather than within (author's interviews, 2002–2003).

Robert Putnam (1993) focused on the differences in governance between southern and northern Italy; after eliminating several other factors, he concluded that measures of civil society, such as the density of voluntary associations, voter turnout, and the like, predicted the quality of government responses to policy challenges far better than did standard explanations such as economics. Areas with less social capital—defined as less dense interpersonal networks, lower levels of trust, and fewer cooperative norms—had governments that were less efficient and more corrupt. The strength of horizontal associations, whether bocce clubs, choral groups, or sports leagues, strongly affected the lives of local citizens in multiple ways. Later work extended these claims to the United States (Putnam 1995, 2000).

Out of this initial work grew an enormous literature that illuminated how civil society is formed: rather than the quality of civil society impacting the institutions of government (and hence the economy), these scholars argued, the form of the state influenced the shape and power of civil society.[15] Many of these works adopted the perspective that the state can (and should) improve levels of social capital to enhance its quality of governance. Jonah Levy (1999), for example, posited that the French state's continual and deliberate diminishing of civil society deprived it of valuable feedback and counterbalance mechanisms when it sought reform through decentralization schemes in the late twentieth century. Without strong associations and groups that could critique the state's economic and social plans or, alternatively, work to implement them effectively, the French government's policies languished. Gianpaolo Baiocchi (2002) showed that in the Brazilian village of Porto Alegre, rather than civil society structuring the ways the city government worked, the state could

---

15. At the same time, other scholars, such as Sheri Berman (1997), criticize the argument that social capital is correlated solely with positive outcomes in governance; Berman shows that Germany in the 1920s and 1930s displayed strong measures of horizontal ties and civil society, and that these ties created networks of supporters for the Nazi regime (see also Koshar 1986).

increase mobilization and citizen participation through new policies. Theda Skocpol (1996, 1999) demonstrated how the structures and activities of the U.S. federal government strongly shaped the form and activities of voluntary associations, both directly and indirectly. The state directly encouraged the formation of civic groups with local or regional ties and often provided them with start-up funds. American federalism provided organizations with a blueprint for organizing at local, state, and federal levels. Further, with the advent of additional congressional staffers on Capitol Hill, advocacy groups could better get their messages across to senators and therefore increased their presence in Washington. Susan Pharr (2003) and Wilhelm Vosse (2000, 2003) demonstrated how the Japanese state guided civil society's formation through strict regulation and active monitoring.

This book builds on the burgeoning field of civil society research to emphasize two key points. First, state selection of host communities and strategies for handling contention pivot on the strength of local civil societies. Although the state does mold and affect civil society to some degree, this book complements the original work of Putnam and shows precisely how, over time, the density and membership of groups within civil society alter state plans and policies. More precisely, though some scholars emphasize the ways in which civil society reflects state policies (Kitschelt 1986; Pekkanen 2000a, 2000b), I focus on how states alter policies in response to civil society: state decision makers base their choice of locations for controversial facilities and of harder or softer policy instruments on the density of networks within civil societies. Because of the distributional asymmetries of controversial facilities, weak civil society enables authorities to carry out related policies efficiently and engage in lower-cost, often more coercive strategies for siting. When authorities seeking to locate public bads can avoid strong civil society, they do so.

Second, as a result of the critical role played by civil society, governments encountering strong resistance over time develop more subtle and sophisticated techniques for handling contention than states with weaker, more passive citizenries. To many policymakers even today, coerced solutions appear to be best because they are cost-effective and efficient, but given global trends toward resistance, they are not sustainable in modern democracies. Citizen pressure—both domestic and international—pushes states toward better, more enduring strategies for handling contention (Khagram 2004).

I measure civil society within localities in terms of both its *quality* and its *relative capacity*.[16] The quality of civil society reflects the depth of connections

---

16. Tilly (1994) argues that the strength of movements depends upon their worthiness, unity, numbers, and commitment. My concept of "relative capacity" builds on research by Sheingate (2001) and parallels Tilly's interest in numbers; "quality" combines unity and commitment.

among individuals in a community and their willingness to extend themselves beyond bare minimums of social interaction. Areas with a higher quality of social capital create stronger community solidarity and can overcome collective action problems because individuals better monitor each other and enforce existing norms. However, although individuals enmeshed in civil society may be tightly bound to one another, their numbers may be very small relative to their broader environment, and their impact on state policies and decisions may be negligible. For example, the Little Tennessee Valley was filled with small, rural towns where "[m]ost social activities centered around the church," which both "maintain[ed] community cohesion and prescribe[d] individual behavior" (Wheeler and McDonald 1986, 52). But since many towns had populations of only no more than 100 people, even if an entire town mobilized to block a proposed dam or other local bad, residents quickly recognized their limited ability to influence regional and national policies.

Thus I also take into account the relative capacity of relevant groups in civil society to measure their strength vis-à-vis their environment. As E. E. Schatt-schneider (1960, 2) pointed out long ago, the number of people involved in an activity strongly determines its effects. Because the size of associations strongly correlates with their outcome (Fung 2004), it is "not insignificant how big they are" (Ekiert and Kubik 1999, 85), both absolutely and in relative terms (Sheingate 2001, 27). For decisions about policy tools, states judge the strength of civil society not on the basis of on a single locality or interaction with anti-project groups but rather on interactions over time with numerous towns and civil society organizations active in the policy field.

## Prior Approaches to Facility Siting

Much earlier work on facility siting adopted an actor-centered approach. Social scientists investigated conflicts over unwanted projects primarily from the viewpoint of citizens, zeroing in on the motivations and drives of anti-facility groups and social movement organizations. Rather than dismissing the reactions of local communities as "not in my back yard" NIMBYism or local arrogance (*chiiki ego* in Japanese), these researchers explored citizen opposition from the bottom up. Their primarily qualitative approaches often drew conclusions from extended case studies of or participant observation work within citizens' and social movement organizations in the United States and Europe (Wellock 1978; Nelkin and Pollak 1981; Touraine et al. 1983; Garcia-Gorena 1999; McAvoy 1999; Weingart 2001).

Another wave of scholars, focusing mainly on solutions, suggested ways of dampening or avoiding paralyzing anti-facility politics (Kunreuther and Kleindorfer 1986; Ehrman 1990; Brion 1991; Jenkins-Smith and Bassett 1994; Rabe 1994; and Quah and Tan 2002). These analysts used a combination of experimental and case studies, sometimes in coordination with sample surveys and econometric tools, to identify various possible "solutions" to the problem of finding host communities for unwanted projects. Among their suggested mechanisms were reverse Dutch or low-bid auctions (Inhaber 1998, 2001), where authorities offer higher and higher amounts of compensation to communities until one volunteers to host the facility in question. Others recommended providing property-value guarantees to host areas and covering medical costs (Smith and Kunreuther 2001). Some researchers focused on institutional mechanisms present within democracies (Munton 1996), such as enhanced citizen participation in the process and local referenda allowing citizens to vote for or against the facility (Mitchell and Carson 1986).

Other investigators, rather than seeking to "solve" the issue of facility siting in isolation, traced its roots to racism and stigma. This strand of research, often action-based, began in the late 1980s when a study by the United Church of Christ Commission on Racial Justice linked race to the presence of hazardous waste repositories; *Toxic Waste and Race* (United Church of Christ 1987) spawned outrage in communities around the country and led to hundreds of follow-up studies (Hurley 1995; Cole and Foster 2001). Advocacy coalitions and even President William Clinton sought to prevent the siting of controversial facilities in communities of color (Abel 2001). The strongest form of the environmental racism argument posits an active discrimination against communities with higher concentrations of ethnic and demographic minorities (Bullard 1994, 2000). Some scholars have argued that other nations similarly discriminate against ethnic or demographic subgroups, placing facilities such as nuclear power plants near discontented regional minorities (Falk 1982), while others identified conflict over facilities more generally as a result of socially constructed stigma and marginalization (Takahashi 1998).

This book places the issue of siting in the larger context of relations between civil society and the state. Rather than relying on a handful of cases with similar outcomes, it draws on hundreds of cases of siting attempts, both successful and unsuccessful. Instead of basing itself in the narratives and frames of social movements, my approach emphasizes the interaction between government and citizenry: using new data, cross-national observations from Japan, France, and the United States, and three types of controversial facilities, it tests previous theories to illuminate the role that civil society plays in siting public bads.

## Country Focus: Japan

With a few notable exceptions, most studies of controversial facility siting have focused on North American cases.[17] A comparative perspective provides a better understanding of the significant factors because it involves varied institutional and civil society characteristics. This book uses a data set and extended cases from Japan with selective comparisons to siting in France and the United States. Japan provides an excellent case for investigating the siting of public bads because it has a high population density, has used a variety of policy instruments in handling siting, and has had differing levels of success across facility types.

Japan continues to grapple with high population density, with thirty times as many people as in the United States per square kilometer of habitable land, and three times as many as in France. With a shortage of available space, urban land prices in Japan have skyrocketed since World War II, and even after the "bubble economy" of the 1990s burst, land prices in metropolitan areas like Tokyo remain among the highest in the world. With land so scarce, Japanese government officials must work doubly hard to persuade citizens to accept facilities. If officials "pass the buck" to future politicians and bureaucrats, the costs for siting, negotiation, and compensation will only rise.

State bureaus in Japan confronting the problem of siting public bads can use a variety of strategies. Agencies locate facilities through eminent domain or voluntary procedures involving compensation, education, public relations, and appeals to nationalism. The Agency for Natural Resources and Energy, within the Ministry of International Trade and Industry (MITI), handles nuclear power plants; the Ministries of Construction (MOC) and Transportation (MOT) handle dams and airports, respectively.[18] Whereas the Ministries of Construction and Transportation have relied primarily on coercive methods, ANRE has adopted a full spectrum of soft social control strategies to reduce citizen opposition to planned projects. Studies of how Japanese bureaucracies respond to contention provide insights not into the conditions bringing forth

17. Apter and Sawa (1984), Joppke (1993), Cohen, McCubbins, and Rosenbluth (1995), Lesbirel (1998), Garcia-Gorena (1999), and Khagram (2004) focus primarily on non-American cases. Among the best-known American studies are those by Nelkin (1979), Brion (1991), Portney (1991), Hamilton (1993), Rabe (1994), Takahashi (1998), McAvoy (1999), Miller (2000), Weingart (2001), and Hoyman (2001).

18. In January 2001, MOT and MOC were folded into the new Ministry of Land, Infrastructure, and Transportation (MLIT), and MITI was renamed the Ministry of Economy, Trade, and Industry (METI). These mostly cosmetic alterations do not affect my core arguments, and I use the older names as appropriate.

a single dominant tactic for siting but rather into the factors that precipitate a number of different strategies.

Energy dependence has put nuclear power siting dilemmas on center stage in Japan, which has been one of the world's great success stories for developing nuclear energy despite a professed "nuclear allergy" (Pickett 2002; Cohen, McCubbins, and Rosenbluth 1995). It spends the most on nuclear technology among nations belonging to the Organisation for Economic Cooperation and Development, investing more than $58.1 billion since the 1980s with the lowest lead times for nuclear plants (OECD 2001). But in recent decades, Japan, like the United States and other advanced democracies, has faced rising local opposition to nuclear plants. Despite increasing subsidies and soft social control programs, lead times for reactor siting—including negotiations with local communities, licensing, and construction—have increased threefold (Aldrich 2005c). The Japanese government has scaled its energy plans back in several areas, and recent public documents acknowledge the difficulty in achieving "local understanding" over plant siting.

Despite its (increasingly contested) achievements in the nuclear field, Japan has experienced many nonnuclear land-use conflicts, and its sophisticated nuclear power compensation system does not apply to other facilities. Nor is compensation itself a panacea for siting; many localities, despite generous offers from the central government, have stalled or blocked plans for reactor construction (Lesbirel 1998; Aldrich 2005c). Sometimes authorities simply could not avoid violent resistance to the construction of airports and high-speed rail lines (Apter and Sawa 1984; Groth 1987). More recently, residents in Okinawa fought to have U.S. military bases removed from their soil, and those in Kariwa voted against allowing a recycling plant for nuclear fuel (Smith 2000). As a result, Japan's achievements in facility siting must be explained, not taken for granted.

As of 2008, Japan had more than 3,000 dams, 8 international airports and more than 80 regional airports, and 52 nuclear reactors—and the government was planning to build more of each. Japan's "construction state" (*doken kokka*) is often explained by its deferential, low-efficacy political culture (Doi 1974; Lebra 1976; Nakamura 1975; Nakane 1978; Pye 1985), which, it is claimed, acts as a barrier to citizen mobilization. One commentator went so far as to decry her fellow citizens as "sheep" who have forgotten how to fight back or struggle against unwanted impositions (Sakurai 2000); another argued that civil society in Japan was "virtually unknown" (van Wolferen 1991, 17). In explaining the plethora of public works projects, some scholars instead focus on closed hearings and procedures (Cohen, McCubbins, and Rosenbluth 1995) and restrictive regulations that have prevented nongovernmental organizations

(NGOs)—potential opponents for these facilities—from achieving official recognition and tax exemption (Pekkanen 2000a, 2000b; Vosse 2000, 2003, 7; Broadbent 2002, 22; Nakamura 2002). Others emphasize the social welfare function of public works projects: as pork-barrel projects for Liberal Democratic Party politicians, dams and other facilities provide jobs for low-skilled citizens (Hamilton and Kanabayashi 1994; McCormack 1996, 2002; Woodall 1996; Amano 2001; Takahashi 2002). Arguments that Japanese political culture is not efficacious or even existent cannot explain why communities regularly resist public bads. The remaining approaches shed light on some aspects of the issue, but none fully capture the important dynamics between the state and civil society which undergird it.

## Comparative Perspective: France and the United States

Setting cases of facility siting in France, and occasionally in the United States, against those in Japan offers additional insights into the ways civil society can affect state policies. Comparing cases in these countries allows researchers to hold certain characteristics constant while investigating the results of varying others. Government type, bureaucratic structure, and government commitment to nuclear power are constant in the French and Japanese siting cases, but the level of opposition from groups within civil society varies tremendously. Both France and Japan have unitary governing systems and elite professional bureaucracies, and both are dedicated to increasing the role that nuclear power plays in domestic production. As a federal system with politically dominated bureaucracies, cases from the United States illuminate the effects of a federal system, a semiprofessional bureaucratic structure, and far more access for interest groups (see Weaver and Rockman 1993, 19).

In short, whereas the Japanese and French bureaucracies are quite similar in several ways, those of the United States reveal exceptions (Silberman 1993). The civil services in Japan and France recruit from a restricted set of educational institutions and require candidates to pass difficult exams. Once in office, these civil servants enter as generalists and receive socialization through "practical training" on the job (Koh 1989, 188), often remaining in their bureaus for decades, despite regime shifts and political transitions (from Left to Gaullist in France, from opposition to LDP in Japan). Thus these bureaucracies have reputations as autonomous organizations relatively insulated from outside pressures. In the semiprofessional bureaucracies of America, recruitment is a less elite affair, and duration in office is shorter, often coinciding with the start or end of presidential administrations (Pfiffner 1987).

In France and Japan only a handful of civil servants are political appointees; more than 3,000 of the top leaders in American civil service meet that description (Cohen 1998). Civil servants within the United States also demonstrate less unified visions of state goals and are more influenced by both politicians and civil society (see Jasper 1990, 108) than their counterparts in France and Japan (Simonnot 1978).

The parallels between France and Japan extend beyond the similarities of their government structures and the common view of both as "strong states" (Migdal 1988; Zysman 1983; Ōtake and Nonaka 2000) committed to nuclear power (Boyle 1998). Their nuclear programs are sufficiently alike that private nuclear authorities from both countries meet annually as the "nuclear twenty" (N20)—comprising ten delegates from Japan and ten from France—to discuss issues of nuclear power plant siting and public acceptance (author's interviews, summer 2004; see Appendix 3). French and Japanese nuclear authorities began to exchange information in the early 1970s, when both signed agreements on waste reprocessing; they regularly present papers at each other's symposia and conferences. In the early 1970s the French state passed several regulations regarding its agreement with Japan on nuclear energy (*Journal Officiel*, 5 June 1973).[19]

By drawing on cases from three advanced democracies, this book seeks a global context for controversies over facility siting end—recognizing the importance of institutions and domestic factors that can constrain or amplify the claims of groups within civil society—demonstrates the impact of citizens' associations and NGOs on state goals and policies.

## Overview of the Book

Focusing first on how states select sites for often unwanted projects, chapter 1 examines common explanations for patterns of facility siting—technocratic criteria, environmental racism, economic conditions, and political parties—and shows that these standard accounts cannot satisfactorily explain patterns of nuclear power plant, airport, and dam siting in Japan over the postwar

---

19. Some analysts claim that comparisons of French and Japanese nuclear power are ill-founded because of the intimate connections in France between military use (plutonium production for weapons) and civilian reactors, but much research has shown that protests have primarily focused on the civilian, not military, aspects of these reactors (see Szarka 2002, 33). Thus van Der Eyden (2003, 353) argues that "in the French societal debate, "*le nucléaire*" is primarily about energy, and only in the second place about nuclear weapons."

period. Instead, factors related to civil society, such as the relative capacity of horizontal associations and overall community solidarity (plus occasional political interventions) best explain authorities' placement of divisive facilities.

Once it is established that state agencies pay attention to civil society when choosing where to locate these projects, the next step is to show how states deal with conflicts when they arise. Focusing on the key variable of the strength or weakness of civil society, chapter 2 examines when and why state planners use certain policy instruments and not others in furthering their siting goals. Examples from Japanese, North American, and French nuclear power plant, dam, and airport siting demonstrate that states continue to rely on coercive tools such as expropriation and police suppression when the civil society responding to facility siting attempts is judged weak.

A series of extended case studies grouped thematically supports the book's claims about the strategies states employ to handle contentious civil society; these examine the siting of airports (chapter 3), dams (chapter 4), and nuclear power plants (chapters 5 and 6) in Japan and France. Despite the notoriety of the Narita Airport case in Japan, most communities selected as hosts for airports in that country displayed low levels of resistance, as chapter 3 illuminates. Although the Japanese Ministry of Transportation continued to deploy the policy tool of expropriation against airport host communities, it also shifted future locations away from more populated areas to offshore sites built on landfill. In France, anti-airport coalitions that have put up stronger (but still moderate) levels of resistance have encountered hard social control and incentive strategies, not coercion, from the state.

Because dam-siting cases in Japan generated only low to moderate levels of opposition from host communities, the state's dominant siting strategies relied on its monopoly over force. Chapter 4 underscores that as civil society has organized against dams at the national and international levels, the Japanese state has simultaneously maintained the use of these coercive tools even while adopting superficially more "democratic" procedures. In France, anti-dam movements have sustained protest for decades and have built larger coalitions of allies than their Japanese counterparts. As a result, they have been able to alter significantly both the tools and the trajectory of France's dam-siting policies.

Of the three issue areas, Japanese civil society most strongly resisted the siting of nuclear power plants; here, the state moved away from coercion and even hard social control to incentives and soft social control in handling opposition. Chapter 5 demonstrates that, as in other cases, policy instruments have not remained static: the large incentives, expensive educational and information programs, and variety of soft social control tools developed by Japanese authorities to handle anti-nuclear contention have swelled over time to match increasing resistance.

Chapter 6 focuses on cases in France. The French agency responsible for siting nuclear power plants shares several characteristics with its Japanese counterpart, including a unitary government, commitment to nuclear power, and autonomous and professional bureaucrats, but its responses to resistance depart dramatically from the Japanese example. Encountering only acute but short-lived opposition to nuclear power, and able to marginalize resistance from ecologists and from their allies within civil society, the French state continues to rely on coercion and expropriation in the siting of reactors.

The Conclusion extends the discussion of civil society–state interaction into three areas: Machiavellian state behavior, the importance of competition in developing states' toolkits, and the future of siting public bads. Contrary to popular expectations, advanced industrial democracies do not automatically adopt teleological paths toward transparency, openness, and accessibility over time. Rather, states continue to rely on coercive tools when handling divisive problems, creating and using broader and softer state policy instruments only after extended periods of contention with civil society. The Conclusion ends with a look at the next decades of struggle between states and societies over controversial facilities.

# PICKING SITES

HOW AUTHORITIES SITE PUBLIC BADS is a matter of great controversy among observers. This chapter argues that authorities base their choice among technically appropriate sites on the strength of local civil society. In a handful of cases, powerful legislators intervene in the siting process to place these projects in their own districts. Available data from Japan support these explanations over other accounts, including concentrations of minorities, partisan discrimination, and local economic conditions.

## Explanations for Siting

Different observers see dissimilar landscapes when analyzing how authorities choose where to locate public bads. Table 2 lays out six approaches along with their key siting criteria. Whether in Japan, France, or the United States, government officials and developers involved in choosing locations for such projects typically hold that *technocratic criteria*—earthquake-resistant bedrock, sufficient water supply, distance to existing infrastructure—dictate site choices (author's interviews, 2002–2003). Areas that meet such specified technical qualifications as the ability to withstand strong seismic activity, or proximity to electrical grid and transportation networks, are ranked accordingly. Public officials regularly defend their siting of projects on the basis of such neutral technical criteria (Morone and Woodhouse 1989, 75; Denki jigyō kōza henshū iinkai 1997, 278–279; Quah and Tan 2002, 19). These neutral criteria do exclude inappropriate sites, but placement within feasible locations is not random. Once necessary technical features for sites have been taken into account, other factors influence the siting decision.

A landscape centered on *partisan discrimination* might be painted in shades of blue and red (in the United States) or green and red (in Europe) to reflect local political support for opposition or in-office factions. Researchers who adopt this approach argue that in one-party-dominant systems, such as Japan,

Table 2. Six explanations for siting outcomes

| Explanation | Logic | Key siting criteria |
| --- | --- | --- |
| Technocratic criteria | Bureaucrats control siting process, overlooking politics and local feedback. | Hydrology, geology, and meteorology |
| Partisan discrimination | Dominant political party punishes political opponents. | Concentration of political opponents |
| Environmental racism | Racial/ethnic majority punishes minority. | Concentration of ethnic and racial minorities |
| Economic conditions | Wealthy neighborhoods push away facilities; poorer ones seek potential jobs, taxes, and income. | Socioeconomic status of community |
| Political intervention | Strong politicians bring home what they see as pork" or push away "bads." | Number and strength of legislators to intervene in process |
| Civil society characteristics | Mobilization against facilities depends upon quality and capacity of voluntary groups. | Solidarity and relative strength of groups within civil society |

Mexico, and Sweden, towns supporting the opposition party are punished with a higher concentration of public bads such as nuclear power plants (Ramseyer and Rosenbluth 1993, 129). In Japan, for example, towns and villages that strongly support Socialist or Communist parliament members would be saddled with unwanted facilities as payback for their opposition to the dominant Liberal Democratic Party, and communities that have long supported the LDP would be expected to be free of such facilities. Fiona McGillivray (1997, 586) makes a similar argument about high-discipline, majoritarian systems: "The government will inflict costs on party loyal districts while providing protection to industries concentrated in marginal districts. In low party discipline majoritarian systems, such as the United States, industries in marginal seats are the least likely to receive favorable levels of protection." Although past studies have argued for this approach, I find no supporting evidence that Japan's long-ruling LDP punishes opposition-supporting localities.

Proponents of the *environmental racism* argument see controversial and unwanted facilities located in clusters of ethnic, racial, and religious minorities (Falk 1982; Gould 1986; Austin and Schill 1991; Hurley 1995; Pastor, Sadd, and Hipp 2001). Such landscapes center on disadvantaged groups who bear the brunt of public bads. In the United States, for example, many waste repositories and incinerators are found in communities with large populations of African Americans, Native Americans, and Hispanics (Bullard 1994). A variety of community advocacy groups have formed to combat what they see as policies harmful to communities of people of color. Given the small numbers of minorities and the technical requirements for large-scale projects, however, this explanation cannot apply to nuclear power plant, dam, and airport siting in Japan.[1] One can dismiss arguments that Japanese authorities site such facilities in areas with high concentrations of minorities, since in fact they cannot be located in large metropoles. Further, second-level tests of the environmental racism hypothesis uncover no systematic attempts to locate nuclear power plants, dams, or airports in Hokkaido and Okinawa, areas known for their minority populations.

Another common explanation for the siting of public bads focuses on the *economic conditions* in local communities. For example, small towns in rural North Carolina are said to view prisons as public goods because they bring jobs and other economic benefits (Hoyman 2001), despite fears of jail breaks, riots, and negative effects on the neighborhood. Others argue that such facilities as industrial waste dumps and incinerators are likely to be found in communities with lower levels of income (Mohai and Bryant 1992). But I find little evidence that economic conditions determine these siting outcomes, for economic conditions in communities selected for these public bads differ little from those in similar rural towns nearby that were not chosen. Around 41 percent of workers in Japanese towns selected to host nuclear power plants, for example, are in white-collar occupations, on average only 1 percent less

---

1. Of course, this absence does not indicate that siting decisions in Japan never involve racism or discrimination. Finding evidence for siting discrimination against minorities is difficult, as Japan's four recognized ethnic and demographic minorities—Okinawans, Ainu, Koreans, and *burakumin*—together constitute only 6 percent of Japan's population. *Burakumin,* literally "village people," are physiologically the same as mainstream Japanese but have been discriminated against since the feudal era because their ancestors were involved in undertaking, leatherwork, and butchering. The census counts the *burakumin* at approximately one million. Some groups, such as *zainichi* (resident) Koreans, who number close to 800,000, were forced to register with the state as aliens (despite long-term residence in Japan), whereas Okinawans and *burakumin,* for example, encounter fewer official restrictions and physically resemble their mainstream Japanese counterparts. The government numbers the Ainu at fewer than 20,000 and Okinawans close to a million. Many Okinawans remain in the island chain once known as the Ryukyus; indigenous Ainu people are clustered in Hokkaido; Koreans and *burakumin* are often found in urban neighborhoods in Kyoto, Osaka, and Tokyo. Stories of ethnic, occupational, and social discrimination against these groups are common, and many Okinawans argue that they have been burdened with much of the North American military presence because of long-difficult relations with Japan's main island. Given the necessary geologic constraints of nuclear power plants, dams, and airports, however, siting them in densely populated urban areas—which also house many *burakumin* and Korean residents—is impossible.

than in towns that meet the same technical requirements but were not selected as hosts. Studies of waste facilities in Canada similarly dismissed claims that their siting was based on economic disadvantage, whether measured in terms of either income or unemployment (Castle and Munton 1996, 78).

Another map of siting would focus on clusters of powerful politicians to illuminate *political intervention*. Analysts have shown that both politicians and governmental authorities do manipulate benefits and costs to fall on specific constituencies, within certain constraints. As "agenda setting [is] fundamentally biased in favor of those who possess the most resources" (Berry, Portney, and Thomson 1993, 103), powerful incumbent legislators can intervene to alter bureaucratic processes so as to focus costs and benefits on a locality-by-locality basis (Weingast, Shepsle, and Johnsen 1981, 643). In the late 1970s, for example, government bureaucrats at the Tennessee Valley Authority, working to complete the planned Tellico Dam, found themselves blocked by the discovery of an endangered fish in the local waters. Fearing that the Endangered Species Act would terminate the dam plans, Congressman John Duncan offered an amendment to a "sleepy and near empty House of Representatives" that exempted the project from the act. On a voice vote that took less than a minute, political intervention saved the project and provided jobs, infrastructure, and revenue to affected areas (Wheeler and McDonald 1986, 212). Similarly, North Carolina politicians have intervened to guide prisons to their districts even though earlier site selections have not favored their constituencies (Hoyman and Weinberg 2006). Japanese politicians do occasionally intervene when they have sufficient political power to override bureaucrats and siting authorities, but doing so requires that several powerful legislators work together to override decision-making processes.

A final map of the siting landscape highlights the *characteristics of civil society*. This approach centers on the relative strength of horizontal associations, the ties between individuals, and the depth of shared norms and behavioral expectations. Previous research linked how closely local citizens work and play together to their ability to impact projects slated for their backyards. Research on siting in North America has demonstrated that private developers avoid areas of high potential to mobilize against their projects (Hamilton 1993). Authorities recognize that tighter-knit, better-connected communities will mobilize more strongly against proposed public bads than those with looser connections. For example, local areas made up of homogeneous constituents—that is, those with strong horizontal bonds between citizens—are more likely to create zoning policies that exclude unwanted group homes (Clingermayer 1994). The more social capital in a community and the better its networks, the easier it is for antifacility groups to mobilize and organize against unwanted projects. I find strong evidence in Japan that the quality and relative capacity of social capital in localities influence site selection authorities exclude those areas with stronger and more numerous social ties and in favor of localities with weaker connections.

## Siting Decisions, Civil Society, and Proxies

Decision makers choose from an array of sites that meet geographic and geological criteria and then select the localities that seem most likely to cooperate, or least likely to resist, as host communities. State authorities base their estimates on both the *quality* and *relative capacity* of civil society (cf. Tilly 1994; Sheingate 2001). The *quality* of civil society is the strength and depth of bonds between citizens; neighborhood associations with high levels of participation, for example, can better monitor crime, push for upgrades to local facilities, and maintain community standards than those with declining or nonactive memberships. Previous studies have shown that rapid population growth increases turnover (Hammel 1990, 185), breaks apart community connections, and increases alienation (Freudenburg 1984). Rapid population changes that are due to events such as economic development are often associated with broad, negative social impacts such as increases in crime (Siegel and Alwang 2005, 7), increases in gang population (Spergel 1990, 232), and a breakdown in local networks. Areas where population levels have remained stable are more likely to have intact social networks that allow citizens to overcome collective action problems and to mobilize for such purposes as protesting unwanted facilities.

Authorities envision localities experiencing a large influx of newcomers as good hosts for controversial facilities because protest efforts in these communities are more vulnerable than elsewhere and likely to fracture under pressure (Putnam 1993; Munton 1996, 307). When bureaucrats and developers can site in areas where low potential for resistance is due to nonexistent or low-quality social capital, they do so. The Palo Verde nuclear power plant complex in Arizona, for example, optimizes the siting goals of planners, as census and ZIP code data reveal the abutting population to be zero; the reactors literally sit in the center of a desert. Planners for the new Denver airport found an ideal site: 4,450 hectares of uninhabited land in Adams County, located adjacent to the defunct but heavily polluted Rocky Mountain Arsenal site (Altshuler and Luberoff 2003, 159). In Japan, existing nuclear power plants have been placed in depopulating areas with less than one-third the average nationwide population density (Oikawa 2002). Because past research has demonstrated that rapid population change, either up or down, affects the quality of social ties, I measure community solidarity in Japanese localities through change in population from 1950 until the time of the siting attempt in order to capture broad trends in local ties.

The *relative capacity* of social capital can be determined by comparing the size of participating organizations' memberships with that of their opponents and competing groups. For example, Robert Putnam (2000) mourns declining membership and participation rates in community, fraternal, and civic organizations as signs of disengagement from political and public life. Sheingate (2001, 27) emphasizes that organizations with higher relative capacity maintain advantages over competing groups because they can better capture limited resources. As in previous studies of facility siting, the relevant civic groups most likely to be active in siting processes for controversial facilities are cooperatives made up of farmers and fishermen (cf. Lesbirel 1998; Garcia-Gorena 1999). Because the technical requirements for nuclear power plants, dams, and airports regularly place these facilities in rural areas, these primary-sector workers often participate in siting processes and, more important, regularly join together in collectives and associations. In Japan, fishermen's cooperatives (*gyogyō rōdō kumiai*) hold veto powers over the siting process (Tsebelis 2002); for the plant to proceed, a majority must agree on a contract with site developers (Lesbirel 1998; Aldrich 2005a).[2]

Furthermore, the concerns of fishermen and farmers have been heightened by past accidents and by the potential impact on their livelihood. Developers sited all Japan's nuclear power plants near the ocean, where the process of cooling the reactors draws in ocean water and expels waste water at a temperature 6 degrees Celsius higher than that of ambient water. Fishermen became alarmed over this practice after studies showed that the plants were releasing not only hot water but radioactive elements into the ocean (NGSK 10/2 [1966]; *AS*, 23 March 1972; CNFC 36 [2002]: 3). Along with fears about direct effects on their jobs and health, fishermen and farmers regularly express concern about "nuclear blight": that is, the contamination of their produce and harvests, and sales lost because of fears or rumors of radioactivity (see Tabusa 1992, 244).

The Japanese government and utility developers have long recognized the importance of studying the concentration of fishermen in potential public-bad sites. When the Tokyo Electric Power Company (TEPCO) worked with MITI to site reactors in Fukushima prefecture in the early 1960s, it measured levels of commercial fishing and took into account membership in local

2. Savvy politicians such as Prime Minister Kakuei Tanaka (who served from 1972 to 1974) quickly recognized the importance of properly handling, through redistributive payments, the fishermen involved in nuclear power plant siting attempts (Tanaka 1972).

fishing cooperatives. Argument for siting in the area of Futaba-machi hinged on the point that it was "not an important area for fishing" (NGSK 8/6 [1964]: 21). Similarly, when Chubu Electric Power Company began to survey the Ashihama district near the Kumano Sea, it predicted that the area would be more amenable to nuclear power plant siting than the nearby village of Os-hiraike because it had fewer fishermen's cooperatives (NGSK 8/8 [1964]: 42). Nuclear plant developers bemoaned the fact that even though they had done their best to pick rural areas where resistance would be low, local fishing coop-eratives would likely cause "problems to arise over new projects." Fishermen sought to move beyond local issues when they organized a national forum of fishing unions to discuss the problem of siting (NGSK 10/11 [1966]: 15).

Political power can increase with both absolute (Acemoglu and Robinson 2001; Fung 2004) and relative (Sheingate 2001) group size. Larger groups can amass more votes and donations, as well as letter writers and protesters, and can better pressure state leaders and decision makers. When facing off against competing civil society organizations, relatively stronger groups can better achieve their goals. Smaller groups, conversely, are less powerful, less able to bring political power to bear on decision makers.[3] In reviewing potential host communities, however, I found that the long-term capacity of voluntary asso-ciations, not just the size of relevant groups at the initial siting attempt, forms the core concern for state authorities: facilities such as Logan International Airport's additional runway in Boston and the Higashidōri nuclear plant in Japan can take up to three decades to site (AP News, 18 April 2005; Lesbirel 1998). Siting authorities analyzing potential sites for atomic reactors in Japan, for example, calculate that villages suffering from problems such as depopu-lation of fishermen, low community solidarity, and pollution are less able to resist siting attempts, which might still be going on in twenty years.

State authorities and developers can forecast the mobilization capacity of Japanese fishing and farming collectives using a variety of signals identifiable before the siting process begins; these range from changes in the volume of fish catches over time to demographic trends in the area. Ideally, investigators would

---

3. Scholars have long argued that small interest groups are easiest for the state to handle. For example, they have focused on the fact that industrialized nations regularly protect farmers, perhaps because of interests in "food security," nostalgia for the farm sector, or sympathy for a clearly rec-ognizable group. Lindert (1991, 56) takes a different approach, viewing farmers as one interest or pressure group among many that compete for rents; he argues "Part of the logic is that appeasing a smaller group is cheaper." That is, if the state must pay off certain groups through redistribution, its costs are lower with smaller target populations. The size of the subsidized group is an important factor in determining its effect on policies. Size matters, and not just in the short term.

have access to data that describe changes in membership in local fishermen's and farmers' cooperatives vis-à-vis competing interest groups across Japan for five decades. Measuring change in the relative strength of civil society groups is important, since static membership numbers would not reflect potential shifts in environmental and demographic conditions over a siting process that could take decades. These data were not systematically available, given both the extended time period for the study and the lack of consistent record keeping; instead, I measure the change in the percentage of workers employed in the primary sector from 1980 through 1995 as a proxy for the quantity of social capital.[4] This somewhat cumbersome formula uses the best information available to reflect the relative strength of relevant civil society groups in the locality.

Calculations show that in such localities less than 1 percent of the primary sector is involved in practices other than fishing or farming, such as mining; therefore this figure captures the capacity of farmers and fishermen in the locality. Furthermore, because of economic and social pressures on farmers and the fact that joint fishery rights and licenses for operations are granted almost exclusively to fishery associations (Ruddle 1987), membership rates in cooperatives and associations for Japanese farmers and fishermen are well above 98 percent (author's communications with Aurelia George Mulgan and Kenneth Ruddle, 11 February 2006). Utilizing the change in percentage of employment in the area captures the relative strength of relevant anti-facility horizontal associations vis-à-vis their communities and potential opponents over the fifteen-year period. Fishing or farming that has precipitously decreased over time, relative to other areas of employment in a given village, indicates that the primary sector is losing its standing and thus its political power in the community. Though not ideal, this proxy provides a high-quality estimate of over-time capacity of fishing and farming cooperatives; that is, it captures the strength of groups within civil society most likely to participate in and perhaps block siting attempts (see Appendix 2).

## The Data Set

To evaluate patterns systematically in siting public bads, I created a data set of approximately 500 Japanese localities from 1955 to 1995, using a variety of

---

4. Previous research on siting choices relies on similar proxy variables when other systematic data is not available. For example, Hamilton (1993, 107) uses the percentage of the voting age population that voted in the 1980 presidential election "to measure the potential for residents to overcome free-rider problems and engage in collective action."

sources (listed in Appendix 1). The data set contains only localities that meet the technical (geographical and geological) criteria for siting, such as land impermeable to water and resistant to seismic shocks for dams (see Takada 1954). A full or even random sample of some of the 3,000 villages and towns across Japan would not provide much leverage on the problem, as one does not find nuclear power plants located in downtown Tokyo or Osaka, or airports on the tops of mountains. To exclude technically inappropriate sites, I filtered cases through a matching process using GIS (Geographic Information System) data.[5]

I used an *equal-shares, choice-based* sampling method (see King and Zeng 2001a, 2001b; King, Keohane, and Verba 1994, sec. 4.4.2) with politically defined localities (towns, cities, and villages) as the units of analysis; this process generated 475 observations across more than 250 variables, including temporal, political, demographic, and economic indicators. I deliberately selected observations to include the entire universe of facility-host communities in which state agencies played a major role. By collecting observations in localities where attempts were made to site a nuclear plant, dam, or airport (which may or may not have been completed), along with carefully matched observations in localities that shared the same geographic, geologic, and temporal characteristics but where no controversial facility was proposed, I achieved greater analytical power with fewer total observations.

Along with variables capturing aspects of the six main approaches to siting, I controlled for a variety of factors, such as district magnitude, population density, the area of the village or town, and time period, as seen in table 3. Appendixes 1 and 2 provide additional details on the sources for the data set, the creation of the data set and variable proxies, and weighting correction.

In analyzing the data set, I have built on previous work (Hamilton 1993, 102; Lesbirel 1998; Hamilton and Viscusi 1999; Wolverton 2002) that models the siting of public bads and controversial facilities as the function of a variety of factors. Research has confirmed that nuclear plants, airports, and dams come with different levels of perceived risk, nuclear power being the most feared, dams second, and airports third. Although analyzing these different nuisance facilities as a single group would provide greater confidence about predictions, it would simultaneously obscure the effects associated with each facility type. Therefore, I took facility type into account along with

---

5. Landlocked prefectures are not suitable for nuclear power plants, nor are areas with high concentrations of alluvial soil, which would require extensive reworking to support the weight of such facilities. Airports require some distance from heavily populated areas and access to land transportation networks. See Appendix 2 for a full description of exclusionary criteria.

Table 3. Descriptive statistics of siting data, 1945–1995

| Variable | Description | Mean | Standard deviation | Min. | Max. |
|---|---|---|---|---|---|
| *Dependent Variables:* | *Siting Outcomes* | | | | |
| Inclusion/exclusion | Dummy variable; 0 if no attempt, 1 if attempt | 0.494 | 0.500 | 0 | 1 |
| Overall siting outcome | Three-step ordinal variable; 0 if no attempt, 1 if attempt failed, 2 if attempt succeeded | 0.875 | 0.935 | 0 | 2 |
| *Independent Variables:* | *Civil Society and Powerful Politicians* | | | | |
| Civil society quality | % Population change from 1950 until the siting attempt | 0.01 | 0.707 | −0.78 | 6.378 |
| Civil society capacity | Change in percentage of primary sector employment, 1980–1995 | −0.32 | 0.216 | −0.88 | 0.623 |
| Powerful politicians | Number of LDP members serving 6+ consecutive terms | 1.644 | 1.010 | 0 | 4 |
| | *Political, Economic, and Demographic Characteristics* | | | | |
| Post 1975 | Dummy variable; 1 if siting attempt in or after 1975, 0 if before | 0.625 | 0.485 | 0 | 1 |
| Town area | Square kilometers | 136 | 139.203 | 3 | 869.1 |
| Population density | Population per square kilometer | 509.2 | 1321.484 | 5.6 | 14652 |
| District magnitude | Number of Lower House seats | 4.097 | 0.816 | 2 | 6 |
| Economic growth | Change in tertiary sector, 1980–1995 | 0.155 | 0.193 | −0.4 | 1.368 |

*(continued)*

Table 3—cont.

| Variable | Description | Mean | Standard deviation | Min. | Max. |
|---|---|---|---|---|---|
| | *Majority Party* | | | | |
| Over time support | Average prefectural LDP vote share in Upper House elections, 1956–1989 | 0.517 | 0.084 | 0.27 | 0.678 |
| Percentage in Lower House | Percentage of seats from the district held by LDP members | 0.639 | 0.188 | 0 | 1 |
| Number of Reps in Lower House | Number of LDP seats in Lower House | 2.566 | 0.840 | 0 | 5 |
| Presence of Prime Minister | Number of LDP politicians in office during siting who served or would go on to serve as prime minister | 0.114 | 0.332 | 0 | 2 |
| | *Opposition Party* | | | | |
| Socialists in LH | Number of Socialists in the Lower House | 1.002 | 0.616 | 0 | 3 |
| Communists in LH | Number of Communists in the Lower House | 0.087 | 0.282 | 0 | 1 |
| Other party members in Lower House | Number of seats held by other parties | 0.417 | 0.685 | 0 | 4 |
| | *Minority Concentration* | | | | |
| Minority representation (1) | Dummy variable; 1 if siting attempt in Hokkaido, 0 if not | 0.072 | 0.259 | 0 | 1 |
| Minority representation (2) | Dummy variable; 1 if siting attempt in Okinawa, 0 if not | 0.017 | 0.129 | 0 | 1 |

other factors, usually analyzing each class of public bads by itself. To do so, I used both rare-event logit (*relogit*) and ordered probit (*oprobit*) analyses to tease out the individual effects of factors related to civil society and powerful politicians along with economic, demographic, and political variables on a data set of technically appropriate sites.

This data set reveals both how localities are chosen for sites and whether or not those siting attempts succeed. One way to envision this siting process is to see it as occurring in two stages. Authorities make an initial choice of a host from among technically feasible areas. If excluded, a locality is out of the picture; if it is included, the process moves forward to the next round where local political, demographic, and temporal factors shape the outcome and determine whether the siting succeeds or fails. I used two separate (re)logit models to illustrate this two-stage approach. Logistic regression involves a binary variable (selected / not selected in the first stage; successful / failed attempt in the second) and follows the Bernoulli probability function. The events studied here are rare—that is, in most instances Japanese towns were not selected as hosts for controversial facilities—so the standard logit form provides biased estimators. It was to address this concerns that I used a relogit model developed by King and Zeng (2001a, 2001b).

Another way to view the siting process is as a spectrum. Depending on the strength of organized civil society, siting authorities can view some localities as willing to accept the facility in question, others as less willing, and some as completely unwilling to do so. I used this second model to confirm that the coefficient estimates were not strongly affected by the two-stage *relogit* model type. To reflect this approach statistically, I carried out an *oprobit* analysis with a three-category ordinal dependent variable. The three categories were (0) not being selected for a controversial facility; (1) being selected for a facility but failing to complete the project because of resistance; and (2) being selected for a controversial facility and allowing it to carry through to completion. Imaging a continuum from areas where authorities forgo siting because they believe the town will be resistant, to towns where authorities are more willing to site even with some probability of failure, to a guaranteed success shows that an ordered probit model may better capture the actual dynamics of the selection process.

Instead of unreadable conventional tables of coefficient estimators, I provide simulations and confidence intervals that produce more intuitive displays of the variables (standard coefficient tables are available on the author's website). Confidence intervals "express the appropriate degree of certainty around... quantities," whereas simulation techniques allow one to "extract the currently overlooked information" and "interpret and present it in a reader-friendly manner" (King,

Tomz, and Wittenberg 2000, 341). The predicted probability of interest is displayed as a solid line, with dotted lines bounding it on either side to show the 95 percent confidence intervals. For these simulations I set all independent variables at their means except for the quantity of interest. Weighted estimators are considered more reliable than prior corrected estimators because of the possibility of model misspecification, but in many cases analytic limits prevented the proper calculation of estimators using the actual weight correction (i.e., .0016). The smallest weighting value that would resolve computationally was far larger, at .006, than the actual frequency in the population. The graphs found throughout this text are based on the results from the prior corrected estimators.

### Results: Siting Nuclear Power Plants in Japan

In general, my statistical work demonstrates that civil society proved to be the most significant factor in site selection. Within a pool of technically appropriate sites, developer's selection of host communities for nuclear power plants in Japan has been based on the quality and quantity of civil society. In some cases, where powerful politicians can override decision-making processes, political intervention draws these facilities into constituencies of longtime Liberal Democratic Party incumbents. The data do not support arguments about siting based on political discrimination, economic conditions, or minority concentration; for example, no larger-than-expected numbers of nuclear power plants are found in prefectures such as Hokkaido and Okinawa, which have large concentrations of minority groups. Instead, as predicted by the civil society approach, authorities were most likely to attempt to site reactors in communities with low community solidarity and diminished or decreasing levels of social capital.

Authorities looking ahead to potentially decades-long processes of siting focused closely on civil society measures; in the Japanese context these turn on indicators of relative strength over time in fishing and farming cooperatives. Areas that would lose or were already losing farmers and fishermen at high rates were judged to have weak civil societies and were targeted as potential host communities. Figure 1 displays the predicted probability that a technically suitable town or village in Japan will be selected as a host community for a nuclear power plant, depending on the shifts in the relative capacity of groups in civil society. The numbers on the x-axis indicate the change in the membership of civil society groups: 0 indicates no change; .5 indicates a 50 percent increase in their number, and −.5 indicates a decrease of 50 percent. As the

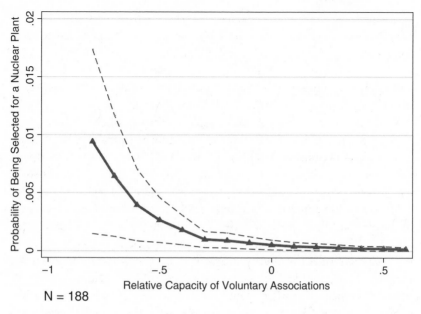

Figure 1. Weaker anti-facility civil society increases probability of selection

figure shows, a village or town that lost 80 percent of its capacity over time was almost one hundred times as likely to be chosen to host a nuclear power plant as one that merely maintained its population of fishermen and farmers.

Fishermen and farmers perceive reactors as causing "nuclear blight": either actual damage to health, produce, and livelihood or fears among food purchasers about radioactive contamination of food. As long as local fishing and farming cooperatives could at least maintain their relative strength over time, they were judged as effective at fighting off proposed public bads as those areas that increased their membership. On the other hand, in areas where the fishing and farming cooperatives were losing capacity, their chances of being chosen as a site rapidly increased, as indicated by the steep curve rising from the point where relative voluntary group strength drops by more than 20 percent. For example, in the village of Tomari, on the northern island of Hokkaido, those cooperatives experienced drastic relative losses. Initially, a third of the village workers belonged to them, but by 1995 less than 5 percent remained engaged in those occupations (with little shift in overall population). With fewer association members available to resist, Tomari ended up being selected for not just one but three nuclear plants. By contrast, in the nearby village of Taisei, also on the northern island of Hokkaido, close to one-fourth of the working population continued as fishers and farmers over the same period, and because of this stronger social capital, it was not selected as a host community. Notice also that for local communities, strengthening farming and fishing employment—that is, increasing the strength of these local groups within civil society—had no more impact on warding off proposed plants than merely maintaining the current levels of those groups.

Along with the quantity of social capital, the quality of civil society played a role in siting decisions for nuclear power plants in Japan. Areas with lower levels of interpersonal trust and fewer interconnections and local networks were more likely to be chosen as hosts than those with stable, intact networks, which were better able to fend off selection. Figure 2 shows that areas that either lost overall population or maintained it were far less likely to be chosen for plants than those where population rose by 80 percent or more. As mentioned previously, a large sociological literature on "boomtowns" underscores the alienation, fragmentation, and lack of unity that accompany population increases. The threshold for this effect was close to 100 percent; that is, the village or town needed nearly to double in population for the boomtown effect to take place. For Japanese towns and cities close to the nation's larger cities, a doubling of population is not uncommon. For example, the town of Ōmiya

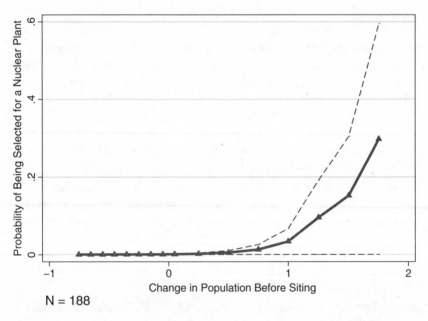

N = 188

Figure 2. Decreasing community solidarity increases chance of selection as host community

in Saitama prefecture more than doubled its population over two decades, this surge weakened existing ties between neighbors, and the influx of newcomers made it difficult to establish the bonds and then strong ties needed for old and new residents to work together against a facility. Given its fragmented populace, developers selected it as a host community. Similarly, Kumatori near Osaka, once a village of only around 10,000 people, found its population swelling by 30,000 new residents over the pre-siting period and, like Ōmiya, was selected as a host for nuclear power plants. Cities and villages that experience a burst in population, finding it difficult to maintain the social networks and ties that facilitate collective action, are less able to present a united front against siting, and their resistance is more likely to fragment under pressures such as offers of compensation.

Although estimates of civil society strength (both quality and quantity) drive siting decisions, powerful legislators can intervene in the process and skew it to pull projects *into* their districts. In Japan, powerful LDP politicians who have served six consecutive terms or more are usually promoted to cabinet-level positions. These conservative, pro-growth politicians, known as *daijin,* regularly traveled to communities resisting nuclear power plant siting to support pronuclear mayors and urge local residents to see nuclear power as safe and necessary (*Nikkei,* 17 March 1981; NGSK 3 (1981): 35). Figure 3 shows

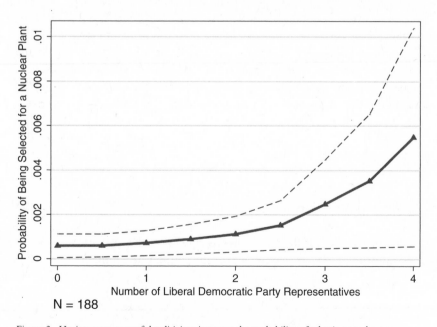

Figure 3. Having more powerful politicians increases the probability of selection as a host

that communities without powerful politicians were only one-sixth as likely to be chosen as their counterparts with four or more such LDP representatives.

In the early 1980s, LDP members also formed national pronuclear organizations within their party headquarters in the early 1980s to assist in siting new nuclear reactors around the country. Folk theorems—often premised on the American electoral system—argue that powerful politicians should shield their constituents against these often dreaded facilities (and instead bring in such facilities as docks and bridges), but in fact, support from the business community pushes politicians to seek them out. As one researcher argues, "Many local politicians in Japan... actually benefit politically and electorally from actively promoting noxious facilities in their own electorates because of the economic benefits yielded" (Lesbirel 1998, 8). In many interviews, LDP Diet members discussed their strong support for these projects and argued forcefully that they should not be seen as unwanted or controversial facilities (*meiwaku shisetsu*). Powerful politicians, such as the former prime minister Kakuei Tanaka, openly discussed their successful drives to bring nuclear projects to their electoral districts (Tanaka 1972; Schlesinger 1997, 72, 103).[6]

The town of Kashima in Shimane prefecture lost only about 17 percent of its fishers and farmers, and its population dropped slightly, yet it was selected as a host for nuclear power plants—evidently because its four long-term, incumbent LDP representatives in the national legislature held sufficient power to override siting authorities. The politicians from Kashima included Noboru Takeshita, who would become a powerful prime minister, and some less-known, long-term incumbents such as Yoshi Sakurauchi. Similarly, the town of Kariwa in Niigata prefecture had four *daijin,* including Kakuei Tanaka and Shin Sakurai, an LDP member who later served as head of the Environmental Agency. Kariwa and its sister city of Kashiwazaki eventually hosted seven reactors. Interestingly, electing just one powerful legislator who becomes prime minister is not enough to bring a reactor to an area (I tested this hypothesis); making that happen actually takes several powerful legislators.

## Siting Airports in Japan

When the divisive facility being sited is an airport, the quantity, but not the quality, of local civil society strongly affects siting decisions. As is true for

---

6. Tanaka displayed his savvy at pork-barrel politics when he set up the Local Development Subcommittee in the House of Representatives in 1949 to help site hydroelectric dams and other public works projects in home districts (Calder 1998a, 301).

nuclear power plants, once authorities have excluded nonsuitable sites, their decisions are not influenced by minority group concentrations, political discrimination against minority opposition parties, or local economic factors. Instead, the Ministry of Transportation pays close attention to the strength of important groups within civil society, primarily local associations of farmers and fishermen. Figure 4 shows that areas where the relative capacity of these groups is weakening are far more likely to be selected as host communities than their counterparts with stronger fishing and farming communities; a community that has lost more than 75 percent of its relative strength in members of cooperatives and unions is more than ten times as likely to be chosen as the site for an airport.

Because airports need vast open spaces, authorities regularly expropriate available farmland; thus farmers make up the largest segment of civil society affected by airports. Authorities most often locate airports in low-lying areas, and it is hard to find similar land for relocating local agricultural families. (Finding replacement land for dams is easier, because nearby mountains can literally be leveled to create more space.) Hence, areas with stronger local civil society, as measured by healthier first-sector employment, are better able to mobilize allies to fight against airport proposals. Allies and political insiders greatly assist societal movements in opposing airports (Giugni 2004).

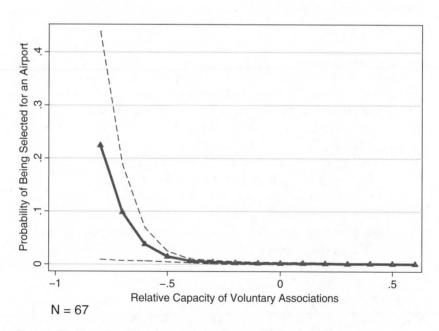

N = 67

Figure 4. Having weaker civil society associations increases likelihood of selection for airport

The deeply rooted and potentially explosive social capital held by farming associations was most visible in the notorious Narita Airport siting case. In Chiba prefecture, where that airport is located, the agricultural sector actually grew over the decades before the airport was proposed. After World War II, many demobilized soldiers and repatriated colonial families were brought to the area called Narita, which was partly an imperial estate, to work as farmers. In an uncommon display of violent resistance, these communities mobilized quickly to resist the siting of the New Tokyo International Airport, stalling its opening by more than seven years and bringing about nearly thirty years of conflict with state security forces (see chapter 3). This level of conflict is unusual, but not the fact that an increase in the farming population made it better able to work in concert against the facility.

Powerful politicians and overall levels of community solidarity play a smaller role in site selection for airports, compared with siting nuclear plants. I believe this is so because the associated levels of dread and fear are far lower than for nuclear power plants; thus, extraregional groups within civil society are less likely to mobilize as allies. Researchers have noted the difficulties in forming anti-airport coalitions even in the United States, where airport expansions and sitings have faced repeated opposition (Altshuler and Luberoff 2003, 163).

## Siting Dams in Japan

In decisions on siting dams, the weakness or strength of civil society and the presence of powerful politicians rarely have much impact. Similarly, theories about political or minority discrimination and economic conditions are not supported by these cases. Instead, the size of the locality and the time period in which the dam is proposed best explain which locality will be chosen, and when, from among a pool of similarly suitable sites.

A town of 800 square kilometers, then, is ten times more likely to be chosen for a dam project than a town of only 200 square kilometers; larger towns likely have more unused land and lower land prices. Larger localities are not any more likely to have water nearby, however. Perhaps most important, larger towns generally have lower population densities; with fewer people per square kilometer, they may find it hard to rally local individuals to take collective action, whereas smaller and hence more densely populated towns and villages may have more individuals living in close proximity to one another and to the project and be better able to raise consciousness and activity levels about proposed dam projects. Still, as the quality and quantity of civil society and town area have virtually no correlation, the underlying relationship between town area and siting decisions remains unclear.

Communities considered after 1975 were *more* likely to have been chosen for dams than those considered in earlier periods. Interestingly, this finding contradicts earlier beliefs. Some speculate that over the postwar period, Japan gradually decreased investment in public works projects; although a standard argument was that authorities were more cautious about siting controversial projects after a shift in citizen consciousness in the mid-1970s, instead, in the 1980s and 1990s, towns were almost twice as likely to be selected as areas that had similar technocratic criteria in the pre-1970s.

There is no evidence that the groups within civil society most active in nuclear power plant and airport siting—cooperatives of fishermen and farmers—influence the siting process of dam projects. Even though some farmland may be lost to flooding, the bureaucracy regularly creates new farmland in the immediate vicinity by leveling nearby mountains (author's site visit, 2003). This is not possible with airports and nuclear power plants, which are often built in lower-lying areas where it is harder to create similar patches of new land ex nihilo; hence, perhaps because of the mitigation strategies used by the Ministry of Construction, the associations that might have fought hardest against those facilities are not doing so against dams.

## Success or Failure of Siting Attempts

Following investigation of the role that civil society plays in the selection of sites for nuclear power plants, airports, and dams, the next question is whether the same factors affect the completion or failure of the proposed projects. If states avoid siting in areas with strong local horizontal associations, enhanced social networks, and few powerful politicians, how do these same characteristics affect the *outcomes* of siting attempts? This question has not been thoroughly explored. For example, it may be that states cannot accurately forecast resistance based on estimates of social capital, and that areas with stronger civil society may be no better equipped to fight off the proposed facility than those with weaker social ties.

If a developer seeks to place a divisive facility in an area with relatively strong horizontal associations, how will it fare? As predicted by arguments about the impact of civil society on a state's policies, figure 5 shows that localities in Japan with high quantities of civil society are best equipped to fend off attempts to site all three types of facilities.

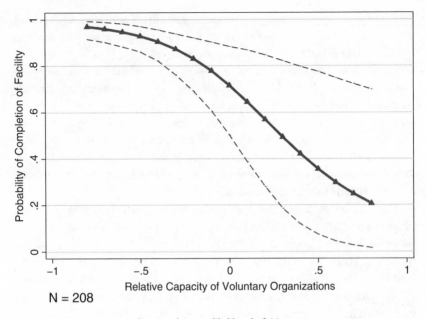

Figure 5. Having stronger civil society decreases likelihood of siting success

Areas where farming and fishing cooperatives have grown or stayed relatively strong are less likely than others to see a proposed public bad come to fruition in their locality. For example, an area that has increased the relative strength of its cooperatives by half has a 70 percent chance of stopping a project. But one that has lost close to three-quarters of its initial relative capacity of farmers and fishermen has a nearly 95 percent chance of seeing that facility come on line.

Another important factor in determining the outcome of siting attempts is the history of other public bads in the area. Once an initial public bad is located in a town or village, the chances of additional public bads being successfully located in that area jump drastically. As shown in figure 6, localities with an existing facility were most likely to see a new facility come to completion. An area that already has one nuclear power plant is far more likely to allow the siting of additional plants than those that have none. This figure shows that moving from having no prior public bads to having a single one increases by more than 20 percent the probability that a new proposed facility will be completed successfully. After an area hosts two controversial facilities, the success of future attempts is all but assured, which helps explain the large clusters of public bads, especially nuclear power plants, in towns in Japan: groups of six or seven reactors are often located within the same community, as in Kashiwazaki-Kariwa in Niigata prefecture.

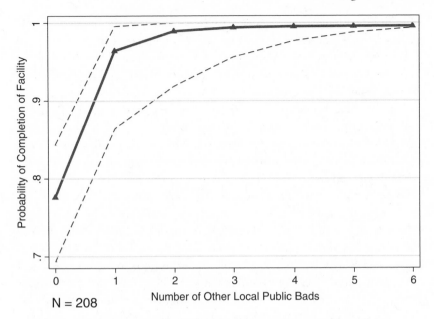

Figure 6. Presence of other public bads increases likelihood of future siting success

This clustering may be due to habituation: additional projects no longer entail large political costs because locals have become used to the idea of such a facility and engage in less opposition to new proposals. There may also be a sense of fatalism: the belief of community members that they will not be able to stop future projects dampens their activism. Alternatively, the community may have developed "skill sets" from its experience with siting the initial project: if locals know how to extract additional rents and revenues from the central government and how to overcome small but vocal opposition, later projects encounter less resistance.[7] Citizen activists criticize as "addiction" the tendency of local communities to get used to higher-than-normal budgets, thanks to the additional income brought by new public bads (Hasegawa 2004, 27). To maintain their spending levels and avoid going into debt, they are forced to take on additional projects.

Localities that have a strong civil society, in both quantity and quality, represent the biggest challenges to long-term siting plans. Such localities become more expensive targets for state authorities and developers in terms

---

7. Some describe local government officials learning how to extract additional resources from the Japanese central government under threat of sabotaging or stalling additional facilities.

of both time (contacting, negotiating with, or coercing the individuals) and money (if redistribution is used). On the other hand, areas with weaker civil society—perhaps because of worsening local environmental conditions, shifting demographics, or altered market conditions—present ideal targets for such projects as nuclear power plants and airports.

This chapter encapsulates the first of two arguments at the heart of this book. Using the best available data, I have argued that from a set of technically feasible sites, states initially base their choice of locations for controversial facilities on measures of civil society's local strength. Especially with the most dreaded and contested projects—nuclear power plants—civil society proves to be the most critical of several possible explanations for how sites are chosen. The relative capacity of associations, such as fishing and farming cooperatives, and the solidarity between neighbors in a community regularly and measurably impact state siting policies. States around the world, such as the United Kingdom, undertake similar investigations to estimate potential opposition within civil society, sometimes through straightforward surveys (Rüdig 1994, 84). American authorities seeking to place controversial facilities often carry out "windshield surveys": a surveyor drives through potential host communities looking for signs of weak community mobilization and fragmentation (Sherman 2006). French authorities may have selected several localities in Normandy because survey research showed that towns there were more favorable to siting than towns in other regions (data reproduced in Hecht 1998, 248). Even in France, known for its closed decision-making processes, bureaucrats sought to place nuclear power plants far from areas of potential resistance. Anecdotal evidence from multiple nations supports the findings from the Japanese cases: civil society vigor serves as the core siting determinative—though sometimes a sufficient number of powerful politicians can override this standard siting logic to draw in projects that they—whatever most of their constituency believes—imagine to be beneficial.

If technically possible, the state will place the project in an area with absolutely no local anti-facility civil society groups, often a remote location or offshore. The majority of Japanese airports built between 1998 and 2008, for example, have been either placed offshore or built on artificial landfill or floating islands or in an area already containing a public bad (such as another airport). The Japanese government now avoids "green field" siting of airports by siting facilities offshore or converting existing facilities.[8] In the United States, developers tend to place public bads in sites almost completely free of

8. Many of the large-scale airports managed by the Ministry of Transportation are former military bases converted into civilian airports. Haneda Airport in Tokyo—one of the area's first international

population: the Palo Verde nuclear power plant complex is in Arizona's desert, and the present Denver airport lies 25 miles (40 km) from downtown. Yucca Mountain sits on empty, federally owned land near sites where nuclear weapons have been tested both above- and belowground for five decades. Authorities recognize the benefits in avoiding areas with the potential for significant opposition, and scholars have argued that, for example, "all of the new airports built in U.S. urban areas during the 1960s and 1970s" were sited to avoid potential resistance from local civil society (Altshuler and Luberoff 2003, 204). For less dreaded facilities, such as dams, nonpolitical characteristics of the local community, such as available land, have an impact on selection. Approaches that emphasize local economic conditions, minority population, or discrimination against minority parties were not supported by my data.

Once a location has been chosen for a public bad, the strength of social capital again impacts state policy by increasing or decreasing the probability that the facility will be completed. Areas with strong civil society groups better resist siting attempts than those areas where groups are losing members. A community's history of having already accepted one public bad makes it less able to resist further siting attempts and more likely to receive future controversial facilities. This model maps well onto empirical observations of communities in North America and Japan that have "clusters" of public bads.

But, as the old saying goes, "Man plans, and God laughs." Despite avoiding communities with strong levels of social capital, state authorities often find themselves locked in a struggle even with carefully selected local communities and their extralocal allies. Whether states use coercion, incentives, or social control as tools to manage contentious political groups is a critical question for social scientists interested in state-society relations.

---

airports, though over time it became a primarily domestic hub—began operations in the early twentieth century as a flight school; next it became a Japanese military base and then an American base until it was turned over to civilian control (Tsuzaki 1980, 25). Similarly, the Nagoya Airport, which began as a military airfield in 1940, was used after the war by the American occupation forces; it was reopened to Japanese citizen use in 1952 (Nagoya Kūkō Birudingu Kabushiki Gaisha 1999). Osaka International Airport was built in January 1939 as an airfield, used by occupation forces as Itami Airfield until 1959, and then returned to Japanese use (OKK 1990; Gresser, Fujikura, and Morishima 1981, 164). Matsuyama Airport in Ehime Ken began as a military airfield in 1941, was utilized by the occupation forces in the postwar period, and was returned to Japanese custody in 1952 (Kokudokōtsūshō Ōsaka 2003).

# 2

# A LOGIC OF TOOL CHOICE

DEPENDING ON THE CHARACTERISTICS of organized civil society, the policy instruments that state agencies can select for handling conflict vary in visibility, power, and time scale. This chapter breaks new ground not only by presenting a viable framework for classifying and analyzing a state's toolkit but also by connecting the state's strategies to the characteristics of its civil society opponents.

Ever since Max Weber, social scientists have distinguished states from other political and social organizations by their monopoly over physical force. Force defines a state, as Machiavelli suggests in *The Prince;* however, he continues, it must be both a lion, to frighten wolves, and a fox, to recognize traps. A state that relies solely on force may fall into traps set by civil society opponents.[1] Although modern states remain coercive organizations, successful states do more than just use power; they also structure, pay off, and persuade. The modern state is distinguished from its ancestors not so much by its accumulation of power, which is considerable, as by the incredible scope of its powers. Yet not all states can, or do, choose to be lions or foxes as appropriate to the accomplishment of their plans; some nondemocratic nations, known as predatory states, do little more than extract resources and protect the interests they need in order to survive. Even some democratic countries have the reputation of steamrolling civil society, but others regularly accomplish a diverse array of public works despite considerable citizen resistance—and without resorting to force. Machiavelli's metaphor poses a central conundrum in understanding the spectrum of modern states: all states are part, if not all, lion, but not all states

---

1. "Lions cannot defend themselves against traps, and foxes cannot defend themselves against wolves. You have to be like a fox to see the traps, and like a lion to terrify the wolves." (Machiavelli 1532 [1999], chap. 18). Civil rights activists in the 1960s deliberately sought out media opportunities where local law enforcement would use hoses, police dogs, and truncheons on unarmed marchers, thus providing sympathetic nationwide media coverage. Some authorities learned from these experiences to avoid direct confrontation with protesters, thereby denying the movement media attention (Kryder 2000b).

are part fox. Why do some states develop the capacity to be foxes, while others do not? The answer to this question can deeply enhance an understanding of political development. It may also explain why some states are more successful than others in handling contestation without resorting to violence.

States are a unique organizational form, able not only to set policy goals that may conflict with those of civil society but able also to change and structure the political arena. States monopolize not only coercive force but also resource allocation, juridical power, arenas and regulations for deliberation, and political symbols of suasion. Therefore, they have many possible ways to pursue their designs. To take one example, when states seek to carry out costly and unpopular endeavors, such as war, they can do so coercively through a draft or by calling for a volunteer force. In 1793, France's Committee of Public Safety initiated a *levée en masse,* drafting peasants, farmers, and shopkeepers to create an army of more than a million men. Although the American military used a draft through the Vietnam War, backlash shifted its doctrine toward an all-volunteer force that relies chiefly on persuasion and patriotism to maintain its complement.[2] A state's tools or strategies are commonly taken to be simple functions or manifestations of its accumulated resources. In this approach, the amount of state resources matters more than how those resources are ultimately adapted, updated, and applied; the implication is that two equally equipped states should experience similar success when handling movements. This is not always the case, however, as the comparison of the French and Japanese nuclear power cases demonstrates (chapters 5 and 6).

### Conventional Theories of Tool Use

Previous investigations of policy tools have provided admirable descriptive categories for various instruments but little analytical leverage. While some researchers continue to define policy instruments as either "accommodative" or "oppressive," more detailed research has classified policy tools into categories of authority, incentive, capacity, symbolic, and learning (Schneider and Ingram

---

2. Instead of continuing to use its coercive powers to push younger Americans into the often dangerous and difficult job of soldiering, the state began to fund upbeat ad campaigns ("Be All That You Can Be"); supported financially or administratively the production of glamorous, promilitary movies (*Top Gun*) and television shows (*JAG*); and offered financial incentives (payment of existing student loans, additional support for future degrees) to pull them into the military. Here we see a lion transforming itself into a fox.

1990). Similarly, Mark Lichbach (1995) has laid out the ways in which states can raise the barriers to collective action for partisans and dissidents but has not provided a framework for predicting when certain tools will or will not be applied. That is, whereas these approaches lay out the broad range of tool types available to state authorities, these groupings are not accompanied by a logic of use. They provide a typology of labels for the tools available to decision makers but not the conditions under which the types of tools are more likely to be applied or avoided.

Some researchers have sought to link state characteristics to the strategies and policies that decision makers use in handling critical problems. Social scientists argue that "strong states" use toolkits different from those of "weak states" when dealing with economic and political phenomena. States with strong, centralized bureaucracies and few access points for citizens, such as Japan and France, may use a different set of tools than do nations that have less professionalized civil servants and more openings for citizen involvement, such as the United States and England (Zysman 1983; Ōtake and Nonaka 2000). For example, John L. Campbell (1988) argued that France and Japan hold more policy instruments for advancing commercial nuclear power than their counterparts in the United States. Sheldon Garon (1997) posited that Japanese authorities, far more than most Western nations, regularly use moral suasion as one of a variety of tactics of "social management" to bring citizen preferences into line with state plans.

Certain investigators argue that the existing juridical environment makes some states more likely than others to use particular approaches in managing contentious publics. Political institutions and legal frames affect the ways that states handle contentious politics, so that certain nations dampen the motivation for certain types of activity against the state and push activists toward other, sometimes more radical strategies (Boyle 1998; Upham 1976, 1987). And some scholars connect selected time periods to state use of policy instruments: they see particular historical periods, often those involving public unrest, as generating specific responses from the state, such as compensation, whereas other periods have seen no application of incentives (Calder 1988a). Similarly, normative arguments about state tool use posit a correlation in recent decades between increasing citizen consciousness and higher expectations with more transparency and democracy in state tactics. John Noakes (2001), for example, argued that since the 1960s, police departments in the United States have moved from aggressive handling of protest toward a more hands-off, "managerial" style. Most observers imagine that governments over time have moved away from police violence and coercion toward softer ways of handling contentious civil society.

Although these earlier approaches provided insights into individual phenomena across states, they cannot explain the variation found cross-nationally, cross-temporally, and across same-nation cases in the siting of public bads. Distinctions between weak and strong states cannot provide leverage on the issue of tool use because "weak" states (e.g., the United States and Britain) have used the same tools as "strong" states (e.g., France and Japan) in managing contentious civil society.[3] In handling dam siting in the United States, nuclear power plant siting in France, and dam siting in Japan, coercion is often the norm. Nor can national "bureaucratic culture" explain tool use: the three Japanese ministries I studied recruit from the same schools and have similar spending and retirement patterns but use completely different sets of tools. Whereas the Japanese Agency for Natural Resources and Environment utilized incentives and soft social control in handling nuclear power protest, the Ministry of Transportation relied primarily on coercion and the Ministry of Construction on coercion with occasional incentives. Likewise, time periods cannot explain tool use because in the same time period in the same country, different tools—coercion, hard and soft social control, and incentives—have been used to handle contestation. Furthermore, rather than states decreasing their use of coercion in handling resistance, some have continued over time to use expropriation against unwilling landowners.

Rather than seeking to connect policy use to state characteristics, a few researchers have investigated links between the characteristics of civil society and governmental policies. William Gamson (1968, 180–182) based some basic hypotheses about the conditions under which authorities use policy tools to manage groups on the groups' levels of trust. I build on Gamson's ideas to investigate the ways in which the characteristics of civil society impact the state's choice of tools. Given their theoretically limitless options, it is still not clear how advanced, democratic states decide which tools to use or create. For developed nations with large toolkits, there is never a single solution to a problem. North American bureaucracies have used simple policy instruments to limit public participation, control the venue, and set the agenda (Campbell 1988, 83); Japanese ministry officials have sought to change local preferences about nuclear power through complex institutions and tools (Aldrich 2005a); and their French counterparts have relied on secrecy, censorship, and the consistent use of coercive police force against those who opposed nuclear power plant siting (Nelkin and Pollak 1981). To explain this variation, I argue that

---

3. Similarly, scholars have pointed out that systematic attempts to link state response to political opportunity structures have failed (Flam 1994c, 307).

the core determinant of state policy instruments is the strength of relevant groups within civil society over time.

All states need to carry out policies that go against the preferences of some citizens. Consider tax collection, waging war, speed limits, and deregulation, as well as the siting of controversial facilities. As states pursue their goals, certain communities must bear the burden of those decisions. More specifically, modern societies require the presence of necessary but controversial facilities, such as waste dumps, incinerators, nuclear power plants, and airports. Although these facilities may be public *goods* in the sense that they provide benefits to the majority, if not all, of the citizens, they are often simultaneously public *bads* for the local communities where they are situated.[4] States are charged with regulation and entrepreneurial control over many such facilities because private companies themselves cannot make them work.[5] States also need to avoid electoral backlash, and though some constituents may see such facilities as pork-barrel projects—some sort of benefit or reward for electoral support—others do not.

As they seek to implement policies that create negative externalities for some citizens, states have access to the shortest route: force. But democratic states, more than nondemocratic ones, cannot always do what requires the fewest resources and least amount of time—that is, apply coercion to enact their desired policies. If faced with potential backlash from electoral and other sectors, decision makers cannot rely on the highly visible coercive tools that guarantee quick and certain outcomes. Even if democratic states use immediate, direct, visible, and hard methods to carry out the "national interest," feedback mechanisms such as future elections, protests, and strikes can impose heavy penalties. This is the heart of their problem. Such feedback can, however, help states develop more sustainable policies: the process of contestation with protest groups and civil society may push a state to develop new policy tools and improve or discard old ones.

## Categorizing State Policy Tools

Three main characteristics define policy instruments vis-à-vis civil society: their *mode of power* (hard or soft), their *level of visibility* (seen or unseen) and

---

4. Paehlke (2003) refers to the attempt to balance economic development with social and environmental protection as "Democracy's dilemma."

5. That is, private companies cannot provide facilities like nuclear power plants on their own because of the heavy research and design, legislative, capital, and upkeep requirements. Since firms cannot recoup their investments in them, these projects typify market failures that must be assisted, if not managed, by the state.

their *time to effectiveness* (whether their effects are immediate or delayed). State tools can be differentiated along these three axes and further grouped into categories of coercion, hard social control, incentives, and soft social control. Note that simply categorizing state policy tools does not presume that certain tools, such as persuasion, are ethically superior to others, such as coercion. Recognizing the "depth and complexity" necessary to carry out such judgments (Grant 2006), I hold instead that strategies rooted in coercion are less sustainable over the long term.

Recent work on soft and hard power shows that, especially in the international arena, states have great discretion in how they attempt to meet their goals (Nye 2004). In domestic interaction with contentious political groups, states can use coercive force such as arrests, detentions, beatings, threats, and the confiscation of previously granted or promised resources (such as loans or grants to local communities). Or, authorities can appeal to patriotism and civic duty by using soft social control tools, including school curricula, suasion, and targeted media messages. Casual observers regularly view soft tools as more legitimate than those based on force but should remember that, by law, states hold legitimacy over force as well.

Tools can be quite visible (such as dispatching police or military service personnel to sites of contention), or they can be invisible, hidden to all but their designers (Howard 1997; Hacker 2000). Higher visibility makes institutions and policies more likely targets for opponents, whereas those instruments that lie submerged can often remain so for decades without interference. United States bureaucrats allowed public utilities to expropriate land; when citizens refused to sell their homes and property for nuclear power plants, police forced them off (Nelkin 1979, 51). Such tools sit squarely in the visible spectrum and provide excellent media coverage for facility opponents who hope to make the issue more salient. Other tools, such as a "submerged" tax on electricity use in Japan to fund pronuclear institutions, are all but invisible and are hard for activists to locate and display to the public in hopes of criticizing the state.

Further, tools require different amounts of time to take effect. The arrest and intimidation of opposition leaders impact their targets immediately; redesigning school curricula to be more favorable to a pronuclear state policy, however, requires multiple steps between state action and its results. State functions such as policing are immediate (i.e., causally proximate); others involve indirect consequences and indeterminacy. Jailing anti-airport protesters during the Narita conflict immediately removed them from the protest arena, for example, and reduced the number of opponents the state had to face, but moral suasion, symbolism, and community relations take longer to alter the

Table 4.  Clusters of policy tools

| Type of policy tool | Goal | Mode of power | Examples |
|---|---|---|---|
| Coercion | Punish resistance | Hard | Police coercion, land expropriation, cutting grants |
| Hard social control | Block citizen mobilization, set agenda | Semi-hard | Closing licensing hearings, making NGO registration difficult |
| Incentives | Reward cooperation | Soft | Offering subsidies, side payments, and grants |
| Soft social control | Change preferences | Soft | Education, habituation, awards ceremonies |

preferences of local communities and make them more likely to volunteer as hosts for noxious facilities. The longer the time until a policy instrument will become effective, the less certain its results.

Table 4 summarizes the types, goals, and modes of power of four clusters of tools and gives examples.[6] These four clusters of tools available to the state for handling citizen resistance to controversial facilities can be organized as concentric circles. Tools at the bull's eye constitute coercion; the tools of hard social control form the second circle, and incentives the third; at the outermost ring are soft social control tools, which involve a longer time to affect their targets, rely completely on soft power, and are far less likely to be seen as intrusive or worthy of media coverage. Figure 7 graphically represents these circles of policy instruments within states' toolkits.

The contents of these tools range across the three primary scales identified above: from hard to soft power, from visible to invisible, and from immediate to long term. Researchers have found regularities in the clusters: there are many hard, immediate, visible tools such as expropriation, and numerous soft social control, often overlooked tools such as educational curricula. The tools within a circle may display the same characteristics, but it is not a theoretical necessity. A state could utilize soft-power tools that are quite visible: in a

6. This classification builds on Gamson's (1968, 116) three categories of types of social control, incorporating more such principles.

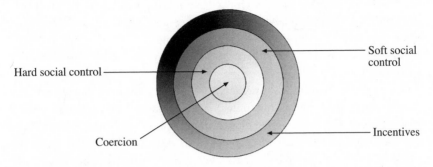

Figure 7.  Clusters of policy tools

national campaign for nuclear power an administration could buy full-page ads in popular newspapers to promote nuclear plants as protection against both excessive carbon dioxide emission and destruction of the ozone layer. Few of the soft social control tools, however, spark the outrage that arose over land expropriation, police suppression, and surveillance even in the 1950s and 1960s; therefore, they are less visible. Generally speaking, as tools move outward from the center, their characteristics shift across all three axes (from hard to soft power, visible to invisible, and short term to long term).

*Coercion*

All states hold coercive tools in their toolkits; they need them to survive as they compete against opponents both domestic and foreign. The clearest examples of these sorts of tools are the state functions of border protection (performed by the military), crime prevention (the police), and revenue extraction (the tax collection agency). Some theorists see this circle as containing policy instruments that reflect the first face or dimension of power: not only the direct impact of corporal or lethal force but also more subtle inducements, such as economic or social disincentives (Lukes 1974; Gaventa 1980). Anne Schneider and Helen Ingram (1990, 514) would likely include these types under the category of authority tools, those that "grant permission, prohibit, or require action under designated circumstances." John Kenneth Galbraith (1985) might envision this category as entailing "condign power," which "wins submission by inflicting or threatening appropriately adverse consequences." These instruments reflect the state's monopoly on both the creation of legislation and policy and its implementation of them through coercive force, if necessary. When the state uses coercion in its interaction with civil society, the social preferences of targeted actors remain the same, but their incentives for action are altered. By confiscating land from local residents who resist the siting of controversial facilities, the state does not attempt to "win their hearts and minds" but rather forces them to rethink their opposition by increasing its cost.

As a primary tool in most democracies, police and other uniformed authorities provide a means not only for maintaining order through arrest, physical force, and coercion but also for intimidation, surveillance, and information gathering. Among other strategies of coercion which play a role in siting controversies, an excellent example is Japan's Narita Public Order Law (*Narita Chian Hō*), which the central government enacted specifically to handle the violent opposition to the Narita Airport from the farmers of Chiba prefecture and their New Left allies. The law granted the Ministry of Transportation broad powers to prohibit the use of buildings by citizens deemed "violent"; it allowed officials to enter, seal up, or even raze the buildings such individuals inhabited, without extensive legal groundwork or evidence. Using this law, state authorities moved quickly to demolish the "resistance towers" that anti-airport activists had built near the runways in the hope of stalling the airport's opening. The law also allowed representatives of the state to ask individuals for identification, with minimal "probable cause," in an attempt to prevent the anti-airport opponents from mobilizing. Authorities at Narita still regularly stop individuals traveling in the vicinity if they fit the "profile" of students or radicals, and more than 1,500 riot police remain stationed at the airport.

Police can use tear gas, batons, stun guns, and water guns as disincentives in their attempts to keep protesters from marching. French riot police (Compagnies Républicaines de Sécurité, CRS) regularly use tear gas and stun grenades against anti-nuclear demonstrations. The CRS killed one protester during the now infamous demonstrations protesting the Superphoenix fast breeder in the late 1970s. Analysts have argued that these extreme responses from the French state sapped much of the commitment and strength of the anti-nuclear movement, which was unwilling to risk lives in future confrontations with state authorities (Boyle 1998).

### Hard Social Control

Analysts such as John Gaventa (1980) and Steven Lukes (1974) would envision hard social control approaches as containing the second dimension or face of power, for they set the agenda: the state structures institutions so that alternatives to its preferred plans will not likely be raised or considered. These sorts of tools require less time than soft, preference-changing social control but take more time than direct coercive responses. The payoffs from these tools are more obvious and usually more likely than those of habituation and education.

States utilize hard social control primarily to frustrate citizen opposition. By making it more difficult for civil society to intervene in state processes, the state raises the cost of opposition in more subtle ways than with coercion: closing access points to maintain control over who gets into the arena where policies are debated, or blurring the locus of decision making so that citizens feel they have no specific target for their resistance. The state can thus impede or deflect struggle. (Interestingly, contentious political groups in Japan themselves use a similar tool in their fight against facilities by buying a plot of land and dividing it among hundreds, if not thousands, of individual owners in what is called the *hito-tsubo* strategy.)[7] Citizens are often left in the dark about how the decision has been made to site a project in their community, and the state uses its control over both the agenda and the political arena to obstruct their mobilization.[8]

One example of hard social control comes from the American bureaucracy that was originally responsible for promoting and regulating nuclear power plants: the Atomic Energy Commission (AEC). Its regulatory framework for siting reactors allowed the process of locating plants to remain invisible until long after authorities had decided on a site for the reactor and purchased the land. In 1966, for instance, United Illuminating Company bought land for a nuclear power plant secretly through a third party; bureaucratic procedures allowed the entire approval process to remain opaque to citizens until the construction permit was issued (*New York Times*, 20 August 1968). Local citizens could not protest against a project they knew nothing about.

When initial protest against the planned Tellico Dam upset government planners within the Tennessee Valley Authority, the agency headed off

7. The *tsubo* is a Japanese measure of floor space or land, one (*hito-tsubo*) is approximately 3.3 square meters or 35.5 square feet. By blurring ownership of desired property and forcing the state to contact each and every owner of a contested piece of land, however small, anti-nuclear and anti-dam opposition groups in Japan and France seek to make it more difficult for the state to carry out its job. For example, anti-dam activists in the Shimouke and Matsubara Dam cases regularly exchanged ownership of the land targeted for dam siting in order to muddle bureaucrats charged with forcibly expropriating it (Shimouke Matsubara 1972, 267–278). Similarly, to delay attempts at siting a nuclear power plant in the coastal community of Kaminoseki, activists there sold each individual tree in a plot near the planned area (author's visit to Kaminoseki, 4 November 2002).

8. Franz Kafka (1925) captured this feeling of helplessness in the face of ambiguous but powerful authority in his surrealist work *Der Prozess (The Trial)* when the character Joseph K., a bank clerk, is ordered to appear in court, but the time (and place) of his interrogation is left unspecified.

opposition by providing no information about its final decisions on the project. When landowners wrote letters seeking to clarify whether their lands were to be taken by the project, the TVA responded, "We have no immediate plans for the project," even though it had made formal requests for construction funds. So until 1963, "landowners in the area remained uncertain, confused, and generally silent." A well-known activist who showed up at the TVA planning building seeking information "was given the cold shoulder—and no information" (Wheeler and McDonald 1986, 41, 130).

Residents of neighborhoods marked for "slum clearance" and other forms of urban renewal in U.S. cities have not always been notified of their impending eviction and destruction of property until right before the event; in fact, such programs have "operated... in relative secrecy, so that those affected often learned of projects just before the bulldozers rolled" (Altshuler and Luberoff 2003, 22). Similarly, the Japanese state restricted access for NGOs; a social movement or nongovernmental organization could gain benefits like cheaper mailing rates and tax-deductible donations only if it registered with the state, which entailed accepting an ex-government official as a member of its board (Pekkanen 2000a, 2000b; Vosse 2000). These kinds of procedural obstacles have prevented Japanese anti-nuclear groups from gaining a foothold and slowing down the licensing process. Their American counterparts had far more access points, despite attempts to limit their participation (Cohen, McCubbins, and Rosenbluth 1995).

In Japan, the Ministry of International Trade and Industry (MITI) has set up a process for public hearings designed to provide the appearance of citizen involvement and input in nuclear power plant siting. At these meetings, preselected citizens with prescreened questions are given an allotment of time to voice their opinions before being cut off by the moderator. French bureaucrats use a similar system: local citizens able to prove that they live within 5 kilometers of a planned nuclear facility are invited by "public use" commissions to enter their opinions in a record book—which then has no impact on the actual process itself. State decision makers use these soft social control tools to provide citizens with the illusion that they are involved in what remains an insulated and top-down process.

States can also use hard social control tools to punish localities that do not cooperate with their goals. When central governments hold tight financial control over peripheral localities, threats to cut or actually cutting funds from these communities provide a strong way of ensuring compliance. The Japanese state punishes localities that refuse to accept facilities such as dams by slashing local spending on the other construction and maintenance projects that provide employment for many locals. At risk of losing construction jobs, and with older roads lying in decay, such villages face enormous "administrative pressure" (*gyōsei appaku*) to support the state's goals. Because the Japanese Ministry of Construction regularly builds a wide variety of projects in rural areas, including the concreting of river beds and construction of new highways, the MOC can withhold such standard projects from local communities as a form of hard social control. Several Japanese villages that publicly refused to allow dam sitings have faced such administrative pressure, losing promised funding and construction assistance (Fujita 1999).

Eminent domain lies at least partially in this category of hard social control. National governments have long used the power of expropriation to further their construction interests over those of uncooperative citizens.[9] When citizens refuse to comply with eviction notices, the police publicly remove them; thus this tool juts across the circles of coercion (forcibly taking land from reluctant citizens) and hard social control agenda-setting (creation of a maze of bureaucratic procedures against which citizens are powerless). Because eminent domain is so important a tool in siting controversial facilities, especially in Japan, it is worth describing in some detail. Japanese law long protected individual property rights, but both the Meiji and postwar constitutions provided a mechanism whereby the government could override citizens in certain cases. Quite a wide gap lies between the procedures involved in a voluntary sale of land to developers or the central government, for the purpose of a public works project, and involuntary loss of land to expropriation by the state. As figure 8 demonstrates, citizens have essentially no procedural rights within the land expropriation structure.

In 2001, MOC bureaucrats further revised the Land Expropriation Law to allow, among other things, a more rapid prosecution of the expropriation process.[10] Most troubling for citizen groups, the 2001 revised version allows the government to more easily overcome the *hito-tsubo* strategy described earlier.

The revised expropriation law also assists bureaucrats in dealing with the common activist strategy of rejecting compensation offers from the government; in the past this rejection forced the ministry or project developer to

9. For a critique of the implementation and practice of eminent domain and other "taking" land-use legislation developed during and after the New Deal era in the United States, see Epstein (1985, 1993). The American Supreme Court recently ruled that local governments can confiscate land, homes, and businesses even for use by private developers (*The Economist,* 19 February 2005; *New York Times,* 23 June 2005).

10. Officially, the revision allows "more satisfactory loss compensation" and creates "a simple system for arbitration of compensation." In interviews, bureaucrats expressed three primary reasons for the revision: to promote understanding among local citizens, to ensure the smooth and efficient implementation of eminent domain proceedings, and to promote an environmentally conscious society (author's direct communication with MLIT bureaucrats, spring 2003).

Involuntary Land Acquisition

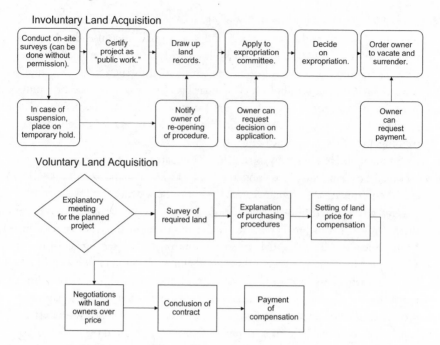

Figure 8.  Comparing voluntary and involuntary acquisition of land in Japan
*Source:* Adapted from Kotaka (1996, 59).

hold additional meetings with anti-project groups and thus further delayed construction (author's direct communication with MLIT bureaucrats, 27 May 2003). Overall, bureaucrats were pleased with the revision because it streamlined procedures and shortened the time they needed to expropriate land; in one case, this amount shrank from thirty-four months to under seven months, and the time period for payment of compensation declined from 180 days to 30. The average process was shortened from over four years to two. Because the expropriation process takes time, citizens who resist it are not only guaranteed to lose their land but could also get less compensation from the state.[11] As a result, in many cases, if the request for use of eminent domain is approved by either the prefectural council and governor or the ministry itself, the authority's mere threat of buying the property in question for less than

---

11. Suzuki (1964) pointed out that even though the MOC had established broad compensation standards by the early 1960s, the actual compensation amount itself was flexible. Matsura (1974, 122) believes there should be no difference in the price of a parcel of land acquired through a standard contractual purchase and through expropriation, but developers who carry the expropriation process through to the end are under no obligation to provide market price for that property. If the value of

market value to encourages citizens to "voluntarily" sell their land (author's interview with Japanese government officials, winter 2002).

The French state also engages in expropriation of citizen-owned land, even in high-profile cases of nuclear power plant siting, something the Japanese authorities have always avoided. The procedures for expropriation in France, like those in Japan, provide few access points where citizens can stall or halt the process. Further, the very process of being notified about a "public interest" project is very restricted, and citizens can provide feedback to state authorities only in written form. The French state primarily uses tools like expropriation and police coercion to construct its nuclear energy program because authorities, working rapidly to upgrade indigenous energy production, envision anti-nuclear protest as marginal at best.

### Incentives

As policy instruments, incentives often rely on "tangible payoffs, positive or negative, to induce compliance or encourage utilization" (Schneider and Ingram 1990, 515). Galbraith (1985, 5) would label them forms of "compensatory power" that "wins submission by the offer of affirmative reward." In Japan's case, these appear most commonly in the form of compensation and redistributive payments to host or potential host communities. The state provides funds for schools, roads, medical facilities, old age homes, and other often desirable facilities as a way of altering the locality's "price" for hosting local public bads. Although citizens may worry about the potential for a nuclear meltdown, the presence of improved infrastructure and new educational opportunities for their children can dampen their enthusiasm for anti-nuclear mobilization. Japan's central government established and continuously upgraded the *Dengen Sanpō* (Three Power Source Development Laws) in the early 1970s to help overcome local resistance to siting nuclear power plants.[12]

---

that land increases after a contract for expropriation has been set but before the land is acquired, the government is not responsible for paying the new, higher price (Kobayashi 1994, 38). By agreeing to sell land to the government but dragging out the voluntary negotiations, a citizen could receive far more than by resisting and having the land expropriated forcibly. For example, in the Matsubara and Shimouke cases, citizens in Kumamoto prefecture who resisted the procedure and thus had their lands expropriated by the MOC received far less than their counterparts in Oita prefecture, who voluntarily sold their land to the MOC. The latter group received, on average, 1.9 million yen for their property, whereas citizens in Kumamoto prefecture whose land was expropriated received only 68,530 yen for the same acreage (Shimouke Matsubara 1972, 164).

12. Japan's central government adopted the same technique to provide funds to local communities that host dams and airports, although these programs are less sophisticated and far less extensive because of smaller resistance to those facilities. For communities that host dams, the Measures for

These laws redistribute electricity taxes to potential and actual host communities to pay for a variety of programs and facilities; a community can receive up to $20 million per year.

It is important to note that the *Dengen Sanpō* do not drain money from the central government treasury, nor do the enormous subsidies sent to local communities appear in the national budget. Because the money for this policy instrument comes from an invisible tax on electricity use, the money is independent of standard political budgetary processes, which are far more visible and open to political intervention. Few citizens know that a portion of their electricity payment is funding the distribution of side payments to communities hosting nuclear power plants; politicians, also ignorant about the instrument, have little power to affect this institution. By structuring the subsidies for host communities of controversial facilities this way, central government administrators assure the program's autonomy and invisibility.

### Soft Social Control

Some analysts would classify these kinds of tools under the third face or dimension of power, as the state uses them to change the preferences of citizens and thus reduce the likelihood of resistance (Lukes 1974; Gaventa 1980). Galbraith (1985, 6) would envision them as forms of "conditioned power" involving "persuasion, education, or social commitment to what seems natural, proper, or right." Such tools seek to reduce civil society's opposition to state plans. Instead of merely raising the cost of resistance through police suppression or denial of resources (as with coercion), or making it more difficult for citizens to protest or more worth their while to cooperate (as with hard social control), instruments of soft social control seek to change the hearts and minds of protesters. For example, the Japanese state provides pronuclear science curricula to schools, along with visits by white-coated scientists, to justify and legitimize its nuclear power program. Additionally, the Japanese government sponsors annual fairs for goods produced by the host communities, hoping to change the ways that farmers view nuclear power, by shifting their vision of the facility from a detriment to a benefit.

---

Water Resource Areas (*Suigen chiiki taisaku*), like the *Dengen Sanpō*, provide funds for a variety of local infrastructure needs. To communities that host airports, the Airport Fuel Tax (*Kūkōki Nenryōzei*) redistributes a tax on airplane fuel. In contrast, the central French government provides no such incentives to nuclear power plant communities and, in fact, blocked attempts by the state-owned monopoly EDF to give additional incentives to local towns.

Capacity tools, which Schneider and Ingram (1990, 517) define as instruments that "provide information, training, education, and resources to enable individuals, groups, or agencies to make decisions to carry out activities," fit within this grouping. Most commonly applied by the Japanese state in siting nuclear power plants and dams, such tools include information tours for citizens from potential host communities, materials and comic books for students in these areas, and workshops for local politicians which teach not only about nuclear power in general but also about how to "sell" the facility to their constituents. Other tools include pep talks from Japanese government officials to discontented local communities, yearly awards ceremonies for conforming local politicians, and safety and promotion days for the general public.

The Japanese Agency for Natural Resources, charged with promoting and regulating nuclear power, also provides "scientist visits." The scientist, often wearing a white coat, visits potential host communities to lecture to local residents and local government employees about the safety and necessity of nuclear power. Many citizens imagine these scientists to be neutral third parties; in fact, they are often employees of the state.[13] Still another tool used to gain legitimacy for state policies is to form alliances with local constituencies: state decision makers seek out or create pro-state policy groups, such as local business associations or powerful politicians, to show that their bureaucratic policies have "broad" support and should be viewed as acceptable to civil society as a whole (Garon 1997; Carpenter 2001). In Japan, state ministries often request that local "supporters" publish open letters in regional newspapers, arguing that those opposing projects in the community are in fact a minority.

The tools in the soft social control class are often subtle and require long-term investment; they are not "one-shot" solutions (like arresting protest leaders, or cutting off funds to an area). Further, the outcome of soft social controls, unlike coercion and hard social control, is often quite uncertain. Attempts to change the preferences of citizens can have highly unpredictable outcomes; even information biased in favor of facilities can in fact raise local resistance. For example, Herbert Inhaber (1998, 38) studied attempts to reduce resistance to controversial facilities by educating the public about risks

13. Researchers uncovered similar soft social control in studies of the creation and dissemination of "social knowledge." In the late nineteenth and early twentieth centuries, social science experts gave their opinions about issues such as industrial accidents, child welfare, social security, and poverty in a variety of forms to legislative and judicial venues, opinions that often formed the "scientific" basis for national policy. By legitimizing and justifying state practices, authorities sought to alter the preferences of citizens—that is, to make these programs more acceptable to those who would bear the burden of them (Rueschemeyer and Skocpol 1996).

and found that they often have a "perverse effect, producing more concern." Nevertheless, though soft social controls may require more resources and take longer, they can result in the highest levels of legitimacy, because providing information to civil society is seen as a natural, legitimate extension of the state's role in education. Some argue that every state seeking industrialization must utilize the institutions of education to promote a national identity (Gellner 1983) or form a unified nation (Garon 1997). Critics may dub these sorts of institutions propaganda or reeducation, but state authorities see the dispersion of information as normative behavior.

## Predictions for Tool Use and Creation

Given the characteristics of the four main clusters of tools, what is the process by which state decision makers choose which tools to apply in which scenarios? The strength of relevant groups within civil society strongly impacts the state agencies' choice of policy instruments for handling contentious localities. In the language of social science, the independent variables—of the quality and quantity of the targeted segment of society—strongly impact the dependent variable, the state's choice of tools.

State bureaucrats facing small or weak groups within civil society are most likely to use coercion. Even if paying off small interest groups would be less costly than providing incentives to larger ones, coercive tools are less expensive to implement against smaller groups in both resources and time. Expropriation is readily available to bureaucracies around the world, and if requires no new tools, organizational structures, or monetary or time investments. Coercive tools may need only a single application, as shown by Elizabeth Boyle (1998), because strong suppression can prevent future protest from forming. One study points out that states are most likely to apply coercive force when target groups within civil society have not yet managed to mobilize larger allies or bring their message to the wider public (Flam 1994b, 348). As a result, anti-facility groups with little social capital, such as contentious political groups that have been delegitimized or marginalized by the state, will be unable to activate allies and are therefore likely to encounter the tactics of coercive force and expropriation.

Using the coercive tool of police repression against small groups labeled as "radical" or "terrorist" brings few repercussions from society as a whole, as French bureaucrats know from experience. Using such strategies against large-scale, legitimate social movements with links to significant segments of society can result in public backlash, however. During the struggles over nuclear power plants in the United States, large numbers of arrests—sometimes over 3,000 per site—led to public outcry.[14] But if states can guarantee the siting of a project through coercion, they may be willing to take on smaller, temporary (electoral, media, reputational) costs for absolute long-term gains (the presence of the facility). In such cases, the state faces less political backlash and fewer negative repercussions because the targeted group is smaller.

The history of French nuclear power plant siting and Japanese airport siting demonstrates the tendency to use coercion against weak civil society. In both cases, small, contentious subsections of the overall civil society found it hard to create alliances and enlarge their membership and relative capacity. The French state marginalized the anti-nuclear movement through coercion and hard social control; a contentious political network that held the potential for wide, cross-societal alliances was thereby reduced to a small number of independent organizations. Despite the notoriety of the Narita Airport siting case, anti-airport siting movements rarely become more than ad hoc social movements in Japan, so bureaucrats encountered little trouble in consistently applying expropriation and other measures to complete infrastructure goals.

When larger subgroups of civil society are involved, bureaucrats can seek to reduce opposition by making it more difficult for citizens to resist. Because the response from civil society will be larger in such a case, less visible tools involving a mix of hard and soft power smooth the way better more than coercive, short-term tools. Dam-siting cases in Japan and airport-siting cases in France match this prediction well. Siting dams involves larger target populations than airports but smaller ones than nuclear power plants. Dams involve the trouble of relocating entire communities (often 100 or more families) that will be flooded by the facility, so authorities will primarily use hard social control tools with some coercion.

It is when states must deal with broader, mobilized associations in civil society which maintain long-term opposition that they will invest resources in developing and updating incentives and tools for soft social control. In these cases, authorities are wary of applying immediate-acting but less "legitimate" coercive tools that could alienate potential allies and reduce the state's future chances at siting. Instead, the state will seek to change first the preferences of affected host communities and then public opinion as a whole. Japan's siting program for nuclear power plants fits these criteria well: bureaucrats

14. Struggles between the Clamshell Alliance and the Seabrook nuclear power plant authorities in New Hampshire resulted in thousands of arrests. In one exchange, police arrested 1,414 protesters over a fourteen-hour period (*Washington Post,* 11 May 1977), and later site occupations involved 3,000 people.

working in that field have developed many soft social controls for their tool-kits. Because anti-nuclear opposition in Japan has been widespread since the events at Hiroshima and Nagasaki and the *Lucky Dragon* incident during the Bikini bomb tests (the so-called third atomic bombing of Japan), the state has strenuously avoided expropriation and coercion and instead moved primarily toward soft and hard social control.

These predictions for tool use are general ones. In initial interactions with civil society where state agencies face unusually sharp negative feedback, bureaucrats may temporarily refrain from applying coercion. Such "learning cases" may push the state to better disguise its future uses of force. Interestingly, most representative democratic theorists imagined that rising citizen expectations for involvement and transparency over the twentieth century would reduce the state's dependence on coercive and hard social control tools, but that has not been the case. Instead, states such as France and Japan continue to employ these tools wherever contentious political activity is low.

Returning to Machiavellian terminology, one can now better understand when bureaucratic agencies will act as foxes and when they will act as lions. The choice of policy tools is not determined by factors such as national bureaucratic or political culture, juridical environment, time period, or increasing citizen expectations about democratic procedures and instruments. Rather, tool choices depend heavily on the strength of contentious political opponents within civil society. On the one hand, where state authorities face well-organized groups that can sustain widespread opposition over a long period, they are most likely to utilize soft social control. Such tools rely on invisible, soft-power-based approaches that seek to alter citizen preferences, By using a softer approach, state agencies avoid alienating potential allies and ensure an image, if not the actuality, of democratic procedure. On the other hand, if planners encounter contentious groups that are fragmented and without societal allies, they stick with older, coercive tools based on the state's monopoly over force. Such coercive policy instruments as policing, disincentives, and expropriation raise the cost of opposition but do not win the hearts and minds of civil society.

Because state policies are a function of civil society, states that encounter only weak protest over time will not develop a full repertoire of strategies available to authorities engaged with longer-term, more acute contestation. That is, although state agencies control an enormous array of resources and venues, they may not actually have access to all the tools of *both* lion and fox. The toolkits of certain bureaucracies may contain only expropriation and licensing-control approaches, with no policy tools that seek to alter preferences.

Dam-siting authorities in Japan, for example, did not develop the soft social control tools that were available to their counterparts handling nuclear power in the 1970s, and those agencies handling nuclear power in France have actually restrained the Electricité de France from doing so. Why some offices but not others—even within the same government—operate with different toolkits is an overlooked but critically important question that this chapter has sought to answer.

Chapter 1 demonstrated that when the state is selecting communities to host public bads, the strength of groups within civil society strongly determines location. In-depth historical institutional case studies of siting in Japan and France provide empirical support for the argument that civil society also strongly conditions state policies for handling contention.

# 3

# OCCASIONAL TURBULENCE

## *Airport Siting in Japan and France*

IN 1990 THE JAPANESE MINISTRY OF TRANSPORTATION announced plans for a new international airport to be built offshore near Nagoya in Ise Bay, Aichi prefecture. The airport—known as the Chubu, or Central, Airport—would absorb flights from nearby but aging Nagoya Airport and be the third largest in Japan. By building this enormous facility on artificial landfill in the center of the bay, planners hoped to avoid the delays caused by local resistance that had plagued Narita Airport. The government prepared to raze lush local mountains to provide the landfill material and notified local residents of its intention to acquire land for access roads that would connect the airport to existing highways. Local residents, fishermen, and environmental groups opposed the siting plan, with one local group, the Trust for the Protection of Nature in Hazu, arguing vehemently against it on the basis of potential damage to the ecosystem. Close to 1,600 local residents petitioned against the destruction of local hills for landfill, and thirteen residents divided the land sought by the state into 800 pieces to slow its acquisition. Despite such tactics and the pressure brought to bear by local fishermen and residents, the state expropriated the contested land from the owners in 2003 and opened the completed airport in February 2005.

By investigating the siting of airports in Japan and France, this chapter illustrates how Japan's Ministry of Transportation and its French counterpart, Aéroport de Paris (ADP), responded to comparatively weak and moderately contentious civil society, respectively.[1] Although resistance was occasionally acute and prolonged in Japan, as in the infamous Narita siting case, it was more often weak and short-lived, and as a result, state authorities did not develop new strategies for handling contestation. Used to relying on expropriation, and

---

1. As previously noted, the MOT was folded into the MLIT in January 2001. This chapter focuses on the thirty large, international airports (class 1 and class 2) founded, funded, and managed directly by the MOT; class 3 facilities managed or constructed by prefectural authorities are beyond the scope of this study.

able to use new construction technology to site airports offshore, the MOT set up few, if any, hard or soft social controls to handle civil society. In France, though, the ADP's encounter with moderate levels of resistance from nationally organized groups pushed it away from coercive tools and toward softer social control instruments.

After laying out the problems and benefits involved in airport siting in general, I focus on Japanese airports and then raise the French case to put these experiences in comparative perspective.

Observers of Japan are quite familiar with the horrific battles over the Narita Airport between anti-airport groups and riot police, which left ten dead and thousands more hurt or maimed. From 1965 to 1989, protesters carried out more than 400 acts of sabotage (Sumiya 1996, 62). To this day, a handful of radicals continues to conduct guerrilla warfare against the airport and the firms and individuals involved in its construction. In the context of other airport siting attempts in Japan, Narita is an extreme and aberrant case; no other airport attracted similar levels of violence. Article totals in the *Asahi Shinbun,* Japan's second-largest daily newspaper, show that protests at Narita accounted for 80 percent of all coverage of airport opposition. Narita involved the longest delay (seven years) in the opening of a planned airport and the largest number of riot police (14,000) called out to handle local opposition. During ninety-four other airport sitings in Japan, civil society mobilized to engage in petitions, marches, and litigation, but not violence. Because the externalities of airports are more focused and their benefits more equitable, compared with dams and nuclear power plants, they activate smaller portions of civil society.

## Why Airports Generate Only Mild NIMBY Responses

"Noise, fear of accidents, vibration, and possible air pollution" (Stratford 1974, 60) form the core issues for local residents, but airports, unlike nuclear power plants, tightly focus their externalities on the immediate surroundings and the areas under their flight paths. Like dams, they may require local citizens to relocate, but usually far fewer individuals and families are pushed off of their land. Furthermore, though airports may decrease surrounding property values, they do so to a lesser extent than nuclear power plants (which can drastically reduce the value of local property) and dams (which reduce it to zero, as the land is under water).

Since the infancy of jet travel, noise pollution has been the primary obstacle around the world to siting airports (Stratford 1974, 38; Ashford, Stanton, and Moore 1997, 57; Horonjeff 1983, 153; Hamilton 1991, 85–86).[2] In one court case, the Osaka High Court remarked in finding for the plaintiffs that "noise in the area where we visited at night was devastating when accompanied by the overwhelming and imposing image of a huge airplane descending with full landing lights on" (quoted in Gresser, Fujikura, and Morishima 1981, 168). Nearby communities regularly struggle with noise levels that disrupt normal conversation and cause hearing loss. Studies show that even communities 5 kilometers (3 miles) away experience up to 90 decibels of noise pollution with each take-off. Average noise levels in Narita and Shibayama (more than 1 kilometer from Narita airport), for example, are around 80 to 85 decibels on the WECPNL scale, the most common standard of measurement (Sumiya 1996, 255).

In addition to noise pollution, airports bring the potential for environmental pollution through the accidental release of jet fuel. Even as planners struggled to keep Narita plans from being derailed by violent protests, moderate citizens fought against pipelines for jet fuel (*AS*, 16 November 1971). Eventually, planners began to use a railway line running through Ibaraki prefecture to transport the fuel to Narita, but local citizens continued to protest regularly. Other problems accompanying airports include airplane accidents that threaten the lives not only of the passengers and crew but also of local residents. No Japanese airport has ever experienced a severe accident, but the possibility came into sharp focus on 27 January 2003 when a Japan Airlines jet overran Narita's Runway B by approximately 70 meters, stopping less than half a kilometer from the house of an anti-airport farmer (TBS, Japan News Network, 28 January 2003).

Among studies demonstrating that airports negatively affect property values, one found that the residents of households nearest to the Osaka Airport (Itami) regularly denigrated their property and felt that their location was poor. Two-thirds of the eighty-nine households surveyed regarded their property as undesirable (*yoku nai tochi*), and 85 percent reported that noise was a serious problem (Kōkū Kōgai Bōshi Kyōkai 1973, 5–6). Quantitative studies found that airports somewhat decreased the property values of nearby homes; one reported that each decibel of noise from the airport decreased the property values slightly, by approximately .58 percent (Nelson 2004).

Despite these negative effects, however, fewer risks are associated with airports than with nuclear power plants or dams. Whereas a construction mistake

2. One airport administrator cynically warned his colleagues that noise "arouses people's wrath and is most likely to defy any rational or objective analysis and be exploited for demagogic purposes by pressure groups" (Block 1971, 33).

at a dam could kill thousands, and a reactor meltdown could contaminate citizens hundreds of kilometers away, the primary problem related to airports is noise pollution, which is quite focused over take-off and landing zones. Furthermore, because airports are regularly built offshore or far from existing communities, only relatively small areas are affected by noise. For example, the Japanese MOT sited six airports on the island of Hokkaido in remote rural towns and villages and used offshore construction and landfill technologies to build those such as Kansai and Haneda in the ocean.

In addition, the merits of airport construction are more clear and numerous than those for other facilities, they include increased business, improved transportation, and more exposure in both domestic and international markets for local firms. Some local governments, at Narita, for example, provide additional benefits to airport neighbors such as slight discounts on electricity for local residents (author's interviews, 25 August 2003). Japanese MOT bureaucrats also like to point out that host communities for airports avoid the common problem of depopulation, noting that such communities grew by 8.9 percent between 1980 and 2000, while the national average showed a slight decrease over the same period (Kokudokōtsūshō Kōkūkyoku 2003, 10). Narita City and Tomisato, a village that borders Narita Airport, doubled and quadrupled respectively between 1965 and 1990, while the population for Chiba prefecture doubled (Sumiya 1996, 250–251).

Studies of British airports found that thanks to infrastructure improvements and other public goods, properties out of direct flight paths were not adversely affected (Tomkins et al. 1998). Even some Japanese anti-airport activists agreed in interviews that most citizens see airports as bringing a mix of advantages and disadvantages; early opposition therefore commonly changed to support once citizens were informed of economic benefits and side payments. Despite initial resistance, towns in Chiba prefecture—where Narita Airport is located—eagerly sought to be included on lists of candidate sites for a possible third Tokyo airport. Futtsu City, located ninety minutes by train from Tokyo, frequently petitioned the Airport Bureau of Ministry of Land, Infrastructure, and Transport (MLIT) to support its candidacy.

To summarize, although some residents violently contested airports in well-publicized cases, the accompanying externalities for these projects are sufficiently concentrated that they only rarely trigger broader sustained resistance from civil society. Noise, environmental damage, property devaluation, and potential accidents are by no means minor issues, but only a small proportion of residents experience these directly or acutely. For most, the airport brings economic growth, infrastructure improvement, and access to markets and travel. Some cities seek out airports in anticipation of economic and demographic growth.

Media coverage in Japan bears out those findings. Using a CD–ROM database of material from the *Asahi Shinbun*, I tallied the total number of articles with the words "airport" and "opposition" (*kūkō* and *hantai*). I also investigated to see if "airport" and "opposition movement" (*kūkō* and *hantai undō*) or "airport" and "citizen" (*kūkō* and *jūmin*) were used instead. The results, shown in figure 9, reveal that the Narita conflict generated enormous spikes in the number of articles, especially during the periods of violence in the late 1960s and again around 1978, when the airport opened. Before that case, no anti-airport movements within civil society had received attention from national newspapers; until 1965 the *Asahi Shinbun* ran no articles whatsoever

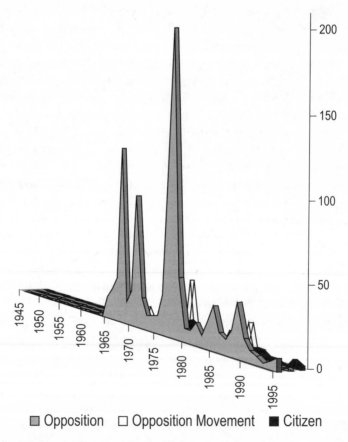

☐ Opposition    ☐ Opposition Movement    ■ Citizen

Figure 9. Number of articles with the key words "airport" and...
Source: *Asahi Shinbun* CD-ROM

on the issue. And even though the violent resistance at Narita sparked public interest in that single case, and enormously increased coverage, eliminating articles focused on Narita leaves only an occasional report in the mainstream media on anti-airport opposition.

## Mostly Clear Skies: Airport Siting in Japan, 1950s to 1970s

Initially, the Japanese MOT encountered almost no resistance in the majority of airport siting cases, but beginning in 1968, its attempts to construct a new airport near Tokyo exploded in unexpected violence. Even though the national government twice switched candidate sites to avoid areas with stronger and better-organized anti-airport civil society, this approach did not prove to be a solution for the Narita Airport: the area finally selected for the Tokyo International Airport—Sanrizuka—mobilized thousands of protesters, far beyond the state's expectations. Despite being well publicized, however, the Narita case is not representative of airport siting in Japan during this or any other period.

The rare, long-term resistance at Narita resulted from several interrelated factors: poor timing, failure to appreciate the area's history, inadequate planning, and hasty maneuvering (Ishihara 1974, 43). It came at the height of the Vietnam War, when large numbers of socially activated left-wing students were available and willing to mobilize alongside conservative right-wing farmers. As one scholar argued, "The left wing students at Narita, and many of the farmers to a lesser degree, saw the Narita conflict as an *extension* of the [Vietnam] war" (Bowen 1975, 599); others have called the struggle over Narita "Japan's Vietnam" (Wilkinson 1999; Libero International 1977). Many students and farmers believed that Narita would be used, as Haneda had been, as a conduit for U.S. troops and war matériel en route to Vietnam (*Zengakuren* 1971, 104).

Central government bureaucrats failed to consider the complicated history of the area and its inhabitants (see Bowen 1975, 601). Members of the War Sufferers' Union, repatriated settlers from Japan's overseas colonies, and other groups of citizens who lost their homes during World War II had been encouraged by the government to settle in the nearby villages of Tennami and Kinone. Pioneers who did so undertook backbreaking labor to cut down the bamboo groves, clear the land of obstructions, and build farms (Narita Kūkō Chiiki 2001, 2–8). Only two years before the siting decision, both prefectural and national officials were encouraging local farmers to begin sericulture projects (Ogawa 1992, 89). Some groups began intensive organic farming in the area in the late 1960s and early 1970s, and as one farmer argued, "It takes about ten years before you really get a feel for the land" (quoted in Wilkinson

1999). Further, in interviews, activists described feelings of group belonging and communal participation that had been strengthened by the day-to-day activities of rice and other crop farming (Nakai 1981, 70–71). Some families had been on the airport site for more than two generations; they saw the government's plan to relocate them as violating an unwritten social contract (author's interviews, summer 2003). Yet overall, expropriation remains a core strategy in the state's toolkit for siting airports. Even in the Narita case the state relied on coercion and hard social control as its main strategies to manage contentious civil society, adding incentives and soft social control only after it encountered mounting pressure.

The 1956 Airport Maintenance Law (*Kūkō Seibihō*) had set up the few incentives, soundproofing and infrastructure development, offered to host communities. These subsidies proved sufficient to handle most postwar siting cases until, in 1962, the Cabinet announced that because of overcrowding, the country needed a new five runway international airport occupying 2,300 hectares near the capital. The Ministry of Transportation identified two potential candidate sites in mid-1963: one in Chiba prefecture, near the villages of Yachimata and Tomisato; and one in Ibaraki prefecture, near Kasumigaura (*AS*, 10 December 1963). Strong local opposition led authorities to back away from the Ibaraki site (Ueno 1966, 50; *AS*, 15 November 1965); as in other cases, they sought to avoid confrontation and locate facilities where civil society was weakest. Since immediate protest in Ibaraki showed organized and highly mobilized citizen groups, the airport planners settled on the area near Tomisato in rural Chiba prefecture (*AS*, 19 March 1965)—but wavered again as local citizens made their anti-airport position clear (*AS*, 26 March 1965).

Bureaucrats stated that technical criteria—airspace, climate, and proximity to Tokyo—made Tomisato the most appropriate site for a new international airport (Ishihara 1974, 44), but the MOT neglected to inform even local government officials of the decision. Chiba's Governor Kawakami did not learn of the plan until the Cabinet secretary announced the government's unofficial "final" decision at a televised press conference on 17 November 1965; only after that announcement did the MOT minister, Nakamura Torata, call Governor Kawakami and urgently request that he come to Tokyo to discuss the matter (Sumiya 1996, 7). Writing about the experience, Kawakami expressed shock that he had heard nothing—even unofficially—about the airport siting until the news came on the radio (Hagiwara 1996, 189); he described it as a bolt from the blue (*nemimi ni mizu*) (*AS*, 1 May 1990). Yet opposition groups had mobilized as early as September 1963, two years before the official announcement took place (Ueno 1966, 47).

Tomisato residents organized large-scale demonstrations and marches on prefectural offices; some 1,500 protesters, including labor union members and Socialist Party activists, broke into prefectural government offices. The town councils of Shisui, Tomisato, and Yachimata also opposed the plan (Apter and Sawa 1984, 217). When MOT officials attempted to hold explanatory meetings in Tomisato, 150 protesters said that they had no obligation to listen and left, shouting "absolute opposition!" (*zettai hantai*). Anti-Narita groups then began using the *hito-tsubo* strategy, dividing up the land among thousands of individual landowners to prevent the government from acquiring it (*AS,* 8 December 1965; 10 April 1966). Airport authorities explained to me that, because of the strong citizen opposition, the Chiba prefectural government adopted a "watch and wait" stance about committing to Tomisato.

Within the Cabinet itself, power brokers turned away from the Tomisato site and pushed for the Sanrizuka site instead, noting that the government already held land there. At Tomisato, 22 percent of the necessary land was owned by the central government and an additional 10 percent by Chiba prefecture, but over two-thirds was in the hands of private citizens—more than at the Sanrizuka site. Some of the Sanrizuka land, 60 kilometers from Tokyo, had been *Goryō Bokujō* (Imperial pasture), held by the government since the 1600s (Narita Kūkō Chiiki 2001, 2). Also, government planners believed that the pro-LDP farmer constituency in the Narita area would appreciate and support the state siting plans (Sumiya 1996, 17). They imagined that compared with Tomisato, Sanrizuka's local organizations would be more willing hosts.

Critics argue that Shōjiro Kawashima, Cabinet member and LDP vice chairman, had a personal interest in pushing the Sanrizuka site. He and his friend Kitoshi Tanazawa owned a golf course in the area which was doing poorly, and siting an airport there would create demand for otherwise unwanted rural plots and push up land values (Kamata 1991, 294–296; Apter and Sawa 1984, 199). Additionally, logistical problems at Tomisato caused several other leaders to speak out against that plan. Construction Minister Kawano noted that no project had ever displaced more than 500 homes, but the Tomisato site would uproot 1,500 households; he thought that such a relocation would be impossible (Ueno 1966, 49).

Whatever its reasons, in 1966 the Cabinet retracted its earlier decision and settled on the Sanrizuka area, near Shibayama Chiyoda and Narita City. Prime Minister Eisaku Sato defended the decision, saying that the state had given careful thought to the large amount of publicly held land in the area and its desire to minimize disruption (Isa 1988, 10). When the agriculture minister asked his Ministry of Transport counterpart if he had sought the local farmers' permission or at least their understanding, the reported response was that whenever the MOT wanted to build an airport, it would decide where, and farmers would simply follow along (Uzawa 1992, 78). Having learned their lesson, however, planners did gain prior consent from Chiba's governor before officially announcing the 1,060-hectare plan for an airport at Sanrizuka (Sumiya 1996, 8). The MOT distributed pamphlets to local households discussing their impending relocation and the state's compensation offers (Ishihara 1974, 45).

Although existing laws provided some incentives, such as grants and subsidies, to airport host communities, the government recognized that the struggles over the first two candidate sites indicated potential future problems and therefore strengthened incentives to get cooperation from the local communities. In 1967 it created the Airplane Noise Prevention Act to help combat noise pollution; it updated the act in 1978. Public and private interests combined in 1968 to organize the Aircraft Nuisance Prevention Association to supplement government measures. Primary among these measures were soundproofing schemes, such as installing double-paned windows and additional insulation, and tightening door and window seals; the state helped soundproof schools, hospitals, and private homes. It also built and maintained local public facilities, parks, and cultural halls and protected television reception (Unyushō 1980, 21). As a result, MOT spending jumped between 1967 and 1973 in the face of initial resistance.

In addition to creating incentives such as subsidies for soundproofing, the central government created an "invisible" tax to support airport host communities. In 1967, the MOT set up an airport tax to fund a redistributive compensation system. Much like *Dengen Sanpō*, which channel electricity taxes to power plant host communities, it is funded by a tax on the private airline companies (Unyushō 1983). Beginning in 1972, the government put into effect a 26,000 yen per kiloliter fuel tax (approximately $85/kL at 1972 exchange rates) called the Kūkōki Nenryōzei, of which 20 percent is funneled to regional governments hosting airports and the remainder to the towns, villages, and communities close to the airport. Other advanced democracies created similar systems of compensation for host communities; the funding for all such programs comes not from standard tax instruments but rather from invisible taxes on facility users. For example, France established in the early 1970s a "noise tax" on airplanes at certain airports and used the funds for soundproofing and sound abatement measures in nearby communities (Unyu Keizai Kenkyū Sentā 1976).

These laws provided some funding to every host community, but in specific cases, and especially for the already-controversial Tokyo International Airport in Narita, the government responded more directly to local concerns and expanded the scale and scope of incentives. In July 1966, when the Cabinet announced its intention to build the airport at Sanrizuka, it initiated a series of ad hoc measures, including compensation, assistance with moving and employment, and work on noise pollution, road construction, and sewers to help site Narita airport (*Kakugi Kettei*, 4 July 1966). The Cabinet promised to quickly complete the renovations of the nearby National Highway 51 and provide funds for roads and infrastructure development around Sanrizuka. MOT planners also provided funds for such projects as construction of a railroad to the nearby Shibayama area and joint-use public facilities in the region.

Within a month of the Sanrizuka announcement, a temporary office for bureaucrats was established in Narita City, but as plans went forward the central government and the airport authority offered local citizens few clear explanations about the airport's progress, even though 250 households, holding a total of 670 hectares of land, had to be relocated. The Narita Airport Authority (NAA), the public corporation in charge of siting, was staffed by ex-MOT officials who "descended from heaven": that is, officially retired from the bureaucracy into these jobs (Tomura 1980, 23); they held an initial public hearing on Narita in late June 1966 and another in January 1967. Citizens were told that they were expected to vacate their homes and properties to make way for the airport, and that some assistance would be available. Airport authorities now refer to this as a "misthreading of a button" (*botan no kakechigau*); they acknowledge that insufficient attention was given to local citizens, who received no explanation of the seemingly arbitrary siting decision that uprooted them from their homes (author's personal communication with NAA, 23 July 2003).

In August 1966 the MOT announced that citizens who sold willingly would be provided new land, on average 1.5 times larger than their initial holdings (Ogawa 1992, 106; Sumiya 1996, 31).[3] About half of the local citizens immediately favored the airport siting plan; an additional 30 percent signed on once the government made such additional offers as management of *omiyage* (souvenir) and food shops within the airport terminal and parking lot ownership nearby (Apter and Sawa 1984, 29). By the summer of 1967, then, nearly 80 percent of residents were willing to negotiate or accept government offers of land exchange (Ogawa 1992, 109). By late 1969 the government had acquired some 560 hectares through purchases (Ishihara 1974, 46). In some cases, airport authorities authorized negotiators to pay far above the market price for land. For example, one resident's property was valued at approximately

---

3. Despite these assurances, farmers who did willingly relocate received far less than they were promised (Kitahara 1996, 97).

1.4 million yen per *tan* (equivalent to $3,889/.1 hectare at the 1969 exchange rate), but he received 6.7 million yen ($18,600) per *tan* (Tomura 1980, 32).

Even though a majority of residents accepted the plan, opposition began with local citizens, Socialist and Communist Party members. Within a week of the announcement in 1966, 1,000 protesters mobilized for a demonstration against the airport (*AS,* 29 June 1966). Local resistance groups combined to form the Sanrizuka Shibayama Rengō Kūkō Hantai Dōmei (the Sanrizuka Shibayama Alliance of Anti-Airport Groups), which had more than 1,400 members by the end of the year (*Mainichi Shinbun,* 17 May 2002). Initial resistance followed standard institutional procedures, with "petitions, a letter writing campaign, peaceful 'sit in' demonstrations throughout Tokyo and Chiba that explained their plight, personal appeals to responsible officials, and court action" (Bowen 1975, 603). Local farmers petitioned the emperor as well (Scott-Stokes 1978b). As time passed, the core anti-airport movement brought in outside allies, expelled those they felt did not assist them, and become more violent. Their numbers fluctuated over time as the struggles dragged on— some accepted the government's offers and left the area; students would arrive from campus on weekends to participate—until by the summer of 1972 some 500 "full-time" core resisters, mostly students and farmers, remained (*AS,* 22 January 1973). Still, the movement easily mobilized 4,000 marchers during its protests later in the 1970s (*AS,* 13 October 1975).

Although the state offered incentives to sweeten the process, the promise of expropriation sat heavily on the minds of citizens, who understood that refusing to bargain early could mean loss of property value. The state used a mix of hard and soft social control strategies, including pressure from friends and family, promises of a better future for children, and threats of expropriation and higher taxes. For example, the state often encouraged pro-airport family members to pressure reluctant or anti-airport homeowners to sell their land quickly. The NAA sent letters to protesters promising new jobs and predicting that their sons and daughters would enjoy better schools should they cooperate (*Zengakuren* 1971, 202). Letters to farmers warned that the NAA already had the approval of the central government to take their land forcefully and asked them to come to the table and negotiate (Sumiya 1996, 36). In one case, the local tax office informed a resisting farmer that he would face an inheritance tax of four times the standard level if he attempted to pass on the property to his children rather than sell it for the airport (Musankaikyū Henshūbu 1992, 246).

As the plans for Narita inched forward, MOT bureaucrats worked simultaneously to complete plans for expanding Osaka International Airport. There, strategies of coercion—whether expropriation, police violence, or threats of expulsion—served well. Under the government's aegis the Itami Airport Association (IAA), responsible for constructing that airport, had been able to purchase most of the necessary land. Local residents in the Katsube District refused to sell, however, and in January 1966 the government began eminent domain proceedings against them (*AS*, 31 March 1966). When the expropriation council approved the government's request to take the land by force, activists built a "solidarity cabin" on the property to prevent the order's execution, and local farmers kept it occupied. Only after the mayor intervened and helped publish a series of memoranda critical of the MOT did the activists agree to vacate (Gresser, Fujikura, and Morishima 1981, 178).

## Major Turbulence: The 1970s to 1990s

In March 1970, as protests against Narita continued, the state created new incentive measures for local residents: it would shoulder the majority of costs for road and river improvements, school and emergency facilities, and agricultural improvement (NKOGG 1980, 44–47). The MOT hoped that such assistance would generate goodwill and unify the host community in its support for the airport project. The same year, it envisioned a detailed plan for the area's overall improvement, which was revised four times before 1977. Despite government promises of financial aid, local governments—especially that of Narita City—continued to bear enormous burdens.[4]

As costs for Narita escalated along with the unrest, ministry planners met with citizen resistance to proposals for a new international airport, this one to be placed in the Kansai region (southwest Japan): they planned to build an airport in Osaka Bay not far from Osaka Airport which would be the largest in Asia at the time (*AS*, 22 September 1970). When the Cabinet approved the Kansai plan in 1984, observers noted that it was "originally planned to be only 1 km offshore on solid seabed, but fishermen protested, and the airport island was moved an additional 5 km above a seabed consisting of 20 meters of alluvial silt and sand" (Dempsey, Goetz, and Szyliowicz 1997, 234). Here again, officials shifted plans away from an area with a high concentration of civil society groups that would be directly affected by the accompanying negative externalities—the fishermen's cooperatives—toward a less contested area. MOT officials had hoped to place the airport near the city of Kobe, but local citizens and politicians refused.

---

4. Between 1967 and 1976, for example, Narita City spent between a third and a half of its total budget on airport-related projects (NKOGG 1980, 59).

Both local residents and governments initially opposed the Kansai Airport. A 1970 "secret survey" conducted by the Kobe Chamber of Commerce reported mixed feelings. More than half the respondents said that they already knew of the planned airport; 39 percent said that they felt "normal" levels of concern; 17 percent felt little. One-third agreed that the airport was not desirable because of potential pollution, and two-thirds believed that noise pollution would affect the local community (Hiraiwa 1979, 15). These concerns translated into rejection of the project by local town councils: in the early 1970s, all twelve local governments near the planned site passed resolutions against it—Osaka's city council, for example, in 1974 (AS, 6 July 1974). Local governments that initially opposed airport construction shifted their position under pressure from the state. Less than a decade later, all but one of the twelve "no" votes had changed into support for the facility.

In 1976 the Ministry of Transportation began surveys off Senshu in Osaka Bay. By 1984 it had received permission from Osaka's governor; in 1985 it held explanatory meetings; and in 1987 it began construction. To expedite the Kansai construction, committees issued more than seven volumes of findings for local citizens. MOT officials explained not only the necessity of the airport itself but also the procedures for siting it (Arai 1995, 25–26). In 1991, twenty-one years after the project began, the MOT announced that it had reached agreement with the local citizens (AS, 15 November 1991). Built on landfill, the airport opened on 4 September 1994 at a cost of around $15 billion. It had faced a series of problems ranging from bribery investigations (Blechinger 2000) and bid rigging (Financial Times, 12 October 1990) to sinking caused by liquefaction. Still, though it ran more than 40 percent over predicted costs, its marine location meant that the Kansai Airport had avoided the kind of anti-airport activism that stalled Narita. Since almost no civil society would be directly affected by noise pollution, placing the airport in the middle of the bay shrewdly evaded confrontation. It is the only twenty-four-hour airport in Japan, unhampered by the "night caps" placed on other airports. As one observer commented, "Unlike Tokyo's Narita, which faced bitter opposition from neighboring farmers and thus did not expand sufficiently to meet soaring demand, Kansai enjoys the support of surrounding communities" (Blustein 1994).

During the initial planning, local officials had warned the MOT that pushing plans through without listening to citizens' concerns would create "another Narita." MOT bureaucrats spoke openly about the lessons they had learned from the initial conflict at Narita (AS, 10 June 1975) and noted the importance of public relations materials that stressed the minimal levels of pollution expected (Hiraiwa 1979, 77, 85). Nonetheless, in the mid-1980s, anti-airport groups bombed offices at Kansai Airport (AS, 4 April 1984).

Local officials worked with central government planners to utilize hard social control strategies against anti-airport protests. For example, in the mid-1990s, anti-airport groups were still demonstrating against Kansai, so in 1995, city officials refused a permit when the National Assembly in Opposition to the Kansai Airport asked to use municipal buildings. Despite support from local governments, the airport's opening was delayed several times for technical reasons and by fifteen months of extended negotiations with fishermen's cooperatives, which had long predicted a deleterious effect on fish harvests (*AS*, 4 July 1981). Ultimately, the twenty-four fishermen's cooperatives received 4.5 billion yen (approximately $20.5 million at 1981 exchange rates) in compensation (*AS*, 1 April 1986).

Although Narita opponents did use some nonviolent strategies, such as subdividing land among many owners to slow expropriation, their campaign became more confrontational, and riot police became a fixture at rallies. Protesters wearing white helmets and swinging wooden boards regularly clashed with black-helmeted riot police holding body shields and bamboo staves (*AS*, 26 and 27 February 1968) Anti-airport protesters also demonstrated against the local citizens who negotiated with the government over land purchase. On 10 September 1969 the central government began land expropriation proceedings against the remaining householders and farmers. In the eyes of critics, Chiba prefectural authorities had not given them sufficient notice (*Zengakuren* 1971, 242). Comparing Narita with international airports in Munich and London, one scholar pointed out that it took on average seventeen years to move from planning to land acquisition for those facilities, whereas in Narita, authorities moved from planning to land seizure in five years (Todoroki 2002).

Once it received permission from the expropriation committee, the government announced its intention to seize property forcefully beginning on 28 December 1970. The most violent expropriation battles between members of the radical left wing group Chūkaku-ha with other anti-facility groups and state security forces took place from mid-February through March 1971 (Phase I) and then again from 16 to 22 September 1971 (Phase II), when struggles between the police and activists involved bamboo poles, steel pipes, Molotov cocktails, and human feces. In the end, these battles between 20,000 protesters and 25,000 policemen resulted in the death of three policemen (Bowen 1975, 598) and several protesters.

Whereas anti-airport groups at Narita used violence in their struggle against the airport, citizens' movements fought the Osaka International Airport in court. On 27 November 1975 they won a ban on all flights after 9:00 P.M., and the case eventually went to the Supreme Court (Unyushō 1980, 21;

OKK 1990). Perhaps recognizing that "night cap" legislation as proposed in Osaka and supported in court would mollify local opponents, in April 1976 the Narita Airport Authority similarly prohibited the take-off and landing of aircraft from 11:00 P.M. to 6:00 A.M. Despite such concessions, when Narita was completed in 1978 (seven years later than originally planned), protesters destroyed the equipment within the control tower and forced Transportation Minister Kenji Fukunaga to delay its opening (Malcolm 1978). Only in March 1978 did the MOT's vice minister invite leaders of the main opposition group Hantai Dōmei and farmers to the first real face-to-face dialogue over land acquisition (AS, 29 March 1978). When the airport finally opened on May 20 that year, 13,000 riot policemen were on hand to protect the important people assembled for the ceremonies (Scott-Stokes 1978a).

That same spring, airport authorities in the Ministry of Transportation sought to create legislation that would allow them to move effectively against the often violent anti-airport activists who had disrupted the state's plans (Kitano and Ichinose 1992). Of all the years between 1978 and 1990, 1978 saw the most acts of sabotage and guerrilla warfare against airport facilities (Sumiya 1996, 62). In this atmosphere, the Narita Public Order Law (Narita Chian Hō) was proposed by a Diet member and turned into law by the Fukuda Cabinet in 1978 after thirteen hours of deliberation in the 84th Diet assembly. It provided the Ministry of Transportation with previously unheard of discretionary powers, according to Kitano and Ichinose (1992), whose work I draw on through this section.

The Public Order Law embodied the full coercive powers of the state. It allowed the minister to prohibit the use of buildings and facilities by people deemed "violent" and gave him authority to seal up facilities and even destroy them when he thought it necessary. Further, MOT officials were granted the right to enter any establishments and facilities deemed dangerous and the right to ask for identification from anyone. Individuals who gave false answers to such requests could pay fines up to 50,000 yen (around $240 at 1978 exchange rates). This law applied to all areas within 3 kilometers of Narita. Analysts argued that the law was put in place to ensure the airport's opening after repeated delays. It also allowed authorities to dismantle buildings constructed by anti-airport groups, where existing laws, such as the Construction Standard Acts (Kenchiku Kijun Hō), did not permit such destruction (Kitano and Ichinose 1992). Despite challenges from citizens movements, the courts upheld the Public Order Law (Kitahara 1996, 174).

The Narita Airport was Japan's main international hub, but by the late 1980s critics were calling it "one-lunged" because of its single runway and lack of high-speed train access (AS, 20 May 1988). Given the strong local resistance to expropriation in earlier phases of Narita's siting, observers might have expected the MOT to shy away from that strategy, at least in handling local citizens. It did not. In 1988 the head of the NAA announced that the government would again be using land expropriation in order to finish constructing a long-stalled second runway (Kitahara 1996, 158). Soon thereafter, in October 1988, left-wing radicals assaulted and crippled Ogawa Akira, the chairman of the prefectural expropriation committee, breaking his knees, wrists, and elbows with metal pipes (Chipello 1991), but only one person was arrested and sentenced to two years in prison (AS, 12 October 1989; AS, 9 March 1991). Shortly after the attack, the entire six-member committee disbanded, ending its long experience of verbal assaults and threats from activists in late October 1998 (AS, 31 October 1998; AS, 12 October 1989; Sterngold 1989).[5] Without a committee in place to approve expropriation, the governor could no longer utilize eminent domain.

Only after years of coercion strategies and expropriation had failed to diminish anti-Narita protest did the state move to institute mechanisms of soft social control. In the late 1980s the airport authorities began a public relations campaign involving posters and newspaper ads, stressing the urgent need for airport expansion and their peaceful attempts to negotiate with farmers (Chipello 1991). The central government also began an investigation into how citizens in the broader public viewed the struggle over Narita. In 1988 the prime minister's office surveyed 7,711 persons and found that 84.5 percent of them knew about anti-airport activities at Narita (Naikaku 1988 19), yet only a small percentage of respondents strongly supported the protesters' behavior. Approximately 45 percent said either that the protesters should cooperate, because of the compensation they would receive or for the sake of society, or that they could not understand such behavior. Only 2.5 percent said the protesters were right; 27.9 percent stated that they could sympathize with and understand the farmers emotionally but that they were unrealistic to imagine they could stop the airport (Naikaku 1988, 21). Despite the coalition that local farmers had built with students, their message and approach did not appeal to the wider public.

This survey showed further that the government could use expropriation without a backlash from broader society. Of the respondents, only 5 percent thought the government should give up on plans to expand the airport, whereas 41.1 percent thought the government should make every effort to solve the problem through negotiation, and 20.8 percent thought that if

---

5. In 2003, the chairman was reported to have killed himself because of the constant pain from his fractured joints (author's interviews with activists, summer 2003).

negotiations fell through, the government should use legal measures (i.e., expropriation) against the protesters. As in the previous question, about a quarter of the citizens interviewed did not give an opinion (Naikaku 1988, 23).

In December 1989 the MOT apologized to the Hantai Dōmei and local farmers for failing to explain fully its reasons for siting the airport in Sanrizuka; at a press conference it announced feelings of regret (*AS*, 4 December 1989). But what happened the next day illustrates the Machiavellian behavior of state agencies: within twenty-four hours of apologizing, the MOT used its powers under the Narita Public Order Law to prohibit the use of the Hantai Dōmei's fortress complex and then ordered it destroyed (Koshida 1989). Laying siege to the iron and wood structure, riot police in full battle gear used cranes to help prevent injuries among security forces as they arrested occupants. Not until late 1990 did the MOT begin seeking dialogue with the anti-airport groups in what would become the Narita Airport Symposium and roundtable discussions (*AS*, 19 October 1990). The Regional Promotion Council (Chiiki Shinkō Renraku Kyōgikai), formed in 1990 under the sponsorship of the MLIT, opened the Symposium in November 1991.

### Into the Wild Blue Yonder: 1990 to the Present

Observers might imagine that the government's experience with Narita Airport would push it away from using coercion and land expropriation and toward soft social control and incentives in future interactions with contentious civil society. It did not. The state continues to use coercion as its primary tool for solving siting difficulties. Some foreign observers mistakenly focused on the government's "*inability* to condemn land under eminent domain power and purchase it for fair market value [emphasis added]" (Dempsey, Goetz, and Szyliowicz 1997, 233) as a reason for the delays at Narita. In fact, the state has accelerated the use of eminent domain for highways, national railways, and large airports (Matsura 1974, 126).

As the Ministry of Transport worked to handle anti-Narita groups in the early 1990s, it began plans to construct Nagoya's Chubu Airport on an artificial 470-hectare island. This new airport would cost more than $6 billion, to be split between the central and prefectural governments and private capital (*Airports International* 36/4 [2003]: 31). Announced in 1990, plans for Chubu called for a single 3,500-meter runway which would absorb flights from Nagoya Airport (AP News, 1 August 2000). The planning committee published thirteen different reports on the necessity of the Chubu airport and its effects on the local business climate, shipping, the environment, and the local construction industry. Citizens concerned about noise pollution as well as potential environmental damage resisted the proposal (Shimazaki 2001, 256). Negotiations with the local fishermen stalled several times, bringing the head of MOT's Airport Bureau to the area for a pep talk to local residents (AS, 20 October 1999). (Government officials make such visits also during difficult nuclear power plant siting cases, where the state hopes its visible presence and appeals will sway local opinion.) As land acquisition difficulties continued, prefectural authorities began expropriation, despite strong protests from locals (AS, 13 September 2002). By the summer of 2003, land had been confiscated from the thirteen individuals holding 90 hectares, and construction on the airport began (AS, 4 July 2003).

In many siting cases, the local community is not unified in its reaction. Groups with strong economic interests in the Sanrizuka area see Narita Airport as a public good, providing jobs, taxes, and international exposure to their town. For example, in April 1999 local business groups formed the Narita Airport Parallel Runway Completion Support Association to push for Runway B, arguing that "lives and local economies depend upon it." The government opened the second runway in April 2002, just in time for the FIFA World Cup soccer matches, but because of local resistance it is some 400 meters shorter than planned, not long enough for large jet aircraft. It ends at an unfinished section on which stand two houses with vegetable patches and chicken coops (AS, 17 April 2002).

As the central government sought to resolve long-standing tensions with local residents over Narita, it also ran into resistance when attempting to expand Haneda Airport, Tokyo's second largest, primarily domestic, airfield. It had grown out of earlier flight-school airfields that were enhanced during the early 1930s as Japan waged war against other Asian countries (Hiraki 1983, 182–183). After World War II the base was taken over by the General Headquarters of the Allies and then was returned in the late 1940s. Some thirty years later, seeking to expand the limited space available at what was then Tokyo's main airport, MOT bureaucrats built three more runways, designated A, B, and C, on landfill farther away from the local population than the original runways (Yomiuri Shinbun, 24 March 2000). Citizen opposition to this expansion delayed their completion until the 1990s (AS, 14 April 1972).

Since then, state administrators have tried to add a fourth runway to increase Haneda Airport's domestic and international routes. As in other recent airport siting attempts, plans to expand Haneda were accompanied by numerous explanatory meetings about landing patterns, noise pollution, and potential environmental damage; officials also said they expected domestic traffic to surpass 73.2 million passengers by 2012. With citizens opposing another runway near the already noise-polluted mainland, planners envision building an offshore island, either floating, on pile-supported piers, or using hybrid construction techniques (*Nikkei*, 22 January 2001).

Until recently, the public had only minimal involvement and access to siting procedures, but demands from citizens who had witnessed more open and transparent government procedures elsewhere pushed the ministry to redesign its siting process, at least superficially. The Ministry of Land, Infrastructure, and Transport (which absorbed the MOT) designed a siting procedure that takes public opinion into account with built-in access points for public voices and opinions (Watanabe 2003, 28). Ironically, because Japan as of 2008 has excess capacity for aviation, no airports are planned for the immediate future.

### French Airport Siting: Moderate Resistance

In Japan, resistance has come primarily from individual, local-level groups seeking to stop airports from being built in their backyards. In France, however, where the state has built some 430 airports since World War II, civil society has mobilized on a broader scale to create anti-airport organizations at the regional and national levels. Among these umbrella groups, ADVOC-NAR (Association de Défense contre les Nuisances Aériennes) UFCNA (Union Francilienne contre les Nuisances des Aéronefs), and CDRR (Comité de Défense des Riverains de Roissy) have led several anti-airport movements, fighting both siting and expansion, over the past several decades. Because of this wider-ranging, extended opposition, the government has used both hard and soft social tools along with incentives when siting airports, as opposed to relying on coercion and land expropriation. French state agencies have gerrymandered site acquisitions to avoid inflaming local landowners and have established newsletters and local offices to smooth their relationships with residents—but in order to dampen the efforts of anti-airport groups, they have also refused to divulge information.

In October 1945 the French government set up the government-owned institution Aéroport de Paris (ADP) under the *tutelle* (guardianship) of the Ministry of Transport and Public Works to construct and manage airports within 50 kilometers of Paris.[6] Two airports, Le Bourget and Orly, which

---

6. The ADP was shifted to the Ministry of State from within the Ministry of Transport and Public Works, but it maintained its responsibilities for airport management and siting (Feldman 1985, 145).

had been built primarily for military use in 1914 and 1937, served the area as commercial airfields until the late 1950s. At that time, French government planners predicted that existing facilities would soon be saturated by ever increasing volumes of passengers. Even though Orly, located south of Paris, was rebuilt in 1954, the ADP soon began to search for a new location for an airport that could handle projected levels of traffic. As with other decisions involving controversial facility siting, the state showed a keen awareness of the potential levels of opposition and, in order to speed up the process, selected an area seen as low in civil society. Bureaucrats chose the Paris-Nord site 30 kilometers northeast of Paris in the area of Roissy-en-France, where low population density minimized the potential for local resistance over issues of noise pollution (Onnée 2004). The area had been used as a training ground for Napoleon's army and remained as relatively unpopulated, very dry farmland for beets and wheat (Feldman 1985, 23). In 1963 the ADP officially announced the decision to site there what would become Charles de Gaulle Airport, which, because the government saw the project as serving the public good, received a *déclaration d'utilité publique* (DUP), or declaration of public use.

The DUP for this third Paris airport provided the state with the legal right to expropriate from local owners all land necessary for the project (Feldman 1985, 24), but French government planners structured the site so they could "acquire the maximum amount of land without taking homes and villages" (Feldman and Milch 1982, 160). As a result of the gerrymandering, only a single farmhouse stood on the site's more than 3,034 hectares, which was divided among roughly fifty families. Yet even though the ADP had taken care in choosing its location and layout, local communities organized against the project early in 1959, even before the official selection was made, bringing in the well-known spokesperson Pierre Dubois and agreeing to divide any government monies among themselves equally. Residents formed the CDRR, an umbrella organization that rallied 4,000 marchers in protest when the airport finally opened on 9 March 1974. The activities of the CDRR and other regional citizen action groups, starting even before the official announcement was made, demonstrated the case's wider significance to civil society and kept the state from immediately using land expropriation.

The ADP, hoping to avoid the controversy that could accompany attempts to use eminent domain, relied on the Finance Ministry to negotiate with local landowners over property issues, using the Government Property Administration bureau (Administration des Domaines) within the Finance Ministry as its proxy. As Aéroport de Paris and the Finance Ministry wanted to ease tensions with residents, they initially offered citizens close to 150 percent of the market value of their land, though the Administration des Domaines objected to the high expenditures. Little progress was made during the first year of negotiations, but by the end of the third year the state had increased its offer to nearly four times the market rate, and only a single owner refused to sell his land voluntarily. His portion of the site was the only one forcibly taken by the state, and construction on the airport began in 1966.

During the process of siting Charles de Gaulle Airport, the state used the hard social control technique of information control when it refused to provide data about noise pollution to anti-airport protesters. Facing a legal requirement to post information about the projected noise levels from jet take-offs and landings at the airport, but desiring to keep local communities from protesting potential noise levels, the state initially resisted releasing information at all. Despite claims from the ADP that it was "impossible to measure noise properly before an airport is operational," it had earlier done exactly that when Italian planners asked it to estimate expected noise levels for the yet-to-open Malpensa Airport at Milan (Feldman and Milch 1982, 138). Eventually, following the letter of the law, the ADP made data on noise curves available but concealed the information in the hands of the local prefect. Citizens who asked officials about the existence of these data were often told they did not exist (Feldman 1985, 42–43). (The French state likewise controlled the flow of information on forthcoming nuclear power plants by placing it in local government offices and making it available only to those who could show that they lived within 5 kilometers of the planned plant. In this way, too, it sought to dampen potential resistance to the project.)

Unlike Japan, where no regional or national umbrella anti-airport groups formed, civil society in France created a number of such institutions. ADVOCNAR formed in 1981; its nearly 2,000 active members across the country worked to organize and connect anti-airport groups (Trenz and Jentges 2005). Along with the CDRR, which formed to fight specifically against Charles de Gaulle Airport, French activists formed UFCNA, whose motto was "mak[ing] the existence and functioning of civil and military aviation compatible with the right to a normal life for people on the ground." UFCNA, like ADVOCNAR, petitioned the government not to build new airports and sought "night caps" to limit evening flying, along with better guarantees for local citizens against noise pollution. Furthermore, anti-airport groups in France found consistent allies in the ecologist political party known as the Greens (*Les Verts*), a luxury not available to anti-airport groups in Japan.[7]

7. On Green parties in the French political system, see Szarka (2002, chap. 3).

Once the Charles de Gaulle Airport was completed and had begun operations, the Office for Expropriation was renamed the Office to Help Airport Neighbors; it offered to purchase the houses of local residents who were bothered by the noise. Residents outside the actual airport property but still facing noise pollution understood that few would want to purchase their homes, given sound levels of close to 100 decibels and their discovery that an expanding amount of land was affected by noise pollution as the number of evening and morning flights increased over time. As a result, some 260 homeowners living nearby sold their property to the state, which demolished their homes to prevent future protest (Feldman and Milch 1982, 163). The French state developed an invisible tool for funding this policy by imposing a Cabinet-level tax on every passenger who came through Charles de Gaulle Airport. Like the Japanese electricity tax known as the *Dengen Sanpō,* which funds pronuclear policies, this submerged instrument of the state cannot be viewed or scrutinized by politicians or citizens through standard policy or budget reviews.

Along with working to avoid contestation by altering the layout of the airport and by offering large markups when purchasing property, the French state set up soft social control tools such as newsletters that emphasized the economic benefits of airport siting. Entitled *Entre Voisins* (Among Neighbors), the newsletter was parodied by local residents; their *Entre Riverains* (Among the Bordering Communities) was decidedly less enthusiastic (Feldman 1985, 42). As another soft social control tool, the government built Maison de l'Environment (Environment House), a structure near the airport that provided information on the "acceptable" levels of noise being emitted from the airport and on the steps that state authorities had taken to "green" the project.

Within a few years after Charles de Gaulle Airport opened in 1974, Le Bourget was closed to international traffic (in 1977) and then to regional traffic (in 1980). But French planners again believed that existing airports would not be able to handle future demand and sought a new site for another international airport (after calling off plans to expand Charles de Gaulle because of concerns about backlash from local residents). The state abandoned its first choice of Beauvillers, 90 kilometers southwest of Paris, when several NGOs—including Amis de la Terre (Friends of the Earth) and Collectif contre l'Aéroport (Collective to Oppose the Airport), along with political parties such as the Greens—attacked the plan (Hayes 2002, 25–26).

In late 2001 the ADP officially announced a site for the third airport for Paris: the town of Chaulnes in the Somne region, 125 kilometers northeast of Paris. It raised interesting questions about the extent of the ADP's jurisdiction, as it has a mandate to build and manage airports only within

50 kilometers of Paris. When reporters asked about the legal basis for its involvement, Pierre Chassigneux, then the ADP president, said that laws "can
be changed" (Frank-Keyes 2002, 8). The village of Chaulnes, sustained primarily by farming, has a population of fewer than 2,000 people, close to half
of whom will have to be rehoused should the airport plans be realized. Of the
8,000 area residents who voted in a nonbinding citizens' referendum in 2001,
90 percent were against the proposed airport. Multiple protests, both in Paris
and near the planned site in the Somne, have regularly brought in close to
5,000 participants, reflecting the ability of national and regional civil society
groups to draw in allies. Anti-airport umbrella groups were able to mobilize
15,000 participants at several rallies against expansion plans at other airports,
such as Strasbourg-Entzheim in Alsace (Pipard and Gualezzi 2002). As with
the siting of Charles de Gaulle Airport, initial movements for Chaulnes show
that the state will seek to move away from the coercive tools used by their
Japanese counterparts and instead use hard and soft social control tools to
smooth the siting of this new international airport.

Extended cases from Japanese airport siting alongside a brief glimpse into
French airport siting provide a comparative perspective on the interaction between civil society resistance over time and state tools. In Japan, the Ministry
of Transportation remained wedded to strategies of coercion, moving to offer
small concessions and incentives only long after the process of siting began.
Resistance against airports in Japan came only occasionally, however, and primarily from local groups, not regional or national ones. The Narita Airport
case proved to be an anomaly, driving up newspaper coverage of the issue and
involving the largest delays recorded in the history of Japanese airport siting.
Rather than imagining Narita's resistance as representative of other cases, bureaucrats in the Ministry of Transportation labeled it as an outlier, believing
correctly that the larger society would not join with affected local residents to
resist airport siting.

Although Japanese citizens in general were aware of anti-airport opposition like that at Narita, few joined with the opponents to create wider bodies
of mobilized civil society that could pressure the government to alter its tools,
if not its overall plans. Only after years of protest and often violent resistance
from farmers near Narita, and their radical student allies, did the state implement some minor social control mechanisms to convince local citizens that the
airport was legitimate and necessary. Such soft tools were the exception, not
the rule. As a sign of the stability of government strategies for siting airports
in Japan, the central government established the core relevant legislation, the
Kūkō Seibi Hō, in 1956 and did not revise it until 1993.

Despite violence over the expropriation of land early in the siting of Narita Airport, the state was willing not only to use eminent domain again with its plans for a second runway there but also to use it regularly to handle resistance in other airport siting cases. The MOT created the Narita Public Order Law—a policy instrument that combines outright coercion and hard social control—to smooth the crushing of anti-airport associations. Because it did not face strong challenges from civil society groups in most cases, the state altered its siting practices only slightly, making them seemingly more democratic, without having to add new tactics to its toolkit for handling contentious civil society. For example, although new procedures for airport siting officially consider local public opinion, no new airports are planned for the immediate future. The money available to host communities, including compensation for noiseproofing, is dwarfed by the huge amounts given to communities hosting nuclear power plants; these small incentives mirror the low levels of resistance from civil society.

Though the Narita airport case did not in itself trigger the creation of new policies for siting future airports, it did change the way Japanese citizens viewed their government and the way the state viewed potential resistance. Authorities have regularly mentioned the "lessons of Narita" in dealings with anti-facility protesters. For example, because of the events at Narita, the National Governors Conference justified the creation of an institutionalized subsidy program for communities that host dams (Aida 1977, 51; Miyano 2000, 171). Planners seeking to site nuclear power plants viewed Narita as a worst-case potential outcome for their own projects and referred to it when they created compensation for towns hosting the plants. During the struggle between Shizuoka prefectural authorities and local citizens over the siting of a new airport there, anti-airport groups framed the issue in terms of another Narita, arguing that if "the Ministry of Land, Infrastructure, and Transport approves this high-handed plan, they'll show that they learned nothing from their lesson at Narita" (*AS,* 13 August 2003).

In France, by contrast with Japan, regional and national anti-airport movements established themselves early on and have kept up pressure over three decades. By bringing in broader umbrella groups such as ADVOCNAR, CDRR, and UFCNA, French communities have pushed the state away from its available coercive tools such as land expropriation and police repression. Rather than utilizing its full available powers of eminent domain, Aéroport de Paris sought to negotiate with citizens through large incentive programs and then used hard and soft social control instruments to suppress opposition. Despite a reputation for "steamrolling" local citizens who disagreed with state plans, the ADP, the Ministry of Finance, and other state agencies stepped lightly during the siting process. Thus they demonstrated how even medium levels of resistance can alter a state's toolkit as they established house-purchasing programs, public relations magazines, and the distribution of environmental information although the French state did also suppress information about noise pollution that potentially could assist anti-airport groups.

French airport siting cases are in fact quite similar to Japanese dam-siting cases of the 1990s, with moderate levels of resistance and alliances with extra-local civil society groups.

# 4

## DAM THE RIVERS

### *Siting Water Projects in Japan and France*

EARLY IN THE SUMMER OF 1952 a representative of the Ministry of Construction appeared at the village of Kawarayu in Gunma prefecture, 151 kilometers northwest of Tokyo, and called a village meeting without any prior explanation. To the mayor and townspeople the official brusquely announced, "We are building a dam here.... This village is going to be flooded out" (Hagiwara 1996, 1). That was how local residents learned of the state's plan to construct the Yanba Dam in their backyard. The project would flood the village, displace approximately 1,200 people, and cover 340 homes and 50 hectares of farm land (KKCKYDKJ 1989). The dam would also submerge historical areas and the spas for which the area had become famous (Nakagome 1978, 104). Although the state temporarily pulled its offices from the town to diffuse the immediate angry reaction, the plan moved forward over local objections. Homeowners who refused to sell faced expropriation of their land at unknown prices. Residents organized against the plan and managed to stall it but had difficulty drawing in regional or national allies and maintaining resistance over the four decades of planning that ensued. As of late 2007, relocation plans were being finalized for many local residents, and construction had begun on the main site. The state offered land to displaced families, but approximately half the village, frustrated with what they saw as higher prices for the "replacement" land, abandoned the area altogether (*Yomiuri Shinbun,* 13 January 2005).

This chapter explores dam siting in Japan and France to show how states handle conflict with civil society once it arises. For most of the period since World War II, the Japanese Ministry of Construction encountered only small-scale anti-dam groups within civil society.[1] Thus even today it relies on expropriation of land and other policy tools based on coercion. In recent years, civil society has mobilized more broadly and decisively against dams, often bringing in international allies, so the MOC has added minor policies—primarily

---

1. Although in 2001, the MOC merged with other ministries to form the mammoth MLIT, this primarily historical case study uses the older name for the agency as appropriate. The MLIT directly oversees ninety-six completed dams; an additional sixty-eight are under construction on Class A

small incentives and a handful of soft social control strategies—to its toolkit in response to increasing pressure from contentious citizens' groups at home and abroad. In France, unlike Japan, anti-dam movements were able to mobilize early, in the 1970s, at regional and national levels to call attention to their causes. Groups within civil society such as the SOS Loire Vivante and the labor union Confédération Française Démocratique du Travail (CFDT) brought in allies including political parties—the Greens and the Socialists—to broaden what might have otherwise been just local anti-dam movements. Resistance movements against French dam projects, including those planned for the Loire River basin, sustained protest for extended periods, in one case occupying a planned dam site for five years. The French state could have expropriated land and used coercive tools such as police repression, yet it did not; instead, it responded to these long-lasting but moderate levels of opposition with hard and soft social control tools and incentives.

Dams are the cornerstone of Japan's "construction state." With 2,734 dams dotting the waterscape and 373 more under construction, virtually no Japanese river flows unimpeded to the sea. (By comparison, even though France has almost twice as much land as Japan, it has built only 250 dams over the postwar period.) Although the government estimates that Japan uses only 37 percent of its hydropower potential (Kokudokōtsūshō Kasenkyoku 2003, 8), some argue that over 90 percent is already being utilized (*Economist*, 19 July 2003). Japan's dams are expensive; in 2002 Japan spent more than $4.7 billion on water-based public works projects (Kokudokōtsūshō Kasenkyoku 2002) and $7.74 billion over the previous two years. For many, dams have become the paradigmatic symbol of Japan's social, political, and economic malaise in recent years (Kerr 2001; Kobayashi 2003).

How can a government persuade the public to destroy nature so utterly? The proliferation of dams in Japan did not happen overnight, nor is it the inexorable result of culture, closed procedures, or deep economic incentives. Rather, it is a political story. The government managed a mildly contentious segment of civil society with institutions designed to dampen citizen resistance. As noted in chapter 1, bureaucrats placed dams in spread-out towns and villages where the population density was low and resistance least likely. Unlike the strategies of their counterparts who handled nuclear power siting, bureaucrats within the MOC primarily used tools of coercion, such as land expropriation and the cutting of subsidies, along with small-scale inducements,

---

rivers. It provides two-thirds of the funding for these usually large, multipurpose dams that cross prefectural boundaries. Dams built under the initiative of local governments and private or quasi-private corporations are beyond the scope of this study.

to handle moderately contentious anti-dam civil society groups. Only when they encountered better-organized and larger organizations in recent years did the River Bureau within the MOC create soft social control tools that spread positive images and information regarding proposed projects.

Dams do not immediately come to mind as controversial facilities that trigger negative reactions from local communities. Unlike radioactive waste dumps or nuclear power plants, dams seem mundane and stable facilities. Engineers usually detect and fix leaks before serious damage results.[2] Although some significant environmental problems remain, dams are not like waste disposal sites, which leak toxins into the groundwater, or like airports, which entail both air and noise pollution (Altshuler and Luberoff 2003, 134). Dams are commonly viewed as quiet and nonpolluting. Dam construction also concentrates externalities more than that of such facilities as nuclear plants, leading to shorter and less acute interactions between state and society. Whereas nuclear plants provoke resistance from distant and even international communities, resistance to Japanese dams comes primarily from the local communities that are flooded out by newly created reservoirs. As a result, nationwide anti-dam groups developed slowly in Japan, in contrast to France. Japan's case is similar to that of India, where coordinated citizen resistance to dams emerged only in the mid-1980s and grew throughout the 1990s (Khagram 2004). International coalitions of environmental and activist movements now regularly ally with local groups to challenge dam construction in Japan and abroad. Still, the lack of a sustained challenge over most of the postwar period permitted Japan's government to meet its dam-siting goals without aggressively or innovatively upgrading its social control strategies.

As resistance to dam construction in Japan was regularly small-scale and localized, civil society's opposition to water projects received little media coverage over the postwar period except for a brief spike in the late 1950s. Early anti-dam movements garnered almost no coverage, with only an article or two a year from 1945 until the late 1950s, when a rare but fierce mobilization of civil society against the Matsubara and Shimouke Dams grabbed the national spotlight. Not until the late 1980s and 1990s did media outlets again focus sustained attention on the issue, as figure 10 shows. On average from 1945 to

2. There are some exceptions to this statement; for example, the 1889 flood in Johnstown, Pennsylvania, occurred when the levee on an artificial lake created for the wealthy boaters of the South Fork Fishing Club collapsed; the resulting 20 million tons of floodwaters killed more than 2,000 people (*New York Times*, 1 June 1889). More recently a 1975 dam failure in China killed 230,000 people (*The Economist*, 19 July 2003); in Idaho in 1976 the collapse of the Teton Dam killed eleven people and caused $1 billion in damage; and a 1988 dam failure in Tokushima prefecture in Japan flooded local homes and villages (*AS*, 8 June 1988). In March 2006, weakened by rain, the Kaloko Reservoir Dam failed on the Hawaiian island of Kauai, killing several residents (AP Wire, 15 March 2006).

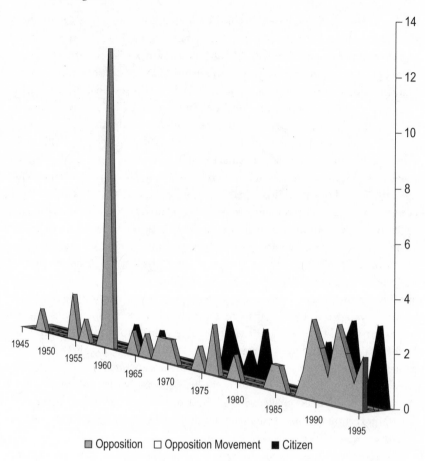

Figure 10. Low level of anti-dam sentiment over the postwar period. Number of articles with the key words "dam" and...
Source: *Asahi Shinbun* CD-ROM

1995, resistance to state dam plans rated fewer than four articles per year in the national *Asahi Shinbun*. This low level of coverage indicates the difficulties that anti-dam groups have had in garnering allies from the larger population and increasing their visibility and levels of contestation against the state.

Though dams involve smaller-scale problems than airports or nuclear plants, three sets of concerns motivate resistance to them. First, local citizens may perceive that they are being unfairly targeted for projects that bring few, if any, direct benefits but can uproot several hundred residents from their homes. Second, resettlement for the uprooted residents creates considerable anxiety and disruption: those remaining near the dam site must face cut-off bus services, relocated and more distant schools, and a sense of isolation (*AS,* 21

February 1976), while those who are forced to move face the triple difficulty of finding new jobs, paying higher prices, and losing their social ties (Nishiyama 1971, 35–36). Third, other citizens—both local and farther away—resist for environmental, ecological, or ideological reasons (Tanimura 1982, 24).

## A Calm Surface: Dam Siting in Japan in the 1950s and 1960s

The early postwar period in Japan witnessed little organized citizen resistance to dam construction, and thus little expansion in the scale or scope of government strategies for managing civil society. The unexpected and rare levels of resistance in the Matsubara-Shimouke case led the state to modify and strengthen its procedures for handling opposition and forced the Ministry of Construction to recognize the potential for future difficulties in obtaining private land for dam construction.

The initial impetus for dam construction came from the Cabinet, which began meeting in the mid-1950s to establish budgets and target water volumes for five-year intervals (Tsugano 1977, 15; author's interviews with Diet members, summer 2003).[3] During this early period the MOC emphasized three reasons for dam construction: low water-resource levels, flooding concerns, and electricity production. Promotional materials still regularly emphasize Japan's vulnerability to droughts and relative lack of precipitation compared with other advanced nations (Kokudokōtsūshō Kasenkyoku 2002, 2003). For example, at a 1995 conference on rivers and development, the MOC's representative argued that in water resources, Japan was still a developing nation (Nihon Bengoshi Rengōkai 1995, 43). Similarly, MOC planners regularly inform critics that the Hoover Dam alone holds more than twice the volume of all of Japan's reservoirs (Amano 2001, 6; Nihon Bengoshi Rengōkai 1995, 94; Tanimura 1997, 9). Additionally, a series of typhoons and damaging floods in the late 1950s and 1960s justified a nationwide program of dam construction under the MOC. Environmentalists and anti-dam activists regularly note, however, that bureaucratic projections of flooding and rains are usually based on improbable or rare occurrences, such as once-in-a-century torrential rains (Takahashi 2002, 170; author's interviews with anti-dam activists, spring 2003).

3. As most existing dams—and some still currently under construction—were planned and built during the economic growth era of the 1950s and 1960s (author's interviews with Diet members, spring 2003), that time is sometimes referred to as the "dam boom." Some of more contested dams—including the Matsubara and Shimouke, the Yanba, (Hagiwara 1996), and the Nagara River Dams (Choy 2000)—were initiated during this period. Some researchers have postulated that the previous experience of American occupiers with the TVA and other New Deal projects heavily influenced the thinking of postwar Japanese planners (Amano 2001, 31).

As the state began expropriating private land for dams and faced little or no public outcry, official compensation levels depended on the type of project. For example, in 1953, the Cabinet set guidelines for compensation for hydroelectric dams, officially flexible enough to compensate for lost jobs and lifestyle changes in addition to loss of land and property (Takase 1971, 43). But early guidelines provided compensation only to those citizens with "legally acknowledged rights": that is, those directly affected by construction or relocation (Naganohara 1954, 68). Despite this legal patchwork, compensation standards for land expropriation were so unclear that relevant ministries set up a deliberation council in the early 1960s to resolve the legal ambiguities (T. Kobayashi 1994, 15). After five years, the Cabinet agreed in 1967 on a unified set of compensation laws (Takase 1971, 45).[4]

Typically, MOC administrators summoned residents and announced that the village would be submerged at a future date, quickly departing after such proclamations. Yanba Dam's "decide, announce, defend" approach forced the state to shut down its local office for more than a decade to let tempers cool (Hagiwara 1996, 1), and in the Shitara Dam case the MOC withdrew for fourteen years to let the anti-dam opposition die down (GDN 11/685 [2001]: 70). Although local authorities announced the Yanba Dam plan to unbelieving villagers in 1952, the villagers thought the plan dead when they heard no further announcements for thirteen years. During that time, however, the MOC quietly carried out preliminary surveys (yobi chōsa) that discovered naturally high levels of acidity in the water and soil which would undermine the dam's structure. Officials used the time to formulate a plan to neutralize the acidity. In 1965, having resolved the issue, the government reannounced its intention to construct the dam (Hagiwara 1996, 8; author's site visit, spring 2003).

Because it encountered only small-scale responses from targeted communities, the Ministry of Construction began to rely on the coercive tool of land expropriation to site dams, starting in the early postwar era. Although MOC planners emphasized that "solving the compensation problem is half the battle" (Ito 1954, 16; cf. Shimouke Matsubara 1972, 5), the forced acquisition of land was a policy tool that lurked at the back of every negotiation: should bargaining over compensation break down, state officials could always rely on the tried-and-true tool of eminent domain. Citizen anger over expropriation

---

4. From the earliest days of dam negotiation, observers understood that although the Ministry of Construction established a variety of methods to determine "objective" compensation standards, they were in no way binding, especially on landowners who were being forcibly removed from their property. Law scholars argued that the Expropriation Council, a necessary institution in any expropriation proceeding, need not be locked into the standard prices set by the Ministry of Construction but could fix prices as it believed appropriate (Suzuki 1964, 241).

only occasionally made it into the mainstream news. In 1954, reporters described the anguish of local residents when state planners received permission to expropriate the land of five homeowners who had refused to sell (*AS*, 10 July 1975). In 1973, MOC officials used the law to acquire land for the Ōmachi Dam and, in 1975, the Sagae Dam project (KHCKODKJ 1986, 955; KTCKGDKJ 1982, 7–10). For the $619.9 million Nibutani Dam, the state forcibly expropriated land from indigenous Ainu people to howls of protest (*AS*, 4 April 1989).

A critical juncture for the state came in the late 1950s as Tomoyuki Murohara led publicized and violent resistance to the expropriation of land for the Matsubara and Shimouke dams. Murohara was a wealthy man living 500 meters from one of the dam sites. The MOC carried out stealthy geographical and river surveys for the projects and announced these dam schemes without explaining their necessity or purpose (Murohara 1971, 81). These two dams, proposed in 1958 and completed in 1972, submerged more than 30,000 hectares of land and displaced some 480 families (author's communication with dam administrators, summer 2003). Murohara's slogan, posted on billboards for all to see, disputed the legality of the MOC's procedures (KKCKCDTKJ 1992, 186). Murohara used his substantial personal resources, possibly spending up to 100 million yen (more than $330,000 at 1972 exchange rates) (Shimouke Matsubara 1972, 106) to build what became known as the Bees' Nest (*hachi no sujō*), a huge wooden structure covering the river banks near the proposed sites from which anti-dam banners were hung (Kashima 1964, 244).

Widespread popular resistance to these dams arose when the Ministry of Construction surveyors cut down cedar trees in May 1959 (Soejima 1969, 66). Although the MOC had received permission from the landowner to remove the trees, other residents objected. Anti-dam activists went on to use the lumber to build the Bees' Nest (*AS*, 14 February 1960). As in other cases, one reason for the anger and violence against the state was the speedy use of land expropriation against those who refused to sell. Parties to the conflict argued that the MOC's rapid reliance on eminent domain—filed only nine months after it set up a branch office—enraged residents (*AS*, 18 April 1960; Shimouke Matsubara 1972, 162). Citizens filed lawsuits seeking to void land expropriation; the government filed countersuits declaring locals' sit-down strikes to be illegal (see *GDN* 653/3 [1999]: 21–23).

In the Matsubara-Shimouke confrontation, conflicts between citizen activists and the MOC often grew violent, and authorities turned to police coercion to maintain order. At one point, riot police were called into the melee to arrest activists attacking surveyors near the Bees' Nest (Murohara 1971, 85; *AS*, 28 June 1988). Photographs show local citizens using forked bamboo poles to keep surveyors at bay, while others hurled stones and splashed water. Murohara and others were arrested on 4 July 1960 because of their interference with and violence against the MOC surveyors, and Murohara was sentenced to ten months in prison (Shimouke Matsubara 1972, 4, 384–386). Over the next decade, police demolished the Bees' Nest forty-four times, but activists rebuilt it. When Murohara passed away suddenly at age seventy, the MOC publicly announced that it would consider his criticisms in improving its future siting procedures; the activists entered into talks with authorities; and MOC officials completed the project smoothly (Shimouke Matsubara 1972, 14).

Some bureaucrats credit Murohara with pushing them to offer additional subsidies and compensation to dam communities (Shinoda and Takigawa 1985, 52), including small revisions to the Land Expropriation and River Laws (Shimouke Matsubara 1972, 160). Yet though casual observers may have believed that the MOC would, in the future, be more open to citizen voices, anti-dam activists argued the opposite. The 1964 River Law strengthened many MOC procedures that had proved inadequate during the Shimouke-Matsubara Dam construction (Amano 2001, 10).

Observers might also imagine that the widespread media coverage of the violent opposition over the Murohara cases would push the Ministry of Construction to stop expropriating private land for dams. But the opposite was true: the annual number of approved land expropriations for river projects grew over the postwar period (though the average number stayed stable, at fifteen to twenty per year). During the 1960s, following the Matsubara and Shimouke cases, the state approved more expropriations than in any other decade. In short, the violence of Murohara's followers did not dissuade state planners from using coercion in siting dams. Instead, bureaucrats saw how limited the scope of resistance was even in the Murohara case; it was indeed an outlier compared with typical dam-siting experiences up to that point. Civil society displayed weakness in response to state plans for dams, as few regional or national allies joined in the often short battles against these projects. Where there was little chance of wide-scale backlash against the state, expropriation provided the quickest and cheapest way to carry out state goals.

According to the 1967 revision of the Land Expropriation Law, moreover, contractors and government officials could conduct land and household surveys without the consent of the property owner (Matsuzawa 1969, 23). (One Ministry of Construction official suggested to his colleagues that when owners refused to allow surveys of their property, administrators should use aerial photography.)

Though fierce citizen resistance was uncommon, however, bureaucrats did slightly restructure their coercive tactics. The resistance at Yanba, Shimouke, and Matsubara Dams pushed administrators to boost the very modest incentives provided to host communities (Shinoda and Takigawa 1985, 52), and the state began to distribute small bonuses. In 1968 the National Governors Committee demanded equitable benefits for local communities from the construction of government-sponsored, large-scale projects such as Narita Airport, which (see chapter 3) was rocked by local opposition (Aida 1977, 51; Miyano 2000, 171). Furthermore, since local government bodies encountered many problems in assisting citizens, the governors sought to reduce the financial burdens for villages, towns, and cities (Takase 1971, 51). Between 1967 and 1973, however, ad hoc committees determined compensation and subsidies to communities that hosted dams.

In 1973 the government set up a small-scale system of incentives known as the Water Resource Measures to provide benefits to the host communities (Maruyama 2000, 2). Initially, a community had to face the submersion of at least thirty houses and thirty hectares of acreage to qualify (Aida 1977, 58–59), but over time these standards were lowered. If a local government applies for these funds, and the Cabinet approves, it becomes eligible for whatever benefits, including grants, subsidies, and loans, are provided by the government (Maruyama 2000, 4). In 1976 a subsection of these subsidies, known as the Water Resource Fund, was provisionally created for the Tonegawa River area.[5] The central government, along with the prefectures and cities that received benefits (i.e., drinking water or water for industrial uses) from dams along that river, pooled resources to provide funds for individual citizens and families (Aida 1977, 63).

## Ripples in the Lake: Increasing Resistance in Japan

The 1970s and 1980s witnessed more regular resistance to dam siting, a phenomenon that led the MOC to streamline its land acquisition procedures and hence upgrade its coercion and hard social control tactics. As a result of increased civil society resistance, the government also deepened its basic incentives, creating more systems of subsidies and side payments, and began using some soft social control tools, distributing pro-dam information and establishing "Water Week" and "Water Day." Officials continued to make such statements as "if you solve the compensation problem, the dam is 80 percent built" (*GDN* 7/537 [1987]: 49), but coercion and expropriation remained

5. Economic Planning Agency bureaucrats created this program specifically to provide assistance to communities that sacrificed some degree of their own lifestyles by hosting dams (Tanaka 1977, 54).

their primary tools for handling opposition. During this period, state officials recognized a scarcity of positive public relations about the benefits of siting (Hirose 1977, 20) and worried that the flood of materials produced by the media and anti-dam groups would make the public widely aware that dam construction had negative consequences (Shinharu Zadankai 1975, 43–44; GDN 1/363 [1975]: 43–44). One MOC official warned his colleagues that when negotiating to acquire their lands for public works projects, "they are not merely purchasing land, they are purchasing the hearts of the people" (Yasuda 1975, 100). Internal MOC documents recommended that bureaucrats make contact with citizens in the presence of local officials and warned them against negotiating with residents during breakfast, lunch, dinner, or favorite television shows.

Though some local residents were very concerned about finding new homes and jobs, many revised their opinion on dam construction once it had begun. For example, one study of the Yahagi Dam conducted between 1970 and 1973 found that although only 18 percent of the villagers had initially supported the project, 46 percent came to describe themselves as "reluctantly supportive" and an additional 26 percent switched from opposing to supporting it. Like other research on contentious political movements, this finding confirms Lichbach's argument that only a small percentage of the population will continually participate in opposition activities (the "Five Percent Rule": see Lichbach 1995, 17), with about 5 percent of households expressing continuous opposition to the project (Suzuki 1977, 196). Citizens facing inevitable expropriation if they continued to resist evidently found it in their best interests to realign their opinions. Surveys following the construction of the Matsubara and Shimouke Dams revealed that 40 percent of respondents had switched from opposition to support. As in the Yahagi case, the number of hard-core anti-dam opponents who refused to change their minds hovered under 5 percent.

In the early 1970s, with the advent of the oil shocks, the government looked to dams not only as water resources but as alternative sources of energy; increasingly, therefore, the Ministry of Construction worked with private companies to create institutions to promote dam construction (NDK 1989, i). In July 1974 the Japan Dam Federation, sponsored by the MOC, became a recognized *zaidan hōjin,* or foundation, complete with special tax status and other benefits. In addition to offering annual awards, conducting public relations campaigns, and setting standards for dam technicians, the Federation hosted workshops and discussions to resolve dam construction problems. It provided two years of workshops on "solving" the compensation problem, tried to improve the Measures for Water Resource Areas, and studied both successful and failed dam siting cases (NDK 1989, 69–88). The Federation regularly convened meetings with experts to discuss the state of public relations for dams (*GDN* 3/581 [1993]: 9) and continues to provide the central government with an independent source of pro-dam information and research.

As citizens became more involved in environmental movements and began to expect more of governmental programs, dam siting—which continued to destroy the homesteads of agricultural families in the mountains—become more contentious. Even in the early 1970s, each of more than half the 450 dams surveyed had submerged between 30 and 400 houses. Hence, in 1977, MLIT bureaucrats moved to create soft social control tools to contain the slowly growing opposition; they designated the first week of August as Water Week and August 1 as Water Day. During Water Week the MOC, along with quasi-governmental organizations such as the Water Resources Development Corporation and the Japan Dam Federation coordinated a series of public relations efforts to promote the importance of water conservation and water resources (*GDN* 9/527 [1998]: 8–12). Reflecting on the difficulties of compensation, one bureaucrat suggested using these promotions to impress citizens with the importance of dams (Sato 1977, 13).

The Ministry of Construction set up two more soft social control mechanisms: habituation, and awards ceremonies. By exposing potential host communities to the lives of towns already hosting dams, the MOC hoped to make local citizens less resistant. By viewing the daily lives of other citizens who had moved because of dam construction and made new lives in new places, citizens concerned about their own future in the shadow of a dam could feel more reassured. For example, many citizens in the Gosho Dam area visited at least one dam during the siting process; one survey put the number who did so at 298 of 300 respondents (KTCKGDKJ 1982, 7–76).

## Cracks in the Dam: National-Level Opposition in Japan since the 1990s

Strong, organized, wider-scale anti-dam movements began to form only in the early to middle 1990s; they received a strong boost from well-publicized local resistance to the Nagara River Estuary in the mid-1980s. One activist observed that until 1988 in Japan, "anti-dam movements were limited to isolated minor conflicts at local dam construction sites and those movements never won the case" (Amano 2000). And according to another activist, before the Nagara River movement, which eventually boasted 16,000 participants with thirty-two branch offices, "each case...was viewed as the problem of only one locality. Each campaign would die out, with the knowledge and experience gained by protesters not being passed on to help other campaigns" (Niikura 1999, 99). Since 1988, though, MOC officials have encountered stronger, organized resistance from civil society at all levels (local, regional, and national) and responded by creating and deepening soft social control mechanisms. Nonetheless, because these protests were still comparatively weak, the state continued to rely primarily on such techniques of coercion as expropriation and grant cutting.

As groups within civil society gained experience and interacted with foreign nongovernmental organizations, by the late 1990s they had begun to carry out more large-scale demonstrations involving local activists and organized, extra-local citizen movements; one was a major rally in Gifu prefecture against the Tokuyama Dam in the winter of 1996 (AS, 23 December 1996). These rallies were so large that Daniel Beard, formerly head of the U.S. Bureau of Land Reclamation, spoke about the "end of the dam building era" at several environmentally focused symposia and meetings in Japan (author's interviews with anti-dam activists, summer 2003). Along with Nagano's governor, Yasuo Tanaka, Beard headed a joint U.S.-Japan committee on Japanese dam building which sought to draw on American experiences with *dismantling* river projects (*Japan Times*, 22 March 2003).

Responding to increased pressure from society, Diet members began to target and cut public works projects deemed unnecessary and unwanted. In 1994, approximately 100 Diet members (primarily Socialist and Communist members) under the leadership of Atsuo Nakamura, formed the nonpartisan Dietmembers' Association for a Mechanism for Public Works Review (Kōkyō Jigyō Chekku Giin no Kai, DAMPWR), a legislative organization that parallels the NGO Association for Public Works Review (NAPWR). Representatives of the DAMPWR visited various proposed public works projects and used their position to grill bureaucrats from the MLIT in open Diet sessions on the prospects for various dam projects (AS, 21 November 2001; *Mainichi Shinbun,* 21 October 2001). As a result of political pressure from both politicians and citizens, several hundred projects, including approximately 100 dams, were reevaluated by the bureaucracy and in many cases suspended or stopped. A 1995 audit showed that construction of at least six dams was halted or ended by long-term citizen resistance (AS, 16 December 1995). In September 2000 the Liberal Democratic Party, in coalition with the Komeitō and Conservative Parties, put forth a list of 233 projects to be reviewed for possible cancellation. It targeted projects that (1) were not started within five years of approval, (2) had been under construction for more than twenty years, (3) were not completed within twenty years after their planned completion date, or (4) were frozen or suspended (Kenshokuso Nyūsu 2000, 1).

In January 2000, activists set up the first citizen referendum (*jūmin tōhyō*) against the Yoshino River Estuary Dam by gathering more than 100,000 signatures (*Yomiuri Shinbun,* 10 February 1999). They succeeded in suspending the project, despite a complaint from the minister of construction that it was a "mistaken exercise in democracy." With 55 percent of eligible voters casting ballots, less than 10 percent of voters supported the project (*Yomiuri Shinbun,* 2 February 2000; Choy 2000). In a nationwide *Asahi Shinbun* survey (1 February 2000), 77 percent of respondents said that the government should respect the citizen referendum; only 9 percent said it should be ignored.[6] During the same period, Governor Yasuo Tanaka of Nagano prefecture declared his public opposition to dams and canceled the three at Ōbotoke, Asakawa, and Shimosuwa. The Asakawa was in fact halfway complete; 200 million yen ($1.9 million at 2000 exchange rates) had already been spent on initial surveys and foundational work. Similarly, the Iwate prefectural governor, Hiroya Masuda, suspended the dam project at Kitakami in 1998 even though 5.2 billion yen ($40 million at 1998 exchange rates) had been spent since its inception in 1980 (Kyodo Newswire, 16 December 1998). These cases set new precedents, as previously no dam construction had been canceled after the central government had provided construction expenses (*AS,* 17 January 1995).

In the late 1990s, anti-dam organizations such as the International Rivers Network, Friends of the River, and the NGO Association for Public Works Review become more deeply involved in what previously had often been only local-level conflicts. Fights to halt various government and prefectural plans for new dams sometimes stretched to over four decades, as at the Yanba Dam in Gunma and the Hosogōchi Dam in Tokushima prefecture. In 1994, Prime Minister Morihiro Hosokawa appointed Kozo Igarashi, a critic of the Nagara River Dam plan, to be minister of construction; he then attempted to stop several dam projects. Governor Yoshiko Shiotani of Kumamoto opened debate on dam proposals. Also, some environmental organizations began protesting Japanese ODA support for overseas dams, such those in India, the Philippines, and Indonesia (*AS,* 18 April 1990; Kyodo Newswire, 5 July 2002).

In response to stronger and better-allied civil society, the MOC expanded its toolkit, deepening its strategies of soft social control by developing pro-dam

---

6. Many local NGOs and anti-dam groups attempted to hold referenda on dam-related issues only to see their efforts blocked by local town councils. For example, the assembly of Hitoyoshi in Kumamoto blocked an attempt by a residents' group to hold a referendum on the proposed dam there, as did the Sakamoto village assembly (*AS,* 29 September 2001).

television programs, movies, and pamphlets along with more programs aimed at women and children. In 1991, "through a public relations campaign designed to improve the image of dam projects and water resources development with the general population," administrators created a television program called "Hong Kong Dream." The show, aired on Japan's national television channel NHK, focused on the relationship between a Japanese dam engineer and a female Hong Kong resident whom he met when he helped build a Hong Kong Dam. Though something of a soap opera, the show stressed the need for dams to ensure the water supply (*GDN* 9/563 [1991]: 42–43).

Other new strategies of soft social control included slogan contests, dam information bulletin boards, dam tours, and landscaping to improve the ministry's image (Takahashi and Seike 1991, 15–20). In the Nagara River siting process, when bureaucrats ran into strong local opposition, the MOC produced and distributed pro-dam pamphlets to citizens, sent information slides to the local prefectural offices (Tanaka et al. 1991, 113, 155), and held numerous press conferences emphasizing the need to complete the project. It also promoted lectures by academics who supported the ecological soundness of the plan (Tanimura 1989).

Dam administrators began more sharply focusing their soft social control tactics on children. For example, at one dam in Okinawa, public relations guides led children through a five-step process that taught them about the necessity and uses of dams. Visiting students first view large panels providing information on flooding, drought, and dams; then they watch a twenty-minute video and receive pamphlets on dams and their importance in Japan. They play computer games about dams and conclude their indoor session in the nature preservation hall with a tape of bird songs. The dam authorities also set up an outdoor tour where schoolchildren could watch a dam being constructed. Such "educational" visits are common and often involve lectures about the need for dams (*GDN* 9/587 [1993]: 12). For example, over a five-month period in 1990 the Ryūmon Dam hosted more than sixty organizations and 622 visitors, among them five school trips bringing some 250 students (Jōtatsu 1990, 26). For younger children, the ministry, in conjunction with the Japan Dam Federation, began in 1998 to publish a Japanese *manga,* or comic book, over thirty pages long, titled *Mizu no bōken* (Water adventures); authorities explicitly refer to it as a public relations magazine (*PR shi*) (*GDN* 7/525 [1988]: 1). (Authorities siting nuclear power plants have created similar educational comics.) *Mizu no bōken* stresses water conservation, the benefits of dams, and the efforts of the administrators to ensure water for all Japanese. With the approval of the Ministry of Education, this "educational" comic book was sent to a variety of school systems in an effort to distribute 120,000 copies to classrooms and libraries (NDK 1998, 100).

Several recent amendments to relevant laws and procedures show that the MOC seeks to be seen as taking its opponents seriously in order to project a more democratic image. To solidify this image, dam bureaucrats often ask local authorities to identify pro-dam citizens and encourage them to write letters supporting the project (Amano 2001, 215–216). This soft social control tool is quite similar to one used in nuclear power plant construction, where the government and the private utility companies insist that they build plants only where local people are willing or request them; any local resistance, therefore, is an aberration. Research shows that supporters are far more reluctant than opponents to express their opinion, so this approach helps publicize support that might otherwise go unspoken (Mansfield, Van Houtven, and Huber 2001). In many cases, though, interviews reveal that most local citizens were not told that an invitation had been sent to the central government; such requests often originated in sparsely attended town councils.

In 1997 the River Law was amended to require that the government consider local opinion when planning projects; in 1998 the MOC adopted a role "mandating a complete audit and evaluation of major projects every five years" (Choy 2000, 2). In 2003 the MLIT unveiled specific guidelines requiring local residents to provide opinions that would be reflected in the details of the plans (Jiji Press Ticker, 1 May 2003). Moreover, in response to increasing national debt and a backlash against wasteful public works projects, the official budgets for siting dams have also decreased since the mid-1990s (*Damu Nenkan* 1998, 6; author's direct communication with MLIT River Bureau officials, 23 May 2003). Still, as dams can be funded from a myriad of sources, these cutbacks may be more show than reality.

Another example of efforts to develop a new persuasive image is the recent attempt to site a dam at Tokuyama. There, when citizens affected by the project protested, the MOC responded by holding a dozen or so meetings to explain the need for the dam (*GDN* 5/667 [2000]: 69–72)—thus deviating from the earlier "decide, announce, defend" approach. The MOC also altered its procedures to allow for the termination of opposed dam projects. In 1995 it set up a Dam Council to review eleven construction plans and concluded that three should be canceled (Niikura 1999). By December 2002 the Dam Council had reviewed 454 projects and recommended that 84 of them be stopped (Kokudokōtsūshō Kasenkyoku 2003, 24).

The MOC has added steps to its core dam-siting procedures; one is convening local deliberation councils on the issue of dam construction, which usually involves local executives (mayors, town councilors) and other notable community members. Critics argue that these local committees are made up of individuals chosen by the prefectural governor, who nearly always favors dam construction, and that despite claims of openness, many committee meetings are open only to registered press club members, not the general public or opponents. In the rare cases where local executives have opposed dams and refused to participate on such committees, dam planners were at a loss and often temporarily suspended their plans while placing pressure on the recalcitrant mayor or village leader. For example, Mayor Megumi Fujita of Kitō Village found that refusing to meet with the advisory council for the planned Hosogōchi Dam effectively halted progress on the project (Fujita 1999; *Shūkan Daiyamondo* 1996, 30). Fujita refused because he felt that the council served as a rubber stamp institution for government projects (*Kumamoto Nichinichi,* 26 January 2001).

When anti-dam groups emphasized possible environmental damages, authorities responded to opponents' scientific claims with studies of their own (Tanimura 1989). The MOC issued "Declaration of Eco[logically sound] Dams" (*Eco Damu Senden*), a document insisting that beginning in the late 1990s, dams would preserve the natural biosphere and increase local flora and fauna (Yasuda, Yonaha, and Aragaki 1997, 5–7). And, instead of ignoring the role played by NGOs and nonprofit agencies, authorities began to allow them access to the decision-making process (Inoue 2002).

When farmers showed signs of resisting, the central government targeted them with soft control strategies. For example, in the Kawabegawa Dam struggle the Ministry of Agriculture, Forestry, and Fisheries (MAFF) encountered great difficulties in persuading enough local farmers to sign off on plans to use their land. The MAFF then obtained a list of farmers who had asked to be released from earlier agreements and directed a public relations campaign at them; the mayor himself went "farm to farm" to ensure that the public works project would be completed (Takahashi 2000, 17, 29).

Nevertheless, though Japanese officials have developed soft social control strategies and larger incentives, these should not be viewed as having displaced older tools of coercion and hard social control. For example, in 2001 the MOC (then merged into the MLIT) applied to the prefectural-level Expropriation Council for permission to forcibly take water-use rights from the fishermen's cooperative at Kawabegawa (*AS,* 12 December 2000). The MLIT's local branch office explained to its superiors that the nearby citizens and fishermen had already received enough explanations about the project and that the stalemate in negotiations over fishing rights compensation therefore warranted the use of expropriation (Takahashi 2002, 168–169). The MOC continued to use its ability to cut funds for the desirable public works projects that provide much-needed jobs in rural areas and to exclude individuals from future participation in irrigation and water resource projects. These hard social control methods, known in Japanese as *gyōsei appaku* (administrative pressure), discourage localities from resisting public works. For example, the Ministry of Agriculture warned that farmers refusing to cooperate with the Kawabe River irrigation project would not receive water for their crops (Kawabegawa 2000, 15–16). And at Kitō village the MOC responded to the emphatic refusals of Mayor Fujita Megumi by cutting off funds to his town.

The MOC had entered Kitō in 1992, without the consent of the residents, to collect boring samples (Fujita 1999, 85). The planned dam would submerge thirty-two houses and also main roads, effectively destroying the village. Local citizens organized against the project and worked with the mayor to publicize their plight. Mayor Fujita lectured around the country on the construction of unnecessary dams (Yoshimoto 2000, 30), and publicly documented the government's deliberate slashing of funds available to his village. The amount of money made available for public works projects in one neighboring town increased by almost 2.3 times, for another by 1.8 times, and for a third by 1.16 times. Meanwhile, however, funds slated for Kitō were slashed to 67 percent of the 1990 amount (Odagiri 1997, 80; Fujita 1999, 108).

Anti-dam activists in Kitō noted other obstacles to collective action: threats were made to eliminate their jobs, and financial aid for their children was cut without explanation (Tamura 1998, 16–17). Similarly, citizens in Okutsu village resisted the construction of the Tomata Dam for more than thirty years; they saw it as punishment when funds from the central and prefectural government for road repairs, facilities, and the like were suspended. After the central government had stalled attempts to build a hall for citizens for more than four years, town leaders charged the bureaucracy with deliberately paralyzing the community. When villagers applied to the Ministry of Construction for permission to rebuild storage sheds and other facilities destroyed by a fire, they were turned down. One citizen said that the government used all its regulatory power to push people out of the village (*AS*, 20 October 1992). Others alleged that deliberate bullying and pressure from the central government pushed out Tomata's anti-dam mayor and reduced the opposition to a single landholder. Once the activists were isolated without broader community support, the MOC invoked eminent domain to seize the land (Amano 2001, 48–49). In the case of the Haneji Dam in Okinawa, the local city administration briefly supported anti-dam activists but gave up under strong pressure from the central government (Urashima 1999, 63).

Despite moves to assuage citizen concerns through new procedures involving soft social control, dam construction remains a process with few access points for civil society. For example, during the Nagara River struggle, local anti–dam activists and the MOC tried to establish channels for working together to bridge their differences, but the MOC refused to implement procedures based on democratic rules of decision making.[7] Similarly when anti–dam activists pointed to the accomplishments of symposia and roundtable discussions in the long-running dispute at Narita Airport, an MOC representative informed them that neither he nor the ministry envisioned such a process taking place at Nagara. Arguing that roundtables placed decision-making power in the hands of all discussants, he declared that in the end, final decisions on dams must rest solely in the hands of the minister of construction (Nihon Bengoshi Rengōkai 1995, 71, 104–105). At the 1992 Brazil summit on the environment, the Japanese MOC representative similarly, announced that the Japanese government does not debate with citizens—and was booed (Amano 2001, 217). Yet even though 90 percent of 55,500 local citizens voted against the Yoshino River Dam, Masaaki Nakayama, then minister of construction, told reporters, "I don't want to let the outcome of the plebiscite determine the future of the project.... I will see that the dam plan is finalized during my term in office" (Kakuchi 2000).

State authorities also use hard social control to discourage collective resistance to dam siting: they may follow the letter of the law to "publicly announce" a dam plan but neglect to notify the affected citizens of the event, or they may make the plan available only for two days in a closed glass case (Takahashi 2000, 15). The MOC often refused to release data on dam projects, arguing that full disclosure would lead to their inappropriate use, which would be "bothersome to the citizens as a whole" (Tanaka et al. 1991, 116). These tactics are similar to those used by French authorities to keep information about planned airport and nuclear power plant facilities from potential neighbors of the projects.

## Change over Time

The social control techniques used by Japanese state agencies to handle resistance to dams "softened" in the 1990s; softer methods increased in both scale and scope in response to increasing contestation. As organized civil society brought its attention to the issue of dam construction, bureaucrats moved from paying compensation only to the legal-rights holders of acquired land

---

7. Bureaucrats rejected calls for *minshuteki rūru ni mototsuite hanashiai wo susumeru* (continuing the conversation based on democratic rules).

(Naganohara 1954) to offering broader-based compensation that also provided for lifestyle transitions. Over time, the Water Resources Fund moved away from providing money solely for house construction to a more comprehensive provision of funds for lifestyle maintenance and job training. By broadening the scope of these funds to address economic and social conditions (*Damu Nenkan* 2001, 25), the state added additional incentives and soft social control to its toolkit. Because of increased mobilization from civil society, however, the average lead time for dams doubled between 1960 and 1990, from eight to seventeen years. Over the same period, the proportion of dams submerging houses decreased from 100 percent to approximately 75 percent. The River Bureau is well aware that although fewer citizens are being forced out from their communities, the increasing lead times necessary for dam siting are still due to rising citizen opposition (Kokudokōtsūshō Kasenkyoku 2003, 26).

## French Dam Siting: Moderate Resistance and Little State Coercion

In France, unlike Japan, anti-dam movements mobilized at both the regional and national levels early in the postwar period, rather than remaining a series of individual, atomized protests, as they often were in Japan. Groups within French civil society (such as the Loire Basin Defense Committee and the SOS Loire Vivant) mobilized tens of thousands of protesters and sustained their opposition to state-sponsored river projects for extended periods by means of rallies and years-long site occupations. Because French anti-dam groups also succeeded in pushing the state away from coercive and repressive tools such as land expropriation, often used by their Japanese state counterparts and in other fields of French public policy, these groups also moved state policies in new directions.

Some of the dam-siting cases right after World War II gave the impression that easily placated residents saw dams as solutions, not problems. One such compliant local community lived near the Serre-Ponçon Dam. French authorities had initially planned a dam there in 1856, and in 1948 the French electricity utility, EDF, finalized a plan for a project that would store water for irrigation and drinking and also produce hydroelectric power.

The dam had an enormous impact: it submerged thirteen communities, took land from 1,000 residents, destroyed more than 60 kilometers of roads, and drastically altered life in the nearby towns of Savines-le-Lac and Ubaye (CFGB 2003). But in planning it, the state recognized the need to negotiate with residents rather than coerce them. It set up a local EDF office in the town and established compensation packages for the citizens affected by construction, even though the project received the *déclaration d'utilité publique* (DUP) from the state, recognizing it as in the public interest. As with airports and nuclear power plants in France, public works projects receiving the DUP can expropriate land as necessary from local landowners unwilling to sell to the state. In this case, coercion was unnecessary. Town officials voted for the project, and citizens put up little organized resistance, perhaps because of the incentives offered and the ways in which the state framed the project as enhancing the prestige of the area (Bodon 2002). After the dam was completed in 1960, Ubaye and the nearby valley became tourist attractions.

Such acquiescence in the face of state plans was not the norm, however. Perhaps more representative of anti-dam mobilization were the struggles over the state's attempts to build a series of barrages along the Loire Valley. Politicians and civil society were quiet in the case of the Serre-Ponçon dam, but they were outspoken here. In 1952, local politicians formed the Loire Basin Defense Committee (Le Comité de Défense du Basin de la Loire), working with newspapers, regional anti-dam movements and representatives to fight state-sponsored plans for multiple dam projects. While regional councils supported the idea of having the Loire Valley provide water to Paris, by June 1957 the Defense Committee, under the direction of Pierre Dezarnaulds and Pierre Cheniesseau, rolled back the DUP that had already been granted for the project, forcing the authorities back to the drawing board (Hayes 2002, 119). But the state revived the plan in 1959 and then again in 1962.

The 1960s saw the creation of several state commissions, including DATAR (Délégation à l'Aménagement du Territoire et à l'Action Régionale) in 1963, and CODER (Commissions de Développement Economique Régionales) in 1964; these were designed to unify and enhance regional economic development outside of Paris through infrastructure projects. Perhaps in response, local representatives in the Loire area worked with the Loire Basin Defense Committee to set up ANECLA (Association Nationale pour l'Etude de la Communauté de la Loire et de ses Affluents) to keep the management of local water projects local. In 1962 ANECLA spun off SEMCLA (Société d'Economie Mixte pour la Communauté de la Loire et de ses Affluents) to carry out geographic and economic feasibility studies for potential dams modeled on those of the TVA in America (Hayes 2002, 120). Those local representatives who had resisted top-down development plans involving dams soon were initiating river projects of their own. In 1969 a local committee worked with the Ministry of Infrastructure to set up a dam for flood control, and over the next decade other commissions in the area approved plans for a series of dams. Yet although local political elites now participated in dam plans for the

Loire Valley, local residents remained opposed. In the summer of 1977, plans to build a dam in Roanne brought out more than 1,000 protesters from local ecological organizations and the Parti Socialiste.

In 1984 the Ministry of the Interior replaced ANECLA's successor organization[8] by working with the mayor of Tours to set up EPALA (L'Etablissement Public d'Aménagement de la Loire et de ses Affluents) to "reconcile interests of local communities" while "taking into account the protection and development of natural and human inheritances." In 1986 the Socialist government—which had often been a partner with the Greens and other groups in resisting large-scale public works projects—signed a protocol authorizing the construction of four dams in the Loire Valley. EPALA and the Direction de l'Eau (Water Management Agency), created in 1992, worked together to draw up a plan for the new projects. Five dams, among them Serre de la Fare, Chambonchard, Le Veurdre, and Naussac were to provide flood control, drinking water, and cooling water for nuclear power plants (Hayes 2002, 6; Lewino 1988). These projects would have broad local effects; the dam at Serre de la Fare would create a ten-mile lake, submerging several communities (Webster 1989). This decision from EPALA and the central government triggered a broad reaction; local residents angrily denounced a project that would rob them of "one of their most beautiful valleys" and add another "tamed" river to the list of the Seine, Rhone, and Rhine (Conan 1988).[9] Locals argued that the project would have many ecological impacts and negatively affect the river itself. Along with local residents, ecologists and other communities formed a series of groups in opposition to the dams (Dupuy 1989).

In 1988, fifteen different local and regional associations merged to form SOS Loire Vivante under the leadership of Christine Jean. Its first public action was a large-scale protest at the public inquiry for the Serre de la Fare Dam, followed by marches against plans for a dam in Le Puy. These activities did not deter the Haute-Loire departmental prefect from granting the latter a DUP and authorizing relevant authorities to begin land acquisition. Citizens decided that direct action was called for. "Six days later, activists from SOS Loire Vivante occupied the construction site, an occupation which was ultimately to last 1825 days" (Hayes 2002, 133). (No Japanese protesters managed to sustain a five-year-long occupation of a dam site.) The SOS Loire Vivante

---

8. ANECLA was disbanded in June 1979 and replaced by an organization with the acronym LIGER.

9. Some commentators have speculated that the valley had a history of solidarity because its large Protestant community had been persecuted by Louis XIV, and that more recent events cemented that sense of community (Monier 1989).

used the tactic of sit-ins again when protesting plans for the La Borie Dam (Debrest 1990).

In addition, French anti-dam movements staged mass rallies: in April 1989, 10,000 demonstrators marched in Le Puy against the planned dam, and in 1992 another 10,000 mobilized in the Aspe Valley. They also sought out allies among local politicians. Polls indicated that more than 20 percent of the local communities—which had previously aligned themselves with right-wing candidates—now supported the openly anti-dam Greens in municipal elections. One survey of the Cevennes region put more than 90 percent of respondents against the planned dam (*La Tribune de l'Expansion,* 11 August 1989), and local referenda regularly opposed construction (Lengronne 1989). As if to demonstrate broad public knowledge of and support for anti-dam groups, some mayoral candidates ran successfully on single-issue platforms of opposition to local dam projects, defeating those who supported the dams (Webster 1989).

By 1990, SOS Loire Vivante had more than 3,000 active members in the region, the support of the Fédération Française des Sociétés de Protection de la Nature, (subsequently renamed the France Nature Environnement in 1990), and the financial assistance of the World Wildlife Fund (WWF) (Crie 1989). The movement understood the need "to construct as wide a coalition as possible by presenting themselves as legitimate representatives of mainstream local opinion"; thus they sought to ensure that core participants in rallies and marches were from the area (Hayes 2002, 136). The WWF worked with the SOS Loire Vivante to organize thousands of petitions against the dam project which were sent to President François Mitterrand (Webster 1989).

Against this broad opposition, EPALA and other pro-dam organizations used tools of soft social control, such as press releases and mailings, in an attempt to sway local hearts and minds. EPALA set aside a large budget to combat the "disinformation" put out by SOS Loire Vivante and other anti-dam groups. In poor rural communities such as l'Allier and Haute-Loire, the state sought to appease residents through large-scale incentive programs (Conan 1988). In the town of Nievre, farmers talked openly of their support for the planned dam project at Veurdre primarily because the state had promised compensation (Vif 1991). But these tools and incentives did not dampen opposition; facing ongoing protest, in July 1991 the government terminated plans for the dam at Chambonchard (Perrignon 1992). And although Jean Royer, head of the regional Loire development authority, allegedly stated that plans for the construction of the dam at Serre de la Fare would not be stopped by "10 nitwits," in 1994 the government officially canceled all plans to build dams in the Haute-Loire area.

Thus the mobilization of civil society on a broad scale kept the French state from relying on coercive tools in handling anti-dam resistance. It also pushed the state toward destroying, rather than building, dams. In 1994, as the state canceled plans for new dams within the Loire Valley, it followed the advice of the ecologist and anti-dam movements and took down two dam projects from the Loire River and one from the Léguer River. The state called its new, "greener" approach to water resources in the areas the Plan Loire Grandeur Nature.

Dam construction provides insights into the ways in which state agencies site public bads. For years, the Japanese Ministry of Construction encountered only occasional, concentrated resistance from civil society to its dam-siting plans. As a result, coercion—either expropriation or cutting off local subsidies—became its standard approach. Even the Matsubara and Shimouke cases, which involved abnormally high levels of resistance and violence, did not deter the state from using expropriation in the cases that followed.

Civil society groups in Japan seeking to stop the siting of dams and airports rarely generated sufficient pressure to push Japanese authorities past coercion and expropriation in handling contentious civil society. As civil society mobilized around the issue of dam siting, the state did add minor incentive tools to its strategies, and by the 1990s, organized resistance had pushed the state to implement new soft social control strategies such as television shows, movies, and various programs aimed at making children and women more accepting of dams. Through a variety of recently developed tools, ranging from comics and educational curricula to complex redistributive systems for local residents, the Japanese Ministry of Construction has sought to dampen anti-dam sentiment and smooth the path of dam construction.

Still, when citizens remain unconvinced, land expropriation offers the state a powerful tool. Administrators benefit from the fact that local citizens find it difficult to mobilize broader groups and rally civil society around an issue that has few, primarily localized externalities. Only recently have citizens formed ties to extra-local allies and created a stronger, more organized civil society that has pushed the state at least to add noncoercive tools to its toolkit—even though it is not backing away from the use of expropriation and subsidy cutting. Notably, while state agencies are adopting more "democratic" and "transparent" procedures such as environmental assessments, local deliberation councils, and review committees, they have simultaneously closed loopholes in expropriation procedures and sped up the process of eminent domain. As Japanese bureaucrats absorbed the lessons learned from their interaction with citizens, expropriation became almost impossible to oppose.[10] By increasing the strength of their powers of eminent domain, bureaucrats can more easily counter citizen resistance.

French anti-dam groups, by contrast, mobilized early in the postwar period and kept the state from using its powers of expropriation and police repression. With politicians, local media, and citizens as allies, SOS Loire Vivante and other civil society groups pushed the state to use hard and soft social control tools and incentives in efforts to win over uncooperative locals. Sustaining their resistance for years, and rallying tens of thousands in marches, the citizens who maintained these moderate levels of resistance pushed the state not only toward softer policy instruments but also toward policies that incorporated local ideas. Hence, rather than continuing old policies of dam building, the French state embraced dam breaking, a move that the Japanese state has yet to incorporate.

One policy area in Japan, however, did force state officials to undertake new ways of managing contentious civil society: nuclear power plants.

---

10. Administrative procedures occasionally ensnared their creators. For example, in the case of the Kawabegawa irrigation project, the revised plan of the Ministry of Agriculture, Forestry and Fisheries had to be ratified by two-thirds of the affected farmers. Because the MAFF could not convince a sufficient number of farmers to affix their personal stamps to their petition, they ended up using the names of thirty-five forged signatures to bolster their numbers (AS, 22 January 1999; Kumamoto Shinbun, 4 September 1999; Kawabegawa Risui Soshō Genkoku dan 2000, 42–43; Takahashi 2000, 15–20). Farmers challenged the MAFF in court, and in the end that ministry's actions were nullified by the Fukuoka High Court, forcing it to halt construction at least temporarily (Yomiuri Shinbun, 23 May 2003).

# 5

## TRYING TO CHANGE HEARTS AND MINDS

### Japanese Nuclear Power Plant Siting

IN EARLY 1981, after initial surveys by the central government had determined that local conditions met the necessary geological and geographical criteria, the private Chūgoku Electric Power Company proposed a nuclear reactor complex for the rural town of Kaminoseki in the southern prefecture of Yamaguchi. Central government bureaucrats assisting with the process learned through phone surveys, visits, and discussions with local politicians that local feelings about the project were mixed. To overcome opposition from fishermen's cooperatives, the utility and the local government used central government funds to fly local residents to visit other communities that were hosting nuclear power plants.[1] The bureaucrats also promised also residents millions of dollars for new roads, medical and old age facilities, and loans and subsidies for new businesses.

As talks bogged down, officials from the Agency for Natural Resources and Energy visited and emphasized to local residents the importance of nuclear power plants for Japan's energy security. The government distributed to households thousands of pro-nuclear brochures stressing the safety of nuclear power and the country's need for new reactors. In their science classes, middle school students used a curriculum written by pro-nuclear central government bureaucrats. Local government officials were flown to Tokyo to learn not only the technological aspects of nuclear power but also how to "spin" it to local residents. Although protests continue, and one fishing cooperative from Iwaishima regularly blocks attempts to survey the area (*Japan Times,* 22 June 2005), the state has never used eminent domain, police presence, or other coercive tools to force the issue. The utility expects the plant to be operational by 2015.

This chapter shows how state authorities in Japan developed strategies of soft social control and complex incentives to handle acute, long-duration

---

1. This is an example of the soft social control strategy of habituation: by traveling to host communities and meeting similar people living in the shadow of nuclear power, the members of potential host communities become more familiar with a technology often perceived as alien and dangerous.

contention with anti-nuclear civil society. Pressured from the earliest days by local and outside anti-nuclear groups because of Japan's World War II experience of nuclear warfare, ANRE, part of the Ministry of International Trade and Industry, developed a wide array of strategies to handle citizen opposition and mold citizen preferences. Though expropriation and other forms of coercion are legal, and the state had relied on those policy instruments in handling opposition to other controversial facilities, the government never used them in siting any nuclear power plant. Instead, ANRE developed targeted strategies intended to overcome opposition and win over the hearts and minds of local subsections within civil society.

## Japan's Relative and Absolute Success at Siting Nuclear Power Plants

Given its firsthand experience of the dangers of nuclear weapons, no nation should be less friendly to nuclear power than Japan, yet it embarked on a commercial nuclear power program almost as soon as the American occupation ended. Against all odds, the only country in the world that ever experienced significant civilian exposure to radioactivity began building one of the world's strongest civilian nuclear programs. Although Italy, the United States, and Germany suspended nuclear programs during the 1980s and 1990s, and even France, known for its commitment to nuclear power, canceled its ambitious Superphoenix program (Kodama 1995, 282), Japan has kept going with plans for fast breeder reactors, nuclear fuel recycling, and new plants (Pickett 2002). Furthermore, despite early and continuing protests, and Japan's purported "nuclear allergy" (*kaku arerugi*), communities continue to volunteer to host plants; others host interim radioactive-waste storage facilities; and additional plants are in the works (NGSK 45/1 [2001]: 6; author's interviews with Diet members, winter 2002). The national political culture and comparatively fewer access points for citizens may explain some of this success, but the state's use of soft social strategies and incentives is most critical in understanding its current nuclear program.

In Japan as in the United States, the private sector undertakes siting responsibilities, but the Japanese government plays a substantial role in the process: in addition to research and design, risk amortization, and open support for nuclear power expansion (Lester 1983, 30), it has "carefully nurtured Japanese industries" through "a huge commitment of technological and capital resources" (Garran 1997, 25). Further, like other nations with nuclear energy policies, Japan faced increasing resistance to atomic reactors over time (Rosa and Dunlap 1994), but it did not respond by placing a moratorium on nuclear power. Instead, it identified potential obstacles—primarily fishing cooperatives, local political elites, youth, and women—and aimed to make them more receptive to nuclear power through a variety of programs.

With the advent of nuclear power, MITI (and later ANRE, formed in 1973 as an agency within MITI) assisted private companies by conducting extensive geologic and demographic surveys of potential host communities. The state remains tightly connected to private utility firms; when anti-nuclear activists argued that plans for Yamaguchi's Kaminoseki nuclear site encroached on wetlands, bureaucratic influence by members of MITI compelled the company to alter the plant's layout. Regular meeting and the *amakudari* retirement system[2] ensure that public and private sectors remain close. In 2001 the Science and Technology Agency (STA) and the Ministry of Education merged into the Ministry of Education, Culture, Sports, Science, and Technology, an organization that regulates the field of nuclear power and educates the nation about it.[3] Still, ANRE continues to play the strongest role in the nuclear siting process (CNIC 82 [March/April 2001]: 9).

Two parallel arcs of state-civil society interaction can be traced over nuclear power plant siting. The first focuses on the evolution of public opinion, incorporating major events and accidents and several cases of reactor siting to detail the evolution of state strategies over time. Opposition to nuclear power resonated with many Japanese citizens who regarded it as a known but highly dreaded technology. Groups in civil society which had been completely local coalesced within a short period and organized into regional and ultimately national organizations. The second arc chronicles how the state targeted narrow groups within civil society, including farmers, fishermen, and local political leaders, with specific policies and programs. Some of these groups hold veto power because they control resources, such as water and land, necessary for the siting of reactors; others have a reputation for opposing nuclear power. Bureaucrats view their agreement, or at least acquiescence, as critical to the success of the nuclear power program.

Japan's historical experiences expanded the salience of nuclear power issues beyond local host communities. Figure 11 reveals that anti-nuclear civil society has garnered more steady attention in Japan over time than anti-dam and anti-airport groups. Reporters covered anti-nuclear movements even between

---

2. *Amakudari*, literally "descent from heaven," refers to a system whereby bureaucrats retire into industries they regulated while in office (Colignon and Usui 2003).

3. Because of the historical context of much of the material in this chapter, I continue to use the older names for these organizations when appropriate.

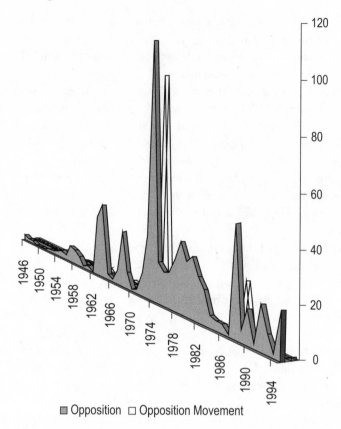

Figure 11. Steady media coverage of anti-nuclear sentiment in Japan.
Number of articles with the key words "nuclear power" and...
Source: Asahi Shinbun CD-ROM

1946 and 1966—a span of two decades during which the few extant anti-dam
and anti-airport groups garnered no reporting whatsoever. As communities
targeted to host nuclear plants responded to siting plans with protest and opposition, they found sympathetic ears in the larger public.

Unlike dams and airports, nuclear power brings with it considerable dread
and other widespread externalities; together, these lower the barriers to wider
collective action. In 1955, for example, millions of Japanese citizens signed
petitions against nuclear weapons after Japanese fishermen were exposed to
radioactivity. Media coverage of anti-nuclear power groups remained steady
between large-scale events such as Three Mile Island—which caused a spike
in the mid-1970s—and Chernobyl, which brought an upsurge of reporting
in the late 1980s. Even between these well-publicized events, however, anti-

nuclear sentiment made it into the national mainstream media. Although airport siting in Japan generated more articles overall, eliminating those focused primarily on the extreme case of Narita reveals more regular coverage even of typically nonviolent antinuclear protest.

## The "Age of the Gods": The 1950s and 1960s

On 13 February 1961 when the opposition party leader interrogated the chairman of a nuclear power commission about the possibility of success, he replied, "Because nuclear technology is still in the age of the gods [*Kamiyo jidai*], God knows whether the program...might be carried through" (NGSK 4/5 [1961]: 1).

The atomic bombings left a legacy of more than the so-called nuclear allergy among the Japanese people (Gale 1978, 1118; author's interviews summer 2002); it includes monuments, annual ceremonies, and constant literary references and allusions to Hiroshima and Nagasaki, along with a recurring distaste for nuclear weapons.[4] Not only is Japan not a nuclear power militarily, but many analysts argue that its nuclear allergy is responsible for public resistance to its nuclear power program.

Despite such trepidation, after the American occupation ended, Japanese authorities quickly moved to ensure sufficient power for industrial and home use. In September 1952, believing that regional companies lacked the capability to maintain facilities sufficient for nationwide energy production, the government created the semi-private Electric Power Development Corporation to guarantee energy production (Ōkawara and Baba 1998, 4). Nevertheless, the EPDC rarely produced more than five percent of the total energy output. At that time, nine regional firms—Hokkaido, Hokuriku, Chubu, Chugoku, Kyushu, Shikoku, Kansai, Tokyo, and Tohoku Electric Power Companies— were made responsible for power generation, distribution, and service in their jurisdictions.[5] But although these private utility companies would be officially responsible for siting and constructing nuclear power plants, the state played an enormous role through policies aimed at smoothing the siting process.

In 1954, closely tied into the affairs of the American government by its occupation experiences, and responding (along with other nations) to President

4. Among the better-known books is Masuji Ibuse's *Black Rain* (*Kuroi Ame*). See Broderick 1996 for a full discussion of the movies on "affected persons" (*hibakusha*), and Treat 1995 for a discussion of Japanese literature on the atomic bombing.

5. In the 1950s, Okinawa was an American protectorate; the power company for those islands— the tenth regional one, Okinawa EPCO—was formed in 1972 as a special public corporation.

Dwight Eisenhower's calls for the civilian use of atomic energy, the Ministry of International Trade and Industry began to debate the use of nuclear energy within the framework of "Atoms for Peace" (*heiwateki riyō*) (*AS*, 9 April 1954). In 1955, MITI set up a nuclear energy division and petitioned the Diet for 5.1 billion yen ($14 million at 1955 exchange rates) for nuclear energy research with the encouragement of the Liberal Democratic Party (*AS*, 5 September 1955). In December 1955, these joint efforts culminated in the passage of the Basic Atomic Energy Law, which established a framework for civilian use of nuclear power (Baba 2002, 17).

In March 1954, before a commercial nuclear program could begin, several Japanese fisherman in a boat named *Lucky Dragon* had been exposed—one fatally—to a Bikini Atoll hydrogen bomb blast. This event deepened antinuclear convictions and spawned the first antinuclear organizations. By August 1955, a women's group based in Tokyo's Suginami Ward had collected more than 30 million signatures against nuclear weapons and weapons testing. Besides increasing antinuclear feelings among the general public, the *Lucky Dragon* tragedy provided the impetus for the formation of *Gensuikyō* (Gensuibaku Kinshi Nihon Kyōgikai), the Japan Council against Atomic and Hydrogen Bombs, which began meeting approximately one year later in Hiroshima (Nakagawa et al. 2004). From its inception, Gensuikyō primarily demonstrated against nuclear weapons, but its members also petitioned and mobilized against civilian nuclear power plants. In 1965, *Gensuikin,* the Japan Congress against Atomic and Hydrogen bombs, broke off from Gensuikyō and later helped form the nationwide umbrella organization Citizens' Nuclear Information Center (CNIC), which coordinated anti-nuclear power activities around the country (Tabusa 1992, 126). Gensuikin has been more active in protests against commercial nuclear power plants than Gensuikyō.

In 1956 the central government formed Genshiryoku Iinkai, the Atomic Energy Commission (AEC) within the prime minister's office to manage nuclear power policy. Members of the AEC and state bureaucrats encountered a portent of things to come when plans for Japan's first reactor met with resistance from civil society groups in the planned host community: opposition from Uji City residents, along with high demands for compensation for nearby urban dwellers, led them to cancel the plan for an experimental reactor at Kansai University (*AS*, 21 September 1957).[6] Vocal resistance to nuclear power plants in potential host communities was joined by opposition parties; in November

---

6. In December of 1960, nuclear promoters within the university did eventually settle on the village of Kumatori near Osaka as the site for the plant (*AS*, 9 December 1960).

1959 the Socialist Party announced its opposition to upgrading the British-model Calder Hall reactor for use in Japan and promised to coordinate its resistance with citizens around the country (AS, 12 November 1959).

Recognizing widespread distrust of nuclear power, the government promoted its development by establishing the first Nuclear Power Day on 26 October 1964 (AS, 31 July and 4 October 1964).[7] This annual observance served as one of the government's first soft social control instruments, disseminating a positive image of nuclear power. On Nuclear Power Day the government sponsors essay contests on the necessity and safety of nuclear power, provides free concerts, and runs commercials in both print and television media to emphasize the need for atomic power. The government also began to open free museums relevant to energy issues, hand out pamphlets and put up posters in subways, and allow the public access to nuclear facilities (NGSK 11/13 [1969]: 30).

Tōkaimura, the site of Japan's major nuclear accident in 1999—a fuel-processing error that resulted in two deaths—hosted the first Japanese experimental reactor, the Japan Power Demonstration Reactor. Sponsored by the Japan Atomic Energy Research Institute, the JPDR came online in 1963. Tōkaimura—a rural village that was losing many fishermen—was also the site for the first nonexperimental commercial reactor, which came online in 1966 under the management of the Japan Atomic Power Company. When MITI selected the location in February 1957, no protest was noted in media coverage (AS, 22 February 1957). In the late 1970s, Tōkaimura accepted a second commercial reactor which came online in 1978, but this time not without protest (AS, 19 February 1973): existing social networks within civil society—in this case, fishermen's cooperatives—mobilized, bringing 130 ships to protest the plant, arguing that negotiations for the siting of the second plant had proceeded without their input (AS, 3 September 1973).

Because of regional economic and demographic stagnation, the local Tōkai community had actively campaigned for the first plant siting with the stipulation that the reactors conform to the "Atoms for Peace" ideology (Hase 1978, 80–81). Through they were initially supportive, in late 1969 fishermen carried out a series of demonstrations against facility expansion: on 4 October, 200 boats rallied in the sea near the proposed site, and on 11 October, 1,000 boats from local fishermen's cooperatives gathered to demonstrate against plans to construct a fuel recycling facility on site (AS, 11 October 1969). And, according to activists, in November 1970 the anti-nuclear weapons group Gensuikin

7. The first Nuclear Power Day was not held in the late 1980s, as some have stated (see Dauvergne 1993, 581).

brought together some 100 protesters to the site from its regional branches (Tanaka 1971, 117).

In the early 1960s the Tokyo Electric Power Company (TEPCO) sited its first complex of commercial nuclear reactors in and around Ōkuma village in Fukushima. (Later reactors were placed in the nearby villages of Futaba, Naraha, and Tomioka.) The village of Ōkuma, like its neighbors, is a small coastal town of fewer than 9,000 people. Town archives show that when MITI and TEPCO announced their desire to construct a nuclear plant, Ōkuma village officials volunteered eagerly. As one observer reported, the town "welcomed the nuclear power plant, then the country's second" because "it meant jobs and tax revenue" (Kelly 2002, 1). In October 1960 a wealthy resident set aside a large plot of coastal shore land for the power plant, land that had been a military airstrip and later converted into a salt plant. As with other public bads, the chosen location for the nuclear complex had few neighbors and had already hosted a public bad—a military airfield. In 1961 the town council formally invited the nuclear power plant through a public vote (TEPCO, direct communication with the author, summer 2002).

For at least a decade beginning in 1960, in an effort to provide a head start to the utility companies, MITI carried out a series of topographical and geographical surveys of coastal areas to map appropriate sites. It spent more than 100,000 yen each year on the process, and each year selected four sites for further testing. These targeted surveys cost MITI 5 million yen (approximately $14,000 at the 1960 exchange rate). In 1968 MITI's survey committee selected three Hokkaido sites as candidates for nuclear power plants. The committee declared that it had considered many technical criteria in selecting sites, including proximity to electricity demand, strong bedrock foundation, few earthquakes, proximity to the sea, small local population, and the ability to insure the site (Ōhashi 1972, 117). (The technical criteria—few recorded earthquakes, abundant water, and aseismic bedrock—remained important official considerations for future reactor sitings (Denki jigyō kōza henshū iinkai 1997, 278–279)—although as shown in chapter 1, geological and geographic criteria may play a role in initial selection, but the choice of sites within technically appropriate localities is best predicted by the weakness of local civil society.)

From the late 1950s until the early 1970s, despite resistance from some local communities and subgroups, many residents were neutral toward their nuclear neighbors: the promise of new jobs, increased tax revenues, and improvement and maintenance of their roads seemed to overcome safety concerns (Hatakenaka 1972, 45). The Japanese state therefore saw no reason to create additional incentives or intensive soft social policy instruments. As one analyst observed, these years "were a time of enthusiasm. . . . The government and industry were making strides, local communities were benefiting from infrastructure development, and little was known of the difficulties that lay ahead" (Pickett 2002, 1349).

Beginning in the late 1960s, the Management and Coordination Ministry (Sōmuchō) initiated a series of opinion polls on energy conservation. These surveys, carried out quite regularly, gauged how seriously Japanese considered energy conservation in their daily lives, and included questions on nuclear power.[8] Figure 12 shows the results of three surveys. Given their wording differences, I compressed responses into three categories: continue building plants, maintain current number or stop building, and no answer. The graph shows

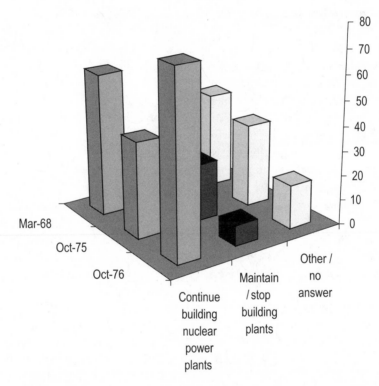

Figure 12. Early support for the Japanese nuclear program. Percentage of respondents who said that Japan should...
Source: Management and Coordination Agency (Sōmuchō) surveys (1968, 1975, 1976)

8. On average, these surveys, carried out by the Chūō Chōsa Sha (Central Research Services), involved at least 2,200 respondents, all over age twenty and located throughout Japan. Several surveys in the mid-1980s had 4,000 respondents; in 1990 there were closer to 7,000. These large, randomly sampled populations provide excellent representation of wider Japanese public opinion.

that through the 1970s the majority of the respondents—close to 70 percent—supported the continuation of Japan's nuclear power plant policies. Notice that the percentage of respondents not answering the question shrank from 40 percent to around 10 percent; some citizens became comfortable with the concept of a commercial nuclear power program. Government assurances and accompanying economic benefits dampened protest and kept mobilization local. Nuclear power seemed to provide an excellent alternative to the difficulties accompanying reliance on oil. Furthermore, no major accidents plagued the industry during that period; nuclear power was still quite clean.

### Moving toward the Boiling Point: The Late 1960s to 1980s

After a primarily auspicious start, during which Japanese resistance to siting was regular but primarily local, the period from the late 1960s through the 1980s brought stronger, extra-local, organized resistance to both nuclear energy and nuclear power plants. Increasing citizen concern over nuclear power issues surfaced when an American nuclear submarine attempted to dock in the early 1960s, setting off nearly two years of debate, with the Liberal Democratic Party weighing in on the issue (Jiyūminshutō 1964). Again in 1964, 1,500 students gathered to protest the presence of a U.S. nuclear submarine (AS, 28 November 1964).

What had been initially been small-scale segments of civil society grew into anti-nuclear associations operating at the regional and national levels. In 1965, 8,000 professors and researchers formed the national Japan Scientists' Congress (JSC) to protest pollution, and in 1972 it established a committee dealing specifically with the dangers of nuclear power. Drawing on support from the Communist and Socialist Parties, the committee met in communities slated to receive nuclear power plants to discuss the issue openly with local citizens, usually bringing in fishermen's cooperatives, environmentalists, and local politicians (Nemoto 1981, 21–22). Other consistent opponents of nuclear power at that time, beyond the "liberal" Diet members of the Socialist and Communist Parties, were labor unions, sometimes even of the power companies themselves (Gogatsusha 1982). Between 1972 and 1977 the committee of the JSC met five times, in Hokkaido, Fukui, Ibaraki, Fukushima, and Shimane—all prefectures where nuclear power plants were planned or under construction.

In 1968, 1,800 local residents signed a petition against a proposed research reactor in Saitama's Ōmiya City. The government rejected their petition (AS, 4 December 1968); nonetheless, by 1973 the experimental facility was dismantled because of citizen lawsuits. Also in 1968, stronger local protests, had began to develop, such as a demonstration against the proposed Hama-oka plant in Shizuoka (*AS,* 21 March 1968). A core complaint among anti-facility groups was the lack of citizen input; in many cases, village politicians "invited" a plant without involving or consulting the public. This procedure was repeated in Tomari-mura in Hokkaido, as well as in Kashiwazaki (Ōhashi 1972, 117). In Kagoshima prefecture a local assembly rammed through its "invitation" to the power company over the strong objections of 2,000 anti-nuclear students and local residents who rallied at the legislature (*AS,* 29 July 1974). In the early 1970s, academics studying nuclear power complained bitterly about nondemocratic plant siting that involved only the governor, mayor, and local notables, put everyone else in the "upper gallery" seats (where they could only view the action), and allowed them no part in the process at all (Tōdai kōgakubu Joshukai 1973, 4).

As local communities and organizations demonstrated against nuclear power, MITI moved to extend its public relations activities beyond its annual Nuclear Power Day. Spending more than 900,000 yen a year (approximately $2,500 at the 1970 exchange rate) through the early 1970s, MITI sponsored the distribution of materials to communities that already had or were targeted for nuclear power plants in order to spread "understanding about the safety of nuclear power" (NGSK 14/10 [1970]: 26).

Despite these attempts to garner public trust and acceptance, the decision to site new reactors in Niigata's Kashiwazaki-Kariwa region set off years of struggle and forced MITI to create more sophisticated strategies for handling resistance. Opposition began in 1969 when the private Tokyo Electric Power Company initiated negotiations with local community members over land purchases and siting. Claiming that the local community had invited them, TEPCO officials indicated their desire to begin construction on a large-scale nuclear power complex (*AS,* 19 September 1969). The proposed location, approximately six kilometers from the nearby town of Kashiwazaki, made many community residents nervous and split the town: the anti-nuclear groups were concerned about the possibility of accidents, radioactive leakage into the water, and health risks; the pronuclear organizations, primarily set up by local businesses, saw the complex as a way to save the village from economic and demographic stagnation.

By late 1969, declaring that the ground under the site was "as soft as tofu," local high school teachers and others in Kashiwazaki formed an anti-nuclear-power union and demonstrated against the plant (Tōdai kōgakubu Joshukai 1976b). In a statement written in 1970, a local fishermen's cooperative angrily accused town officials of inviting the plant in because of the vast sums of money the town would receive in property taxes (Noru 1971, 65). In 1972 anti-nuclear citizens gained a majority on the town council and successfully brought up a referendum that opposed construction (*AS*, 16 July 1972). In 1972 another city, Noto, in Ishikawa prefecture, also held a referendum against nuclear power siting, but prefectural officials there prevented town officials from counting the results by (*AS*, 22 May 1972). Since local citizens' referenda (*jūmin tōhyō*) are not legally binding on politicians, future mayors and local town councils can ignore results without legal sanction.

The Kashiwazaki-Kariwa case in Niigata prefecture prompted central government ministries to develop new strategies. When anti-nuclear groups protested against the Kashiwazaki-Kariwa complex, STA sent in its former minister to give them a "pep talk" (*happa wo kake*) emphasizing the importance for the national energy crisis of building such plants quickly (Kamata 1991, 239). This policy tool, designed to call upon the people's "obligations" to assist the nation toward its energy goal, joined a growing body of soft social control instruments that the state created in response to better-organized, rising opposition.

On 4 July 1974, five years after initial negotiations with local landowners, TEPCO submitted an application to the government to construct eight nuclear power plants near the villages of Kashiwazaki and Kariwa. In 1975, during that same struggle, the central government set up the Japan Science Conference in neighboring Kariwa to convince local citizens that the planned reactors were safe. Recognizing the presence of strong local beliefs concerning the risks of nuclear power, bureaucrats brought in "neutral" experts who stressed the plant's safety. Anti-nuclear activists decried what they felt was the government's deliberate deception, leveraging the "authority" of scholars to undermine their opposition (Tōdai kōgakubu Joshukai 1976b, 8–9). The very legitimacy of these visitors, however, who reassured local residents that nuclear power was safe and needed, provided another soft social control tool.

During this period, when citizens complained about the secrecy of the siting system, MITI developed strategies that seemingly increased citizen input and involvement in the siting procedure but in reality provided little leverage over or access to the process, despite a 1959 Diet bill that mandated public hearings on nuclear plants. But as complaints continued, the state finally outlined a plan to hold "public hearings" when officials in the Atomic Energy Commission felt it necessary. In the summer of 1977, MITI announced environmental assessments and public hearings with the hope that these procedures would overcome local fears and complaints about the lack of access (*AS*, 5 July 1977).

Public hearings are among the hard social control tools in the state's nuclear siting toolkit; at these meetings, preselected citizens with prescreened questions are given a short period of time to present residents' concerns before moderators cut them off. (Anti-nuclear groups have frequently boycotted these hearings, saying they exist merely as pro forma procedures and in fact have no bearing on the actual outcome of the process.) During assessments, bureaucrats must collect the opinions of local citizens to include in ministerial reports. These procedural changes reflected MITI's desire to be seen as responsive to citizen concerns about transparency and citizen participation, but the new procedures have never yet ended or altered a siting process. As even a pro-nuclear editorial writer was forced to admit, the responses from citizens have "not changed fundamental policy" in any way (NGSK 7 [1998]: 3). Nor have MITI and other central government ministries ever denied a license or withheld approval for any nuclear power plant for *any* reason, let alone as a result of citizen responses (author's interviews with electric utility personnel, fall 2002).

In December 1980 after an earlier event had been suspended because of contention, the government and TEPCO attempted to hold a public hearing on the Kashiwazaki-Kariwa power plants. The event attracted 6,000 anti-nuclear activists from Gensuikin, labor groups, and the Socialist Party. Though 2,000 policemen were brought in to guard the building, only eleven of the twenty preselected questioners and 77 of the 250 confirmed observers could enter through the confusion (Kyodo Newswire, 4 December 1980). Despite anti-nuclear sentiment in Kashiwazaki and Kariwa, the plants were completed in September 1985 after almost seventeen years of contestation.

In 1972, in the context of increasing protests against Kashiwazaki-Kariwa and other plants, MITI and STA began establishing branch offices and "atomic energy centers" in potential host communities to demonstrate the government's good intent and to provide the bureaucrats with direct access to their "constituents." These centers allowed citizens to speak directly with local government representatives—often a rare event—and, as soft social control tools, provided local citizens with the feeling that they were not only informed about the process but also able to supply the government with their input. But these centers rarely provide information about accidents, radiation sickness, or the absence of radioactive waste storage and disposal systems. Rather, they focus on the economic benefits for local citizens and emphasize the safety of the plants and their necessity for the national good.

Another tool the government developed to quell public unrest over nuclear power siting was the explanatory meeting, at which bureaucrats and utility representatives described plans to the local citizens. As one nuclear expert observed, however, authorities were "able to hold an explanatory meeting... only under the strict guard of riot police" (NGSK 24/5 [1980]: 2). Those who attended discovered few handouts, little balanced information, and very short time periods for questions (AS, 20 September 1973). And because many anti-nuclear groups sought to disrupt these hearings, riot police were called to keep the peace (AS, 18 September 1973).

In the fall of 1970, MITI proposed legislation that would allow the central government to assist private utilities further in siting nuclear power plants. Concerned about local opposition and striving to ensure that energy goals were met, bureaucrats suggested an intermediate organization that would smooth negotiations with local residents (AS, 7 October 1970). Fearing an energy shortage, the business association Keidanren sought to speed up the implementation of this measure (AS, 3 August 1971). By 1972, MITI's plan to identify those areas supporting the national government's energy plan and assist them with infrastructure upgrades (AS, 24 August 1972) would evolve into the Three Power Source Development Laws known as Dengen Sanpō.

The Atomic Energy Commission had initially sponsored a series of ad hoc local measures for Tōkaimura, the host town for Japan's first experimental reactor, to help build roads, ports, and bridges during the late 1960s.[9] In 1973, after years of urgent pleas from localities that believed they should be receiving some sort of compensation for the presence of nuclear facilities, MITI proposed a Diet bill that would "facilitate the development of local areas near power plants through roads, ports, industrial infrastructure, and radiation monitoring" (NGSK 17/2 [1973]: 30). Under the bill's provisions, the central government would underwrite a large percentage of local costs for infrastructure such as roads or schools in towns that accepted nuclear, fossil fuel, or hydroelectric power facilities (AS, 1 July 1974). Then came the oil shocks, which changed the political landscape for nuclear power in Japan: in early 1973 one barrel of oil went for $3; by January 1974 it would cost almost $12. Consequently, the government's role in facility siting, once fairly limited, expanded drastically (Ōkawara and Baba 1998, 5). Over time, the state increased the amount of money provided by the Dengen Sanpō and the range of projects for which it could be used (Aldrich 2005a).

The early 1970s saw joint mobilization and cross-organizational cooperation among anti-nuclear groups in civil society. In 1972, seventeen organizations

9. Note that I characterize Dengen Sanpō as the institutionalization of previous ad hoc measures; however, other observers have described it as the personal initiative of former Prime Minister Kakuei Tanaka (author's interview with high ranking TEPCO official, 5 August 2002; see also Samuels 1987, 246).

met at Shika City to combine their efforts in distributing information on the dangers of nuclear power (*AS*, 4 and 9 February 1972). Anti-nuclear movements in Mihama and Ōhi became widely known, especially when residents in Ōhi started a recall campaign against their pro-nuclear mayor (*AS*, 4 February 1972). Many members of the Union of Electric Utility Workers, some of them employed at nuclear plants, mobilized to join forces with local anti-nuclear power groups because of the plants' excessive secrecy, lack of proven safety records, and poorly developed radiation standards (*AS*, 6 January 1971). Newspapers commented on the nationwide presence of anti-nuclear groups (*AS*, 1 February 1972). Through legislative wrangling opposition parties in the Diet prevented the AEC from approving plans for construction in Ōhi (*AS*, 10 March 1972), while STA officials reassured the public that problems over waste water discharge had been solved through compensation to local fishermen's groups (*AS*, 9 March 1972). In August 1973, anti-nuclear groups cooperated with the Japan Scientists' Congress to hold a symposium on the environmental dangers of nuclear power; they sent a joint objection to the prime minister and to MITI (*AS*, 27 August 1973). The early 1970s also saw anti-nuclear groups using lawsuits to fight reactors, both extant and planned. In the town of Ikata, residents sued the government and the utility company in 1973 (*AS*, 27 August 1973).[10] Fukushima residents sued the government for approving the use of reclaimed land as a base for the second Fukushima reactor (*AS*, 30 January 1974).

In 1977, for the first time, twenty-three anti-nuclear organizations, including the Japan Consumers' Union, housewives' organizations, and Gensuikin, met in Tokyo on Nuclear Power Day to campaign against nuclear power; they passed out brochures at train stations, met at the YMCA for a "post-nuclear seminar" involving victims of the bombings at Hiroshima and Nagasaki, and gathered hundreds of signatures against nuclear power. Later that same week the Japan Consumers' Union sponsored an open forum on increasing opposition to nuclear power because of its nondemocratic nature (NGSK 21/4 [1977]: 23). On Nuclear Power Day in 1978, anti-nuclear groups gathered to promote their slogan "End nuclear power and coexist with nature" (*AS*, 29 October 1978). One analyst commenting on the alliances between opposition groups in the 1970s argued that although they "began to work together and gained momentum," they "lacked any real policy influence" (Pickett 2002,

10. This lawsuit, like all other such lawsuits, failed in a local court decision set forth in 1978 (*AS*, 25 April 1978); it failed again in two further appeals (*Nikkei*, 18 December 1984; Kaido 1999, 204). See Hasegawa (2004) for a discussion of antiproject movements and lawsuits against developers and the Japanese state.

1349); still, the regular policy responses from the central government suggest that the state was in fact taking their actions quite seriously. In the mid-1970s the central government's Atomic Energy Commission began publishing a variety of public relations documents for local communities, stressing the safety of nuclear power. MITI also publicly debated the possibility of siting nuclear power plants in areas without bedrock—that is, of using different or less strict technocratic criteria—to break the deadlock in local communities with more suitable geographic conditions (*AS*, 6 May 1974).

The mid-1970s saw the creation of two national-level anti-nuclear power groups, which served not only as umbrella organizations for smaller NGOs and social movement organizations but also as sources of anti-nuclear information. In 1975, Professor Jinzaburo Takagi, a nuclear chemist, left his career as a research scientist to start the Citizens' Nuclear Information Center with administrative and financial support from the anti-nuclear group Gensuikin. Under his leadership, the CNIC began publishing Japanese- and English-language materials on the dangers of nuclear power and holding a series of conferences and colloquia about plutonium, reprocessing, and nuclear waste. Its two core publications, the sixteen-page *CNIC Monthly* (in Japanese) and the ten-page *Nuke Info Tokyo* (in English), are distributed domestically and internationally. The CNIC emphasizes data collection, scientific research, and dissemination of information and has regularly challenged the central government's nuclear power plans.

The second national-level anti-nuclear organization that both disseminates information and organizes smaller networks is the National Liaison Conference of the Anti-Nuclear Movement (Hangenpatsu Undō Zenkoku Renraku-kai), formed in 1975 (Tabusa 1992, 125). Its monthly publication *Hangenpatsu Shinbun* (Anti-nuclear newspaper), first published in 1978, has covered not only the activities of various local anti-nuclear power and weapons groups but also accidents and governmental responses to local opposition. Combining profiles of leaders with factual information about the operation of nuclear plants, the paper monitors the government and encourages resistance to national atomic energy policies.

Over time, as anti-nuclear movements increased in number and became better organized, the government decided that a coordinated approach to siting would unify an often fragmented bureaucratic process. While MITI oversaw core licensing and promotion issues, the Ministry of Construction issued relevant construction permits, the Ministry of Finance vetted the budget, and the Environment Agency could theoretically suspend siting on environmental grounds, although it never did so. In December 1976 the government established the Ministerial Council for Promoting a Comprehensive Energy Policy (Sōgō Enerugi Taisaku Suishin Kakuryō Kaigi) under the chairmanship of the prime minister. The council involves a number of ministries, but METI (formerly MITI) dominates the proceedings by providing reference materials and setting the agenda for the meetings (Keizai Sangyōshō 2002). The council initiated two new strategies to promote siting: (1) setting up liaison meetings for the construction of the power plants, and (2) designating power plants as Important Electric Power Resources Requiring Special Measures (Yō Taisaku Jūyō Dengen) (*AS,* 7 July 1977). The liaison meetings involved representatives from the closest regional bureau of MITI, along with local ministerial offices, the local prefectural governor, and mayors of relevant local towns.

Being designated by the committee as an "Important Electric Power Resource" meant that the host locality could receive extra subsidies, up to twice what was normally offered. In 1978, for example, the council applied that designation to twenty-two thermal and nuclear power plants and soon sent government officials to these areas to try to smooth the siting process (*AS,* 11 January 1978). In 1997, twenty-eight nuclear power plants at thirteen sites were given that designation, including a number of contested sites. The council marked Maki-machi, Namie-Odaka, Ashihama, Suzu, and Kaminoseki as areas to receive special subsidies, perhaps because conflicts were ongoing there. These localities each received up to an additional 900 million yen (close to $7.5 million at 2001 exchange rates) over the next five years, while the prefecture received up to 80 million yen (approximately $670,000). In 2001 the right to designate potential or actual host communities was given to the Power Plant Siting Committee (Dengen Ricchi Kaigi).

After the Three Mile Island accident in the United States, March 1979, Japanese authorities on the Atomic Energy Commission reassured the public that "it is almost impossible for nuclear power plants to experience a severe accident" such as that one, a statement immediately attacked by anti-nuclear groups (*AS,* 5 April 1979). Protesters met with MITI officials to argue that the American experience showed how risky nuclear power could be and that Japan should stop its nuclear program, especially because Japan's reactors used the same containment system as that at Three Mile Island. The Japan Scientists' Association asked the government to halt all projects until national consensus could be reached (*WSJ,* 9 April 1979, 7). Hundreds of protesters gathered at rallies throughout Japan to demonstrate against nuclear power. Demonstrators at a government symposium on Three Mile Island grew violent, and police arrested a number of them. Soon, newspapers stated that anti-nuclear sentiment in Japan was gaining momentum at all levels (*AS,* 8 April 1979). MITI began sending out more public relations materials emphasizing the necessity and safety of nuclear power, especially to communities struggling against proposed plants (*AS,* 7 July 1979). MITI also suggested additional subsidies, such as

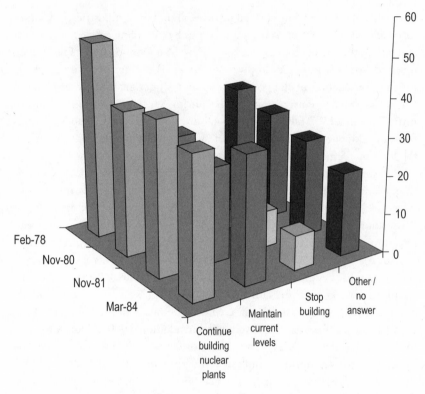

Figure 13. Decreasing public support for nuclear power in the 1970s and 1980s. Percentage of respondents who said that Japan should...
Source: Management and Coordination Agency (Sōmuchō) surveys (1978, 1980, 1981, 1984)

maintenance fees, for host communities, but the Ministry of Finance rejected the plan as unfair because of its single-minded focus on nuclear power plant communities alone (AS, 28 December 1979).

After Three Mile Island, overall support for building new reactors in Japan plummeted. As seen in figure 13, polls in 1980 showed that only 30 percent of citizens were willing to continue building plants—down from 50 percent in February 1979, before the accident. Even though only 10 percent were in favor of stopping current construction, the public was showing widespread concern about nuclear power and a desire to slow Japan's commercial nuclear program.

## Containing a Meltdown: The 1980s to the Present

Recent decades have witnessed a drastic increase in the lead times necessary for construction in Japan, along with many failed siting cases. In the villages of

Koza, Hidaka, Kumatori, Hikigawa, and Nachi-Katsuura, among others, planners who had assessed these communities as suitable for nuclear power plants found that sentiment against the plants prevented their construction. The late 1980s and early 1990s brought a flood of lawsuits that targeted not just the private utility companies but also the central government (Kaido 1999). Citizen referenda stalled some previously approved plants that had been counted in official energy projections. One analyst writing in 2002 concluded, "In Japan today, the general public has a negative view of nuclear power development" (Baba 2002, 16).

As increasing numbers of voices in civil society spoke out against nuclear power in the late 1970s and early 1980s, the Liberal Democratic Party created several organizations dedicated to facilitating the siting of plants and hence increasing Japan's production of nuclear energy. In 1979 the LDP formed the 'Committee for the Promotion of Power Sources' and a year later established the Power Source Siting Promotion Headquarters at its party offices in Tokyo. Operating under the prime minister, the Promotion Headquarters included a former MITI minister and other high officials. For over two decades the committee sought to construct more nuclear power plants, arguing, for example, that Japan "should promote the siting of nuclear power plants as a national policy from the viewpoints of stable energy supply and environmental protection" (NGSK 43/9 [1999]: 5). LDP politicians also visited local communities to stress the importance of nuclear power plant construction. In 1981, for example, several of them, including the party's secretary-general and the chief of the Promotion Headquarters, went to Kubokawa to try to stop the recall movement against its pro-nuclear mayor. LDP speakers emphasized the 3 billion yen ($14 million at 1982 exchange rates) in grants that the local communities would receive should it be constructed (Nikkei, 17 March 1981; NGSK 3 [1981]: 35).

The early 1980s saw the deepening of another tool of soft social control: official visits to local communities. MITI officials decided that their presence, somewhat rare in the affairs of communities far from Tokyo, would make the siting process of unwanted projects more legitimate. Therefore, they began to visit targeted localities to explain national energy needs and to warn of coming power shortages if nuclear power plants were not constructed (OECD 1984). For example, negotiations in Kaminoseki between landowners, fishermen, and the utility dragged on in the 1980s, so MITI officials arrived to give a series of talks about the need for the plants within Japan's overall energy plans. In 1991, MITI began distributing 500,000 copies of a 100-page pro-nuclear brochure in an attempt to "target the moderates" (Perry 1991, 37). In 1992 it raised its electricity discounts for host communities from a range of 10 to 15 percent to 30 to 50 percent (Nikkei Weekly, 5 October 1992).

Major nuclear accidents in the late 1980s and mid-1990s, however, pushed public sentiment even more solidly against nuclear power. Some saw the Soviet Chernobyl disaster in April 1986 as a turning point in anti-nuclear public opinion (*AS* News Service, 23 April 1993). One observer noted that although "the accident did not directly lead to higher levels of radioactivity in Japan, the discovery of radioactive food imports from Europe generated tremendous concern among much of the Japanese public" (Dauvergne 1993, 577). Chernobyl forced Japanese planners to appreciate how much impact foreign accidents would have on nuclear power in Japan (Pickett 2002, 1350). In 1988, 20,000 anti-nuclear protesters gathered in Tokyo's Hibiya Park for a CNIC rally against commercial nuclear power. Figure 14 shows how, over time, more respondents in Japan were willing to abolish nuclear plants, and fewer were willing unconditionally or even conditionally, to build more. In 1988, with organized protests increasing, MITI opened a public relations

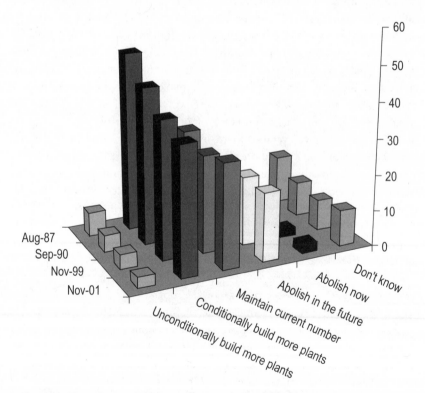

Figure 14. Deepening opposition to nuclear power in the 1990s. Percentage of respondents who said that Japan should…
*Source:* Management and Coordination Agency (*Sōmuchō*) surveys (1987, 1990, 1999); 2001 survey by Agency for Natural Resources and Energy (ANRE, *Shigen enerugi chō*).

center promoting nuclear power generation (Tabusa 1992, 334). In 1992 the agency began to set out safety measures to be utilized in case of an accident, overturning "the government's long standing position that serious accidents cannot occur at nuclear plants in Japan" (AS News Service, 29 May 1992). By moving away from its "unrealistic" position, MITI hoped to defuse worries about major accidents.

In the early 1990s, MITI began to use yet another tool of soft social control: placing advertisements in national papers in the form of articles. At first there was little to indicate that these articles had been authored by MITI, let alone that they were really advertisements; when anti-nuclear groups discovered them, they protested what they saw as subterfuge (AS News Service, 23 April 1993). In 1994, expanding the available incentives, MITI began to eliminate ceilings on subsidies offered to host communities (AS News Service, 27 June 1994).

On 8 December 1995, less than a decade after Chernobyl, Fukui's Monju reactor suffered a major coolant leak. Although the leak itself did not kill anyone, anti-nuclear groups pounded the government for covering up the danger and refusing to admit its seriousness: the Power Reactor and Nuclear Fuel Development, a state-owned corporation that manages Monju, released doctored video footage of the accident and did not report it immediately. The resulting "public outcry and calls for a permanent closure of Monju" (Terazono 1996, 4) were so great that the government was not able to relaunch the reactor until 2005.

Central government bureaucrats still held the tool of expropriation in their toolkits but, in the face of antinuclear unrest, did not seek to use eminent domain because they feared a backlash from wider civil society. Civil servants within ANRE came closest to using it in the late 1990s in the Maki-machi struggle: many years into the siting process of a nuclear power plant there, local citizens successfully brought about a referendum that prevented the sale of land. In 1971, Tohoku Electric Company's announcement of its intent to construct a plant (Nikkei Weekly, 12 August 1996) mobilized more than 600 furious activists who had attended a meeting they hoped would prevent the invitation (CNFC 15 [Autumn 1996]: 16). The subsequent violence brought out the riot police (AS, 19 December 1977). In late summer 1981, when Tohoku attempted to hold public hearings about the reactor, 8,000 demonstrators showed up, and 2,000 riot police were brought in to maintain order (Kyodo Newswire, 28 August 1981). Despite local protests, fishermen's cooperatives in the area signed an agreement transferring fishing rights to Tohoku Electric in return for 3.9 billion yen (approximately $17.5 million at 1981 exchange rates), but the plan stalled because the company was able to acquire only 95 percent of the land it needed for construction. Mayor Sato, elected in 1986, first took a cautious attitude toward nuclear power and then promised to freeze it during his run for reelection in 1990.

In February 1994, however, Tohoku Electric had purchased 97 percent of the property it needed and sought to acquire the remaining land (CNIC 54 [1996]). The government promised residents millions of dollars in property taxes and subsidies once the plant was completed (*Daily Yomiuri* 4 August 1996). Despite this inducement, in late 1994 local residents sought to recall the then pro-nuclear mayor through a petition with more than 10,000 signatures, and Mayor Sato resigned rather than face recall. On 4 August 1996 anti-nuclear residents successfully carried out a referendum—the nation's first involving nuclear power—against plant siting under Mayor Takaaki Sasaguchi, who had been elected in early 1996 on the basis of his commitment to a referendum. Of 20,503 voters (88.29 percent of the eligible Maki residents), 60.86 percent voted against the nuclear plant (Enerugi sōgō suishin iinkai 2002, 19; CNIC 55 [September/October 1996]: 2).

The referendum encouraged Mayor Sasaguchi to sell the 743 square meters of village-owned land that Tohoku still needed to more than twenty anti-nuclear residents for approximately $143,000. Pro-nuclear groups in Maki brought a civil suit against the mayor for doing so but failed to persuade the Supreme Court (Reuters, 24 December 2003). The mayor thus effectively shut down the possibility of plant construction unless the state approved expropriation of the land. ANRE bureaucrats insisted that the referendum's outcome would have no effect on siting plans (*Enerugi sōgō suishin iinkai* 2002, 16), and Tohoku Electric itself demanded that the mayor "promptly restore the sold land to its previous state" (NGSK 43/11 [1999]: 13). Internal MITI memos indicate officials' agreement that the plant would fit under the definition of "public enterprise" and hence the contested land could be expropriated legally; nevertheless, concern over the possible negative reaction, combined with the difficulties in convincing the legal authorities that the plant could not have been located in another spot, prevented them from using the power available to them. In interviews, officials stated their belief that if they had expropriated land for the Maki reactor, they would have alienated future mayors who might otherwise be more amenable. By maintaining that communities choose freely to host nuclear plants and avoiding obvious coercion, authorities hoped to draw more support from rural communities.

During this same period, plans for siting that had been approved by the central government, incorporated into electricity production forecasts, and seemingly supported by local communities were then shut down by local opposition. The TEPCO negotiator in Higashidōri reflected on almost three decades of bargaining: "The days when communities invited us to build nuclear power plants to help combat the effects of depopulation are gone. We must offer something useful" (*Nikkei Weekly,* 5 October 1992). In Ashihama, for example, some thirty years after the nuclear power plant plans were announced, thousands of anti-plant demonstrators gathered at the Nagoya headquarters of Chubu Electric Company, while others carried out sit-down strikes nearby (*AS,* 10 and 11 February 1994). Announced in 1963, the Ashihama plant was to have been located between the towns of Nanto and Kisei in Mie prefecture. Nanto's town assembly voted against the plan a year later, while Kisei voted for it (CNIC 76 [March/April 2000]: 3), and the conflict continued for decades. In 1996, Mayor Inaba of Ashihama gathered approximately 810,000 signatures on a petition against the proposed plant and submitted it to the prefectural governor (*Mainichi,* 1 June 1996). In February 2000, half a year after the Tōkaimura accident, the governor announced that he was effectively terminating the plan, and soon Chubu Electric acknowledged that it was seeking a new location (*Ise Shinbun,* 2 February 2000).[11]

Not long after the failure at Maki, MITI asked for 5.09 billion yen (approximately $47 million at 1996 exchange rates) for its 1997 budget to develop new long-term subsidy programs for host communities (Japan Economic Newswire, 21 August 1996). That same year, ANRE began to put out pro-nuclear television commercials in the prefectures—namely, Ishikawa, Yamaguchi, and Mie—where plants were under attack or had been slowed by anti-nuclear forces. These thirty-second spots were shown more than 5,000 times (*AS,* 28 August 1996). MITI began focusing on the environmental aspects of nuclear power, arguing that "relying on fossil fuels will increase the amount of carbon dioxide emissions, but nuclear energy will help prevent global warming" (Terazono 1996, 4).

In 2000 the MITI minister publicly stated that citizen opposition had made him doubt the government's projected goals of constructing sixteen to twenty new nuclear reactors by 2010 (*Engineering News Record* 2000). Analysts argued that whereas nuclear power had once looked promising, "a series of accidents and scandals have turned public opinion against it" (*Nikkei Weekly,* 10 July 2000). By the turn of the millennium even some high courts were beginning

---

11. Even after Chubu's announcement, some local fishing cooperatives in Kisei pushed to site the plant solely in their village (Naito 2000). Chubu shareholders soon sued the company for paying 200 million yen to local fishermen for the "future fishing losses" expected to result from the plant (which was never built), claiming that the money should be viewed as a bribe (Kyodo Newswire, 19 March 1998). In the spring of 2000, Chubu announced that it would seek to recover 1.5 billion yen from the local fishermen's cooperatives, as the "money was paid on the assumption that marine research would be undertaken" (*Yomiuri,* 21 March 2000).

to acknowledge the negative externalities accompanying nuclear power plants, though continuing to rule that safety processes were appropriate and sufficient (*AS*, 29 October 1992). On 9 September 1998 the Kanazawa branch of the Nagoya High Court stated on the record that nuclear power plants form a "negative legacy" but did not rule in favor of the local anti-nuclear groups that were seeking to suspend the operations of the Shika reactor (CNIC 68/12 [1998]: 11). In 2000 the Atomic Energy Commission's long-term plan, the first since 1994 and the ninth overall, did not specify numerical targets for new nuclear power plants and did not lay out a timetable for developing fast breeder reactors (*Mainichi*, 27 July 2000; *Nikkei*, 26 July 2000). The plan did project that by 2010, sixteen to eighteen reactors would be using mixed oxide (MOX) fuel, which blends plutonium and uranium (*Yomiuri*, 20 July 2000)—part of Japan's overall plan to construct a closed nuclear fuel cycle in which spent fuel is recovered and reprocessed into MOX fuel. This process reduces the amount of high-level waste but simultaneously creates radioactive material that contains four to five times as much plutonium as traditional fuels.

In 2001, the government-controlled Electric Power Development Corporation Ltd. (EPDC, Dengen Kaihatsu Kabushiki Gaisha), established in 1952, finally admitted it had made no headway in its attempts to construct a reactor at Ōma in Aomori prefecture. Initially, the plant was to be a demonstration model of an advanced thermal reactor, but EPDC downgraded its plans and agreed to construct an advanced boiling-water reactor that would use solely MOX fuel. Proposed in 1979, it was still at a stalemate after more than twenty years of negotiations with local landowners who refused to sell 1.2 hectares of land to the company. In December 1984 the Ōma town assembly had agreed to invite the plant into the community (NGSK 1 [1998]: 19). When *konbu* (seaweed) fishermen became concerned about the possible damages to their crops resulting from warm discharge water, authorities "asked these fishermen to go and observe other places where there was already a power plant" (CNFC 3 [Spring 2001]: 16). Ultimately, this soft social control strategy of habituation failed because no other host communities produced seaweed as a primary product. Drawn-out negotiations with these local fishermen's cooperatives, which began in 1985, concluded in May 1994 with each member being granted the unprecedented sum of about 9 million yen (approximately $88,000 at 1994 exchange rates) (CNIC 41/5 [1994]: 9); by 1998, the cooperatives had received three compensation packages worth a total of 15 billion yen (approximately $114 million at 1998 exchange rates) (*Mainichi Daily*, 16 August 1998).

As plans for the reactor changed so that the planned project would take in more cooling water, compensation to the fishing cooperatives was increased an additional 3.60 billion yen ($27.5 million) (NGSK 9 [1998]: 10). Despite progress with the fishermen, in 1994 a local anti-nuclear group, the Peace Labor Union Congress, utilized a *hito-tsubo* strategy that involved dividing up land 100 meters from the reactor core's planned location (CNIC 56 [November/December 1996]: 9). A landowner holding land directly under the planned core itself refused to negotiate; according to one report, "In May 2000, the owner built a greenhouse for strawberries to express his strong will not to sell the land" (NGSK 7/84 [2001]: 16). Despite initial hopes that construction would have begun by 1998, the plan for a reactor in Ōma remains in limbo.

Recognizing the potentially paralyzing power of citizens' referenda, the government responded to recent votes against nuclear plants by increasing its presence on the periphery. METI, established in coordination with officials from other ministries, set up a liaison conference in May 2001 to focus on the city of Kariwa's rejection of a proposal to use MOX fuel in reactors. METI distributed flyers to each household in the village in the name of Minister Takeo Hiranuma, assuring residents that MOX was safe (NGSK 45/6 [2001]: 7). In 2002, ANRE opened a local office in Kashiwazaki City after a referendum voted down the use of MOX fuel. The referendum, held on 27 May 2001, focused on the plan to use MOX fuel in Kashiwazaki-Kariwa Unit 3 operations, but after anti-nuclear groups obtained 37 percent of eligible voters' signatures on an initial petition, 53 percent of the voters (approximately 1,900 people) voted against MOX use. Central government administrators admitted, after seeing the results of the referendum, that they "needed to get to know the public better" (NGSK 46/4 [2002]: 15).

Ministry officials from local branch offices, such as those in Hiroshima, now regularly travel to, or invite bureaucrats and citizens from, towns targeted for nuclear power plants to discuss implementing the planned project. Beginning in 2001, teams of three or four METI officials began visiting host communities in the prefectures of Fukui, Fukushima, and Niigata—those with the highest concentration of nuclear power plants—to carry out ongoing public relations activities. Also in 2001, METI again revised the *Dengen Sanpō* to increase the incentives offered to host communities.

The state has never stood idly by, allowing its various incentive and soft social control strategies to remain frozen in place. The *Dengen Sanpō* incentives were first institutionalized in 1974, but within two years MITI began to update them to meet new community demands (*AS*, 6 July 1976), such as public hearings and environmental assessments. By 2002, of the twenty subcategories of grants and subsidies of *Dengen Sanpō* available to communities hosting power plants, all but one were available only to those hosting nuclear plants; (Keizai Sangyōshō shigen enerugi chō 2002b, 7). In 2001, in addition to the Three Power Source Development Laws, the Diet provided subsidies for road, railway, and port development and improvement projects in areas siting nuclear power plants (NGSK 45/1 [2001]: 12).[12]

MITI has also increased its public relations campaign work through various associated quasi-governmental organizations. The Japan Atomic Energy Relations Organization (JAERO) handles publicity and public relations campaigns for the general public; the Center for the Development of Power Supply Regions (Dengen Chiiki Shinkō Sentā) handles policy instruments focused on host communities. Among other activities, the center publishes monthly bulletins on changes in programs that can assist host communities, and it holds

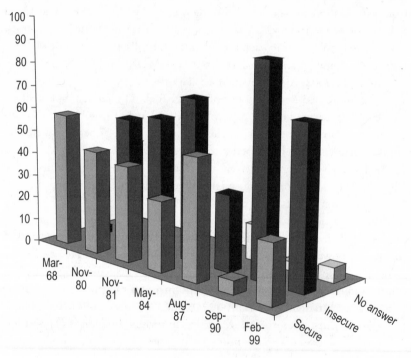

Figure 15. Declining trust in Japanese nuclear power. Percentage of respondents who feel secure / insecure about nuclear power
Source: Management and Coordination Agency (Sōmuchō) surveys (1968, 1980, 1981, 1984, 1987, 1990, 1999); categories "secure" and "somewhat secure" were combined, as were "insecure" and "somewhat insecure."

12. See Aldrich (2005a) for a full description of the changes in incentive structures.

an annual symposium on the development of regions that have power plants. It also publishes large-scale advertisements in popular business magazines such as *Nikkei Bijinesu* (Business Japan), emphasizing the economic benefits for companies that relocate to nuclear power host communities (Dengen Chiiki Shinkō Sentā 1997, 2002).

Yet 2003, despite increasing government outlays for host communities, the mood among private utilities had become grim. One utility manager was quoted as saying, "If we could, we would like to withdraw" from nuclear power generation (*AS*, 19 August 2003). The central government continued to emphasize and promote the use of nuclear power as a vital energy source, despite sagging public support and major scandals involving cover-ups of cracked assemblies at many nuclear facilities (Kyodo Newswire, 14 July 2003). Figure 15 displays the loss of trust in nuclear power from the late 1960s until the late 1990s. The enormous drop between 1987 and 1990 in the percentage of respondents who felt secure or somewhat secure shows how seriously the Chernobyl accident affected trust in nuclear power.

## Targeting Demographic Subgroups

Government authorities seeking to achieve Japan's nuclear power goals had more people to convince than the general public. In Japan, the success or failure of siting attempts rests on the response of key groups within local civil society; fishermen, farmers, students, and local politicians can stop the process through resistance and sabotage. The central state, while wooing the broader population and seeking to prevent ordinary folk from allying with local anti-nuclear groups, focused its strategies on these relevant subgroups to preempt or absorb their resistance. Relying primarily on social control strategies, the state hoped to win over local veto players to ensure its national energy goals (Perry 1991, 37).

### Fishermen

Early on, government officials recognized the power held by existing networks within local civil society. Because Japanese utility companies use ocean water for cooling nuclear reactors, the cooperation of fishing cooperatives was vital to the successful planning of the nuclear power industry. Japanese law requires companies that impinge on a cooperative's fishing areas to purchase its rights in those waters. Transfer of rights requires a two-thirds majority of the cooperative's members, and they must approve compensation plans before they can sell their rights. Without such approval, siting cannot continue. Cooperatives have numerous reasons to resist siting; primary among them the potential loss of their livelihood. Beyond that, however, cooperatives fear that higher water temperatures will negatively affect the aquatic ecosystems on which their livelihood depends.

One common concern expressed by fishermen is that "the warm waste water from the plant will burn you" (CNFC 36 [Winter 2002]: 3), although the government contends that the 6 degrees Celsius difference between ambient sea temperature and the temperature of the discharged water has no lasting negative effects (Keizai Sangyōshō shigen enerugi chō 2002, 95). Further, the utilities used to discharge not only water but radioactive liquids into the ocean, creating additional problems (NGSK 10/2 [1966]). In 1972, for example, the Fishery Agency detected iodine-131 in the discharge from the Fukushima plant (AS, 23 March 1972). Consequently, "antinuclear scientists suspected a strong causal relationship between dead fish and hot water disposed continuously by the nuclear power plant and chemical materials used during the regular inspections" (Tabusa 1992, 286).

Reluctant cooperatives have been the cause of many abandoned projects and lengthy delays. In Yamaguchi prefecture, the continuous refusal of the fishing cooperative at Iwai-shima to deal with government and business negotiators is creating an ever-lengthening lead time for the plant's construction (CNIC 90 [2002]: 10). In Kaminoseki, Chugoku Electric offered eight cooperatives 6 billion yen (approximately $53 million at 1999 exchange rates) in compensation after they had refused to negotiate for many years (Yomiuri Shinbun, 27 December 1999). In Ashihama, Maki, Yamaguchi, and elsewhere, activist fishermen derailed plans for nuclear power plants (see Lesbirel 1998). Anti-nuclear feelings among fishermen's cooperatives in Shimane created "an extremely difficult period for nuclear power" in the village (CNFC 36 [Winter 2002]: 3). Utilities interested in purchasing fishing rights must constantly increase the amount of money they offer—in some recent cases more than 15 billion yen (over $100 million)—but even those incentives have not been a blanket solution to local resistance.

Over time, the Japanese government moved beyond straight incentives to develop more sophisticated approaches when seeking the cooperation of fishermen. The prime minister's office ordered several studies to reassure fishermen that the effects of both temperature increases and radioactivity would be negligible. Beginning in the early 1970s, the government sponsored fish farms that were to be heated by the discharge from the nuclear facility itself, along with studies and lectures to be published and discussed in periodicals read by fishermen; all were to reassure them that the plants would not threaten their livelihood. These studies were published in regular columns in journals such as *Suisankai* (Fishing World) put out by the Japan Fisheries Association (*Suisankai* 2000, 2002).

Most host communities do have fish farms that directly or indirectly use or study discharge water from the plants. Futaba's fish farm in Fukushima, employing thirty-five local residents, was founded in 1982; nearby, another research center, founded in 1983, employs ten. Ibaraki prefecture, host to the Tōkai nuclear complex, built its aquaculture plant in 1972, employing ten (Nihon Ricchi Sentā 2002a). In many cases, MITI contracted such projects to organizations like the Japan Fishery Resources Conservation Association, with budgets of around 40 million yen ($320,000 at 2002 exchange rates) for each fish farm. The Japanese Industrial Location Center, a MITI spin-off that produces public relations materials on nuclear power, copublishes studies of waste water discharge with the Association for the Development of Warm Water Fish Farming. By aiding in the creation of effluent fish farms and greenhouses and by producing studies that downplayed the dangers of waste water, MITI hoped to ensure the cooperation of fishing cooperatives, which would thereby gain not only assurances about safety but also jobs in these fish-farming projects.

*Farmers*

Beginning in the 1970s, MITI realized that farmers held generalized concerns about health alongside fears about their livelihood. Many farmers believed that if their community were to host a nuclear power plant, customers, fearful of radiation in their products, would cease to buy their goods. As one siting authority reported, "They fear that the rumor of an accident at the facilities may cause the cancellation of purchases of their crops or a price reduction" (NGSK 7 [1989]: 4). Industry officials call this concern "nuclear blight" and define it as the "adverse effect of rumors about the nuclear contamination of local products such as seafood and crops" (NGSK 43/7 [1999]: 5). MITI responded with the habituation programs described earlier. Through providing trips to existing host communities, state habituation strategies teach citizens about the normality of life near nuclear plants, allowing them to see how farmers, fishermen, and women coexist peacefully with these facilities (Asahi Shinbun Yamaguchi Shikyoku 2001). Anti-nuclear activists suspected that the village of Kawai in Iwate prefecture was a possible candidate for future nuclear power plant siting when an advertisement in the town bulletin put out by the Kawai Planning Department asked for volunteers to visit Tohoku Electric's nuclear power facilities. The first twenty people to register were to be taken on an overnight trip to the Onagawa nuclear power plant facilities (Kawai Kikaku ka 2001, 10–11).

The state has also worked to alleviate the livelihood concerns of both farmers and fishermen targeting additional soft social control strategies. The Center for the Development of Power Supply Regions, a MITI-affiliated, quasi-governmental corporation, set up the popular annual Electricity Hometown Fair (Denki no Furusato Jimanshi) which showcases products from power plant host communities at the Makuhari Messe Convention Center outside Tokyo. In a clever reversal of fears that the presence of a nuclear plant would drive away customers, this fair heightens awareness of local brands from these communities and thus increases their profits. Instead of seeking to hide the source of these vegetables, fruits, fish, and other products, the fair celebrates them as contributing to the overall good of Japan. The annual fair brings in as many as 138,000 visitors to see and purchase the goods from more than 270 local groups displaying their wares (Ōkawara and Baba 1998, 9).

### Students

Government officials concerned with nuclear energy have spent much of their time on education. As early as 1958, authorities realized that local communities could be wary of, if not opposed to, the idea of atomic power, and they began providing information about it to reduce those fears. The government set up educational centers to do so. Lectures by government experts along with slide shows and movies promoted nuclear power to schools across the nation.

In the early 1970s, JAERO began offering 300 or so free classes and seminars a year to local communities and schools that can guarantee attendance of five or more people. Given three weeks' notice, JAERO will send its trained cadre of teachers to schools, houses, hospitals, and public facilities to provide one- to two-hour seminars on the safety and necessity of nuclear power (JAERO 2002). And, both directly and through JAERO, MITI provides materials and programs for secondary students, ranging from syllabi on nuclear energy and atoms to field trips to nuclear power plants. To teach younger children, JAERO supplies primers that recount events from Japan's history of nuclear power, along with weekly comics (often reprinted or serialized in national newspapers) and thick comic books (*manga*). In addition to offering pro-nuclear information for students, JAERO conducts seminars for local government officials. Its records show that in 2001, for example, educators provided classes and seminars to more than 4,500 people across Japan, ranging from Hokkaido in the north to Yamaguchi prefecture in the south (JAERO 2002).

Beginning in October 1988, soon after Chernobyl, governmental authorities extended nuclear-related educational programs to include teams of nuclear experts, scientists who offer lectures around the country. The government refers to these dispatched lecturing teams as a form of "grassroots public relations" (Science and Technology Agency 1996, 36). Similar teams are sent out after accidents or leakages to explain to the press and the community exactly what happened and why citizens should not be concerned about health consequences. In the late 1980s, as computer use became more common, the Science and Technology Agency developed the so-called "STA Village," an online database accessible to citizens containing information about nuclear power (*Financial Times*, 25 April 1991). In 2001 the MITI branch in northern Japan began to sponsor a national "energy quiz" for high school students from prefectures that were hosting nuclear power plants. Each year, thirty-five students from around the country converge to answer questions about energy use.

### Local Government Officials

Because they envisioned nuclear power plants as generating new taxes and creating new jobs, many local politicians were initially enthusiastic about hosting them in their communities. But when, like representatives in the village of Kubokawa, they discovered that strong anti-nuclear movements could derail their political lives through recall petitions, fewer and fewer volunteered to host new plants. Responding to this reticence, MITI designed and improved several policy instruments to persuade local officials. *Dengen Sanpō,* which can "function as financial incentives for local governments to promote nuclear power" (*Nikkei,* 23 July 1985), gave the state additional leverage to convince officials of the merits of hosting. In 1983, to recapture the support of nervous local politicians, MITI and the prime minister's office began a program to celebrate and reward those local government officials who cooperated with siting efforts. This program, called the Dengen Ricchi Sokushin Kōrōsha Hyōshō, or Citation Ceremony for Electric Power Sources–Siting Promoters, occurs each year, usually in July (Keizai Sangyōshō shigen enerugi chō 2001). The winners meet with the prime minister at his residence in Tokyo and receive their rewards directly from him in front of the national media (*AS,* 28 July 2000). MITI created this soft social control program to encourage mayors from towns targeted for reactors to do all they could to assist the nation in its push for indigenous power supplies (*Denki Shinbun,* 28 July 2000).

Along with praising cooperative local politicians and structuring programs to benefit their communities, MITI began educating and training local government leaders to convince citizens of their important role in the larger energy program. In the 1980s the central government began to invite government officials from areas suitable for nuclear power plants to attend three-day seminars where organizations such as JAERO provide information to the politicians who will decide whether to invite a plant. Along with detailing the funding available, JAERO lays out arguments for the plant and ways to handle negative public reaction. Likewise, MITI set up a Junior Leaders Conference that facilitates the passing of information to town politicians and bureaucrats. Such conferences also bring in leaders from "failed" siting attempts who can explain what went wrong and how to avoid similar problems.

The Ministry of International Trade and Industry holds the same coercive tools of expropriation and police violence in its toolkit as its counterparts in the Ministries of Construction and Transportation, who utilize these policy instruments when siting dams and airports. But it never uses these tools when siting nuclear power plants. Japanese citizens knew firsthand of the dangers of radioactivity from their experience during World War II and the Lucky Dragon incident. Groups within civil society protesting nuclear power were larger and better organized at the regional and national levels than their anti-dam and anti-airport counterparts. Assisted by older groups such as Gensuikin and Gensuikyō, the Citizens' Nuclear Information Center and the National Liaison Conference of the Anti-Nuclear Movement organized local-level groups in potential and actual host communities; they also provided support and information, and helped mobilize allies throughout Japan.

Faced with widespread and long-term resistance from both host communities and larger segments within regional and national civil society, the bureaucrats handling nuclear plant siting moved beyond the policy instruments that had facilitated much of the state's progress in dams and airports. Rather than relying on standard operating procedures from other ministries, civil servants designed new programs specifically targeting farmers, fishermen, students, and local politicians. When fishermen and farmers feared that radioactivity would have negative effects on their crops, the bureau created a yearly fair guaranteed to provide more profits for their products. Nervous local political officials were given new ways to present nuclear power to their constituents and publicly rewarded for their cooperation if they assisted the state. For students, science class curricula focused on the safety and necessity of nuclear power, and communities were visited by white-coated scientists reassuring them that Japan's nuclear program would provide benefits, not harm. The Japanese government thus actively sought to penetrate civil society by flexible and adaptive means.

Interestingly, though, despite years of such programs and enormous expenditures on soft social control instruments and incentives, citizens have become increasingly immune to such techniques. More active and better organized citizens' movements have utilized voter referenda, mayoral and town council recalls, and information dissemination to combat siting efforts by the central government and utilities. Lead times for nuclear power plants have increased threefold since the mid-1970s (Aldrich 2005c), and industry and government alike recognize the likelihood of future siting difficulties. Only about half of all siting attempts within the nuclear power field have succeeded, compared with nearly 80 percent for dams and 95 percent for airports. Nonetheless, for a nation that has experienced major nuclear calamities, Japan's relative and absolute successes at siting nuclear power plants must be attributed primarily to the strategies and tools that state agencies have developed to manage contentious civil society.

Unlike the Japanese state, which has never relied on police force or expropriation in responding to anti-nuclear movements, the French state regularly engages in these hard social control and coercion strategies in pushing its nuclear agenda because of the short-lived and fragmented nature of anti-nuclear opposition in that country.

# 6

## DAVID VERSUS GOLIATH

### *French Nuclear Power Plant Siting*

SOUTHEAST OF PARIS, near the Swiss border, lies the small rural French town of Creys-Malville. On its outskirts in the early 1970s, foundation and con-struction work began on the site of a secret new facility, but few locals under-stood its nature. The French government set up a "public inquiry" to receive citizen opinions about the project—actually the world's largest experimental, highly enriched plutonium-using Superphoenix fast breeder reactor—but almost no citizens were notified of its existence, and no local groups were consulted. Any opinions voiced by the few local citizens attending the inquiry were duly written down by the overseeing panel, but they had no effect on the plan. By the time anti-nuclear groups penetrated the veil of secrecy and succeeded in reopening the hearings to broader participation, construction was well under way, and the French courts overturned citizen lawsuits that sought to have the pre-inquiry construction declared illegal.

Furthermore, the plant had received a statement of public interest (DUP), so it was officially recognized as an undertaking for the good of the people, giving the state the right to expropriate land for the project. With no institu-tions responding to their appeals, and no one trying to alter their perceptions of the facility, antinuclear activists began daily marches and demonstrations against the plant, bringing in tens of thousands of protesters from around France and from Germany as well. Special French anti-riot police, known as the CRS (Compagnies Républicaines de Sécurité) responded to the marches with batons and tear gas. Ultimately, violence erupted, and state police killed one demonstrator and wounded an additional 100. With the death of an ac-tivist, national anti-nuclear power protests became further marginalized by the state and quickly died out.

This chapter examines how the French Ministry of Industry, faced with short-lived but often acute opposition, relied on highly coercive and hard social control tools against anti-nuclear opponents within civil society. At best, these groups could maintain their high numbers and strong unity for no more than seven years; some analysts argue that they were strong for only three years, from 1974 to 1977 (Rucht 1994, 136). Unable to maintain broader alliances and to sustain long-term resistance to the national government's plans, protest groups remained weak and primarily local. Without a strong challenge, the state maintained its narrow toolkit for handling anti-nuclear contention throughout the postwar period.

The French state has created one of the largest commercial nuclear programs in the world, with fifty-nine nuclear power plants and close to 80 percent of its electricity generated by nuclear power.[1] The Ministry of Economy, Finance, and Industry and the Ministry of the Interior used police coercion, surveillance, and land expropriation to handle anti-nuclear resistance, along with hard social tools to control information flow and procedural access points. The state delegates much responsibility for siting to the publicly owned monopoly Electricité de France, but struck down its attempts to provide additional incentives to host communities. Although the EDF is a state-owned entity, its administrative structure and day-to-day practice indicate that the relationship is often fractious. The General Directorate for Energy and Raw Materials (Direction Générale de l'Energie et des Matières Premières, DGEMP) within the Ministry of Economy, Finance, and Industry sets overall nuclear policy for the EDF.[2] Representatives of the state constitute about one-third of the management board including the EDF chairman (IAEA 1998, 184). The firm does not receive state funds but does receive bonds and tax relief. Despite these strong connections and EDF's "public role" (Pean 1978, 59), its behavior is similar to those of other profit-maximizing firms. In interviews, both EDF personnel and state bureaucrats argued that the utility acts as an autonomous organization that cannot be treated as a mere "extension of the state."[3]

EDF directors note that the state's lack of strong vision allowed them to take the initiative for nuclear policy (Boyle 1998, 154; Delmas and Heiman 2001, 446). The EDF and the state engaged in numerous disputes, including initial battles with Commissariat à l'Énergie Atomique (CEA) administrators over technological decisions and later struggles over providing side payments

---

1. In terms of percentage of energy production, France is second only to Lithuania which, as of late 2006, derived slightly more 80 percent of its electricity from nuclear power. In terms of kilowatt production, France (59 reactors; 63,000 megawatts of annual production capacity) is second only to the United States (104 reactors; 98,000 megawatts). France, in fact, has an overcapacity of production: that is, it produces more electricity than it consumes and sells power to neighboring nations.

2. This book focuses primarily on the activities of the energy bureaus within the Industry section of this ministry.

3. French commentators have in fact labeled EDF a "state within the state" (état dans l'état) because of its autonomy, large size, organizational structure, and financial and administrative resources (Pean 1978, 59; Libération, 29 May 2004).

and information to local communities.[4] Since EDF and the French government are not synonymous, EDF actions must be viewed separately from those
of state authorities, especially in light of their strategies for handling contestation. When EDF administrators encountered resistance to siting schemes,
they instituted new strategies of soft social control and incentives much like
Japanese ANRE bureaucrats, whereas the French ministry never enhanced its
policy tools in any meaningful way, continuing to rely on its security and
police forces to back up state-ordered expropriations and to use surveillance
alongside tight control of public information.

### The "Golden Age": Smooth Siting from 1945 to 1969

The French state built its early nuclear plants under a veil of secrecy because of
their dual military/civilian use: they produced meager amounts of electricity
alongside refined, weapons-grade nuclear materials such as plutonium.[5] Providing few, if any, incentives to host communities, and relying on expropriation and other coercive tools, the state's approach to siting nuclear power
plants during this initial period set the tone for the next forty years. With
the public unaware and the state tightly controlling information, "the initial
implementation of French nuclear expansion [did] not prompt... any public
debate" (Boyle 1998, 154). Reflecting the lack of organized opposition, academic articles discussing the siting of nuclear power plants in France and other
European nations did not raise issues of local opposition or citizen fears about
radiation and waste (Hoffman 1957). Hence the "Golden Age" (l'âge d'or).

After World War II, Charles de Gaulle set up the Commissariat à l'Énergie
Atomique CEA,[6] and the government nationalized the utility company EDF,
which was built in 1946 out of private electricity companies. The state made
CEA an organization accountable only to the prime minister with its own
budget and administrative policies; it was to "research the practical applications of atomic energy" (Christensen 1979, 345). In April 1955, to further
centralize decision making, French officials created the advisory commission

---

4. One study notes that the state promoted the nuclear program but left the responsibility of
defending it to the EDF, though it regularly limited the information that it allowed EDF to provide
(Lamiral 1988, 231).

5. Anti-nuclear activists continue to argue that the national defense characteristics of nuclear
power plants combine with the interests of the EDF in maintaining its "industrial secrets," with the
result that the public receives little useful information about the nuclear industry (Marignac and
Pavageau 1998, 7).

6. Ordinance number 45–2563 of 18 October 1945.

known as PEON (Production d'Électricité d'Origine Nucléaire, abandoned in 1981), which coordinated policy between EDF, CEA, top ministerial officials, and the executive branch (Debeir, Deléage, and Hémery 1986, 306). Many saw PEON as the ultimate "technocratic" decision-making body (Colson 1977, 61). Reporting directly to the prime minister, this council, composed of EDF and CEA managers, government ministers, and industrialists, helped the government in the early 1970s drive toward a "total nuclear" strategy (Hecht 1998, 80–81; Delmas and Heiman 2001, 446; Sené 2002, 1).[7]

The state showed early signs of its intention to rely on expropriation and hard social controls; even before experimental nuclear power reactors could be brought on line, the National Assembly considered a law that would provide state officials with the right to expropriate land during exploration for minerals, such as uranium, used in generating atomic energy.[8] Soon after, in 1951, another law confirmed that, as in foreign affairs, it was necessary that the state maintain "absolute power" (*pouvoirs absolus*) over nuclear energy, and expropriation would be carried out as deemed necessary.[9] The first push to develop nuclear power reactors came with the "five-year plan" adopted on 23 July 1957 (Dorget 1984, 299; Colson 1977, 57); however, despite government interest, low oil prices undermined alternative energies such as nuclear power (Fox 2000, 155). Still, state planners viewed nuclear development as a symbol of France's recovery more than as a serious alternative to oil and coal (Hecht 1997, 506; Klein 2002, 93).

Between 1955 and 1960, the state, through the CEA, built three demonstration reactors in rural Marcoule near Avignon in the south of France. In the 1960s, the CEA's sole control over nuclear power shifted to responsibility shared with EDF, which worked with CEA to construct an additional six reactors (even offering its expertise for a "turnkey" reactor in Spain).[10] These nine reactors, spread over four sites, constituted France's initial foray into nuclear power. Authorities planned cautiously, remembering the negative reactions from larger towns. When siting one of the EDF's first reactors at Chinon, managers selected a "sparsely populated region," as they were "anxious to avoid alarm or confrontation"; similarly, for the Marcoule reactor they

---

7. Initially, PEON merely validated the plans that EDF and CEA put before it, but as the conflict between EDF and CEA grew, it came to serve as an "objective arbiter" for competing approaches to the nuclear industry (Hecht 1998, 287+).

8. *Assemblée National Constituante loi* 1196, 18 April 1946.

9. This was prospective bill 13177 in Assemblée Nationale, session of 10 May 1951.

10. This was the 500-mW Vandellos-1 plant, built completely by France. It commenced operation in 1972, stopped in 1989 because of major protests following a large fire there in October 1989, and was shut down officially in 1990.

chose a spot "away from a metropolitan area" (Hecht 1998, 166, 182). EDF acquired the Chinon land through negotiation without expropriation (Lamiral 1988, 213) because it had only a few opponents and offered incentives for local citizens (*Le Monde,* 30 April 1980), but the Marcoule projects involved expropriation. Local reactions to nuclear power were mixed: on the one hand, when the mayor of Bagnols, a town near Marcoule, heard of the construction plans, he envisioned a means for "revitalizing his town's economy"; officials in Véron, on the other hand, reacted with "tempered interest" and "expressed concern about the potential dangers from radiation" (Hecht 1998, 211, 221).

The state showed no qualms about using coercive strategies and expropriating land from many unwilling citizens. For example, at Marcoule in the early 1950s, while carrying out the initial survey work, it quickly expropriated properties and began ground and seismic testing. Those tests involved uprooting local vineyards, cutting down trees, and forcing people to abandon their farmhouses (*Le Monde,* 22 March 1955). Locals lamented the misfortune suffered by a Madame Vigié, for example, who lost acres of vineyards to the project (Hecht 1998, 249). In 1967, continuing under the veil of secrecy, a CEA laboratory director sought to skip the public stages of the expropriation process in order to expedite the construction of a nuclear laboratory at Saclay. Raoul Dautry, the CEA leader, hoped to carry out a "surprise" expropriation of land, justifying the action under the category of an "urgency" clause within the DUP procedure (*L'Aube,* 21 March 1967). In interviews, participants noted that the only outcome of local opposition was an increase in the price of land.

Additionally, hard social controls kept citizens from interfering in state plans. Many local landowners learned that they had lost their homes and property only when they read it the local newspaper or happened upon it in the state publication *Journal Officiel.* During surveying and feasibility studies the state is under no obligation to inform citizens of its plans; only when the DUP and construction are scheduled must they be informed (Colson 1977, 108). When CEA authorities began surveying for Chusclan and Codolet, for example, locals learned of the process from a press release. Some town councils, offended by the high-handedness and lack of information, adopted statements opposing the plant in their towns (Hecht 1998, 251). Other localities, such as Erdeven, were unhappy with the EDF's haughty attitude and with government officials who refused to mix with locals and explain their presence (Frappat 1974). For early reactors like Marcoule, the CEA offered no inducements to local communities to gain their cooperation. In fact, these quasi-military projects were deliberately exempted from *patente,* a tax based on production that usually provides money to local communities. Communities such as Codolet and Chusclan "realized in the mid 1960s that the only way to *extract* money from the CEA was by imposing a municipal tax on its electricity consumption [emphasis added]" (Hecht 1998, 253).

The Avoine case provides additional insights. When EDF announced its intention to construct a plant there in the early 1960s and many Avoine land-owners were "reluctant to sell the land that ensured their livelihood" to the EDF, their property was expropriated (Hecht 1998, 258). Recognizing the potential for long-term damage from alienating the community, the EDF had many of its managers and employers go live in Avoine to gain the trust of local residents (*Le Monde,* 9–10 February 1975, 21–22). Once the reactors were complete, the Avoine residents faired well, at least economically. Since 1963, its 1,200 residents have received subsidies because of the *patente:* 3,350,000 francs (approximately $600,000 at 1971 exchange rates) yearly, more than twelve times the town's annual budget of 270,000 francs ($49,000). With the money, the town purchased a new fire truck and garbage facilities, built gyms, and planned a swimming pool. Anti-nuclear leaders admitted openly that these payments made it difficult to mobilize resistance. Town administrators were so happy about the benefits from the plants that without input from the town council they authorized the construction of two large (180-meter) cooling towers (Georges 1975). These kinds of benefits became a function of EDF's oversight; where the Ministry of Industry has controlled project siting, it has shown far less flexibility in handling opposition.

The state's enthusiastic and strong support for nuclear power did not im-mediately permeate into public opinion. In 1948 a poll showed that 42 per-cent of the French believed that nuclear power would be more bad than good; 34 percent felt the opposite, and 24 percent had no opinion (Beltran and Carré 1991, 307). Less than a decade later the majority opposed the theoretical siting of a nuclear power plant in their area. Interestingly, the surveys demon-strated that only one region had more favorable than unfavorable responses to nuclear power—Normandy and Brittany—yet in the 1970s this area pro-duced the most opposition.[11] Even absent statistical data about the patterns of nuclear facility siting, this 1950s opinion poll indicates that French govern-ment authorities were following the same logic as their Japanese counterparts:

---

11. Many argue that residents in Brittany share a regional consciousness far stronger than their counterparts elsewhere, and that their resistance to proposed projects such as nuclear power plants thus rises from opposition not only to the projects themselves but to Paris-sponsored development (see *Le Monde,* 12 February 1980, 40; *Le Monde,* 8 March 1980, 20). For example, when city of-ficials in Brittany heard that EDF intended to site a plant in the area, it warned EDF to carry out surveys discreetly and avoid contact with locals to avoid inflaming them (Lamiral 1988, 223–224). For a theoretically grounded investigation of siting and other local-central conflicts in Brittany, see Lecourt (2003).

siting facilities where resistance would be lowest. Since polls indicated that Brittany and Normandy seemed pro-nuclear, the state looked to those areas as potential host communities.

In France the process of expropriation for a nuclear power plant begins with the granting of a declaration of public interest; it brings along several hard social controls beyond the obvious overruling of individual property rights. Once a nuclear operator identifies potential sites according to technical criteria, such as the availability of cooling water and aseismic rock, it applies to the Ministry of Industry for the DUP, which applies to all facilities, whether publicly or privately owned, that purport to serve the public good.[12] Once authorities successfully complete the local survey or inquiry, called the *enquête d'utilité publique,* the Conseil d'Etat (the high court over administrative matters) awards DUP status to the project (Maillard 1992, 215). Since 1976, the law has required builders to apply for a DUP for all nuclear facilities (Fagnani and Nicolon 1979, 187), and this application is grouped with the application for the *décret d'autorisation de création,* or decree to authorize building (Faid 2001, 2). Because the DUP establishes a project as in the "public interest," opponents are considered to be working against the "common good."[13]

Declaring the project a public good allows for expropriation. As the French Civil Code's Article 545 states, "No one can be forced to abandon property unless it is for the public good" (Marignac and Pavageau 1998, 21).[14] So once the DUP is issued, the operator can use eminent domain against unwilling landowners. The DUP not only provides justification for the expropriation; it identifies the project as in everyone's interest and, in the state's view, "legitimates" the plant in the eyes of local citizens (Colson 1977, 126–127; Fagnani and Nicolon 1979, 164).

This assumption builds on an old tradition of land confiscation in which the state's perceived needs are given primacy over those of citizens.[15] As René Carle, the EDF chief of nuclear power plant construction, argued in the 1980s, "We try to associate [with] local inhabitants, we have local inquiries, and we explain things to the people—that's necessary—but the conflict, if there is

12. Some have pointed out that getting nuclear power to be seen as "for the public good" has become a "sacred mission" within the French state (Boy 1999, 236).

13. In interviews, anti-nuclear activists pointed out that this view contrasts with that of operators of nuclear facilities in America, who are often seen as private interests working *against* the public good.

14. An ordinance of 23 October 1958 sets out the ground rules for expropriation vis-à-vis the DUP.

15. *Déclaration des droits de l'homme et du citoyen du 27 août 1789,* art. 17 in Constitution, *annexe* p. 179, *Journal Officiel,* no. 1119 (Fagnani and Nicolon 1979, 181 n. 39).

one, is settled centrally" (quoted in Treuthardt 1987, 1). That is, state interests trump local interests, no matter how strong, and in any conflict the central government imposes its will, through either administrative procedures or the Conseil d'Etat. As one analyst noted, "The public inquiry is the modern form of the so-called 'local inquiry,' a process first introduced in the law to justify expropriations through the demonstration of local interest.... This 'justification' is based on the environmental impact [study] and does not necessarily include social or economical considerations" (Faid 2001, 2). Another analyst contended that "local inquiries required for nuclear installations are, roughly, a joke" (Jasper 1990, 88).

The Ministry of Industry forwards the request for the DUP to other ministries (Interior, Health, etc.) and then authorizes the local prefect to begin the public inquiry procedure by creating a local commission.[16] The prefect, as the organizer for the public inquiry, is to inform both local political elites (mayors, town and regional councils, chambers of commerce and industry) and the public of the siting plans. Information about proposed plants is restricted by a set of hard social control tools. During the local inquiry the head of the DUP commission is legally obligated to invite municipalities within 5 kilometers of the plant to become involved and to place notices in at least two regional and two national newspapers for one week before the hearing begins (Chambolle 1980, 3–7); in 1985, this period was extended to fifteen days (Marignac and Pavageau 1998, 27). For example, when the state initiated the local inquiry procedure for the proposed site at Le Carnet, it purchased eleven inches of space in the national newspaper *Le Monde* (16 May 1987) to make the announcement. Signs are often posted on bulletin boards outside the town halls of the local communes, but despite the advent of the Internet, relevant DUP forms and papers are not available online. Further, individuals or towns more than 5 kilometers from the site (e.g., even 5.1 kilometers) are not given standing in the procedure.

Affected members of the public can consult plans during office hours at city halls if they have proper identification; however, to receive a copy of the documents requires effort and sometimes money. For the plant at La Hague, getting "the public inquiry dossiers was subject to draconian conditions: a charge of 5370 francs (around $750 U.S.)" along with various identity checks and a wait of several months (WISE-Paris 2000, 3). Critics argue that the DUP packet is so thick that the average citizen would need several days to work through it all (*La Gazette Nucléaire* 147/148 [February 1995]: 8), but one cannot copy

---

16. The president of the administrative tribunal recruits the members of the commission. For a complete discussion of the possible biases in the way in which the commission is selected and its operating procedures, see Marignac and Pavageau (1998, 28–32).

or remove the materials. The public is given a maximum of two months to respond—in writing—to the proposed plan; people can either write down comments in a book available at the city hall or mail in their observations. For one standard DUP, the "government's local representative [the prefect] simply collected the public's written comments about the license application, reviewed them, and made licensing recommendations to the authorities" (Delmas and Heiman 2001, 446). This is quite similar to the public hearings held in potential host communities over Japanese nuclear power plant siting; as in Japan, the head of the local French commission has no obligation to actually respond to citizen petitions or questions. Siting procedures in France have evolved slightly over the past decades: an environmental impact procedure, along with a right for "concerned individuals" to seek additional information, was added in 1976; in July 1983 the National Assembly passed the "Bouchardeau" law (named for the environmental minister), which seeks to reform the DUP process; and a public debate procedure started in the late 1990s allows people to express their views in a larger discussion of public works. Even so, practically speaking, little has changed in the overall procedure (Marignac and Pavageau 1998, 24).

### "Life or Death in the Alsace": Sharp Opposition from 1970 to 1985

In 1970, France changed its reactors to use the U.S. light-water type, and the EDF took control of the commercial production of electricity.[17] During this period the EDF sought "public interest" status for most, if not all, its reactors, allowing the firm to expropriate land as necessary (Fagnani and Nicolon 1979, 215). Although the state encountered sporadic local resistance to nuclear plants in these early years, the 1970s—the start of the state's heaviest push for new plants—brought out the strongest reaction from civil society. The government's announced intention to go "all nuclear" in producing electricity provoked the creation of organized regional and national anti-nuclear groups and brought about the heaviest, most sustained, and most violent resistance. But France's nuclear program expanded dramatically during this decade, with the biggest leap in plant construction coming in the middle and late 1970s.

Despite the work of local anti-nuclear groups, public opinion about nuclear energy became more favorable in the late 1960s and stayed that way until the Chernobyl disaster. In 1974, opinion polls showed that more than 75 percent

---

17. The transition from French graphite gas reactors to American BWR types involved a fierce struggle between EDF and CEA, inciting among other things, several workers' strikes.

of the population saw nuclear energy in terms of advantages rather than disadvantages (Christensen 1979, 351), though one poll found that support for nuclear power had fallen to 47 percent in 1978 (Delmas and Heiman 2001, 440), approximately a year after the violence at Creys-Malville. In August 1977, pollsters from SOFRES/*Nouvel Observateur* specifically asked people how they would feel about a nuclear power plant being built near their house: 51 percent of respondents said that they would not oppose it; 30 percent were against it and 10 percent undecided (Colson 1977, 99). In 1984, close to 66 percent of the population felt that the benefits of the nuclear program outweighed its costs (*Financial Times,* 6 June 1984).

Even though the general public acquiesced for the first decade of nuclear power, larger-scale protest by groups within civil society began in force in 1969 and 1970 with demonstrations at Fessenheim in Alsace, and then in 1972 at Bugey and other locations (Goldschmidt 1980, 455), with anti-nuclear movements that focused primarily on environmental dangers (OECD 1984, 29). Under the banner of "ecology" (Lamiral 1988, 214), many of these same contentious demonstrators had become politically active fighting dam construction during the 1960s. In Fessenheim, opponents of nuclear power distributed to the local communities small brochures in French and German with such titles as "Fessenheim—Life or Death in Alsace" (Guedeney and Mendel 1973, 123). Anti-nuclear activists in the area joined to form the Comité de sauvegarde de Fessenheim et de la Plaine du Rhin, or Committee to Save Fessenheim and the Rhine Plain (Dorget 1984, 130); other organizations such as Cobayes de Bugey (guinea pigs of Bugey) arose in May 1970. Although public opinion as a whole was not significantly influenced by anti-nuclear movements, local and independent publications were more likely to be critical of the nuclear industry than the mainstream national media, and scientific journals were likely to be supportive of it (Guedeney and Mendel 1973, 231–233).

Because of its high (80 percent) dependence on imported fossil fuels, France, like Japan, suffered during the oil crises of 1973 and 1974 (Taylor, Probert, and Carmo 1998, 39, 52), when the price of oil more than quadrupled in France (Dorget 1984, 301). In March 1974, responding to the oil crisis and a renewed call for energy independence, the government declared its intention to go completely nuclear with the Messmer plan,[18] known popularly as *tout électrique—tout nucléaire* (all electric, all nuclear).[19] The EDF, working with the

18. Named for Prime Minister Pierre Messmer, who was in office under President Georges Pompidou.
19. For a critique of claims that nuclear power would bring France "energy independence," see Belbéoc and Belbéoc (1998).

Ministry of Industry, began to compile a list of potential host communities that met the necessary technical criteria. It created this list with the assistance of public research organizations such as the Institute of Research for the Exploitation of the Sea, regional universities, and various laboratories of the Pasteur Institute of Lille. Among the candidate sites were Gravelines, Paluel, Audinghen, Dannes, Penly, Englesqueville, Flamanville, Ploumoguer, Plogoff, St. Vio, Corsept, and Le Blayais. The official selection criteria focused on proximity to the large amounts of water necessary for cooling the plant, aseismic land, and connectedness and balance within the existing power grid. The initial internal list included more than fifty candidates and was then narrowed down through interministerial discussions and consultations with the regional and local political interests (Fagnani and Nicolon 1979, 170). Beginning in late 1974 and early 1975, thirty-five sites in twenty-two regions were eventually declared potential host communities (*La Croix,* 23 February 1975).

In 1973 and 1974, along with surveying local communities, the state revised its authorization procedures and improved its hard social control measures to accelerate the process. The revisions ensured that the state could "get ahead of the people," alerting the locality only when the siting decision had already been made (Colson 1977, 103–104, 110), but to balance its image the state also mandated that siting be accompanied by a public inquiry (Goldschmidt 1980, 456). Although bureaucrats believed that the DUP procedure provided "legitimacy" in the eyes of local citizens, it simultaneously allowed expropriation of land for the "national interest" so that protests would be ineffectual.

In late 1974 the Ministry of Industry began a "mass consultation and information campaign," rushing to consult with local and regional councils, a move that had rarely been undertaken during the first years of nuclear power (*Le Monde,* 22 November 1974; Le Saux 1974). This meant that for the first time, local and regional assemblies would be consulted before the state and EDF selected a host community in their region (*Les Echos,* 3 December 1974; Colson 1977, 59). These "consultations" did not give assemblies the option of accepting or rejecting the plant itself; rather, they could provide input as to exactly which site in their region would be most appropriate. In some cases, when the towns chosen as good candidates ended up resisting fiercely, state and EDF leaders wondered if the assemblies suggestions were deliberately made to sabotage the process (author's interviews, summer 2004). Nevertheless, they allowed nuclear authorities to stress that the procedure of site selection was a democratic one (Fagnani and Nicolon 1979, 177).

In April 1974, as the issue entered the presidential campaigns, one candidate, Valéry Giscard d'Estaing, declared that nuclear power plants "will not be imposed on those communities who refuse them" (*Le Monde,* 6 December 1980, 37).

Activists saw no way that this promise could be fulfilled (Colson 1977, 99), and one nuclear industry insider told me the activists believed authorities to be insincere. Some analysts argue that the siting system did undergo a transformation in 1974 and 1975 toward a more "democratic" process in which the feelings of local groups were taken into consideration through *concertation* (dialogues or meetings) with elected officials, based primarily on votes in the local assemblies and councils (Fagnani and Nicolon 1979, 202–210), but such claims were not widespread. By February 1975, six regional assemblies had signaled their willingness to accept a plant; a number of local assemblies and municipal councils, however, such as that at Erdeven, voted against the proposals (Frappat 1974). In the end, only nineteen sites were selected for the fleet of reactors, and observers argue that many of the communities on the "short list" of candidate sites showed little enthusiasm for their role (Goldschmidt 1980, 456). Anti-nuclear activists recalled that in some communities, rather than attending the consultation meetings at a candidate site, fishermen and other groups went to purchase guns.

The ministry wanted to ensure the cooperation not only of local officials but also of the citizens. In discussions with the press in 1974, Minister of Industry, Michel d'Ornano, indicated that he and his staff were working to produce a document on nuclear power for the common people. Stressing that it would be written for nonspecialists, he said that the language was "simple and accessible" (*L'Express,* 16 December 1974). Perhaps this explains why a survey conducted in 1974 found that 70 percent of respondents considered the amount of information they received on nuclear power was insufficient (Dorget 1984, 161).

Scientists were among the first preexisting civil society groups to oppose the government's push for nuclear energy. In February 1975, 400 scientists, many of them professors at College de France and Paris University, signed "an appeal to the French people urging them to object to the government's present nuclear power station building program" (*Le Monde,* 11 February 1975; *The Times,* 11 February 1975). Their attack on the government's 1974 report on nuclear power became known as the "manifesto of the 400" (Lamiral 1988, 216). These scientists raised questions about the possible theft of radioactive products, difficulties in transport and storage, the objectivity of state-sponsored research (which often minimizes risks), and the state's failure to consult with scientists and others. Responding to the new "all nuclear" policy, 4,000 scientists organized to provide unbiased information about the risks of nuclear power. In 1975 they formed GSIEN, Group of Scientists for Information on Nuclear Energy, similar to the Union of Concerned Scientists in the United States (Dorget 1984, 131; Rucht 1994, 141). In 1976, GSIEN began a national magazine on the risks of nuclear power, *La Gazette Nucléaire*. Its bimonthly issues contain information on recent developments, accidents, and local responses to nuclear power in France.

Along with the scientifically oriented GSIEN, conventional NGOs and social movements within civil society such as Greenpeace, Friends of the Earth, the Societies for the Protection of Nature, and Sortir du Nucléaire (Get out of nuclear power) actively opposed nuclear power. Friends of the Earth worked through electoral campaigns and demonstrations; Greenpeace activists staged high-publicity media events to raise public consciousness (Szarka 2002, 40–41). These two largest organizations played "a key role in the new anti-nuclear wave" in the early 1970s (OECD 1984, 29). In April 1975, Friends of the Earth promised four actions: (1) to seek popular control over information and research on nuclear power, (2) to occupy nuclear sites, (3) to block information dissemination attempts by the EDF, and (4) to withhold from payments of their electricity bills the percentage that EDF was investing in nuclear power (*Libération*, 29 April 1975).[20] Many of these activists in civil society worked to mobilize voters for the small Green Party, the only French political party united in opposition to nuclear power. Members of the CFDT regularly participated in anti-nuclear activities, and nuclear workers who were members of that union published the first book detailing the economic, social, financial, industrial, and ecological risks of nuclear power (Dorget 1984, 121).[21]

The anti-nuclear movement's repertoire of contentious strategies such as demonstrations, petitions, and letter-writing campaigns did not measurably alter the state's nuclear trajectory. The strongest voices in the "dialogue" came from the government and the EDF, reassuring the public that nuclear power was safe and necessary. Local papers complained about the "stolen debate" (*le débat confisqué*) over nuclear power (*Le Peuple Breton*, November 1981, 10). Activists were frustrated that they could not penetrate the licensing procedures, as "the government never rejected a licensing request despite citizens' vigorous opposition" (Delmas and Heiman 2001, 446). Also annoyed that elected politicians would not respond to their protests, they resorted to extra-institutional and extra-legal means. As one editorial argued, the only choices left for citizens were resignation or violence (*Le Monde*, 6 December 1980). In 1975, protest groups attacked the nuclear plant in Brennilis, using two bombs.

---

20. EDF stated that it was taking the anti-nuclear protest seriously and would cut electricity to individuals refusing to pay portions of their bill.

21. This book, *Le dossier électro-nucléaire* (The nuclear file), was the first written by nuclear plant workers who had a strong technical understanding of the issues involved.

An additional thirty attacks were made against companies working on the plant at Golfech, and twenty explosive charges there caused 20 million francs (approximately $2.2 million at 1984 exchange rates) in damages (*Financial Times*, 6 June 1984).

Although the state remained steadfast in using hard social control techniques such as closed application procedures and coercive strategies such as expropriation to handle opposition, the EDF worked to ensure that its facilities would provide economic benefits to host communities. The CEA nuclear plants were exempt from taxes like the *patente*, but later plants, especially those sited by EDF, gave financial support to host communities. Over time, the *patente* was phased out for nuclear facilities and replaced by the *taxe professionnelle*.[22] A host community that has four 1,300-megawatt nuclear power plants and 1,000 employees can receive as much as 130 million francs (approximately 20 million euros at current exchange rates) from *taxe professionnelle* each year, with an additional 12 million francs from property taxes (Bataille 1990, 100), and a tax on rent paid by plant personnel living in the area (Astolfi, Brunet, and Ithier 1998, 12).

Though EDF's financial compensation was often quite generous, it was not sanctioned or subsidized by the state. In 1974 the Chinon cities received about 12 million francs from the *patente* and approximately 7 million francs from property taxes for a total of 19 million francs (approximately $4 million at 1974 exchange rates). Currently, the Nogent-sur-Seine plant, which has two reactors, provides 25 million euros a year to the local communities (author's interview with EDF employee, Nogent-sur-Seine, 23 August 2004). In recent years, the EDF provided approximately 1.2 billion euros in *taxe professionnelle* to all host communities. For example, Fessenheim, with two 880-megawatt reactors, has received 9 million euros; Paluel, with four 1,300-megawatt reactors, receives 35 million euros, according to an official at the Government Accounting Office (*Cour de comptes*). In the case of Brennilis, the impoverished town gained 235 jobs at the plant plus 500 jobs at service industries. EDF built a soccer stadium (though one local resident commented that "there aren't enough youths here to play a game") and paid approximately $100,000 per year in taxes, "a fourth of the town budget" (Allen 1987, 1). (EDF also offered the community a high-level nuclear waste dump, but the city council

---

22. In France, local governments (regions, departments, and communes), unlike those in Japan, draw most of their revenue from local taxes. The *taxe professionnelle*, or professional tax, is charged on the professional activities of businesses in the jurisdiction of the local government. The maximum amount of this tax that any community can receive is determined by its population; excess amounts are distributed to the local governments of nearby municipalities (Astolfi, Brunet, and Ithier 1998, 12).

rejected that proposal.) When the plant was shut down, local residents, fearing the economic repercussions, demonstrated to keep it open.

Occasionally, when they put up stiff resistance, local communities receive additional benefits from the utility. The mayor of Valence declared his opposition to a proposed plant, but it was not enough impede the process. In the early fall of 1981, between 5,000 and 6,000 anti-nuclear protesters marched on Golfech, breaking into the site complex, setting fire to cars and buildings, engaging state security forces, and causing 15 million francs (approximately $2.8 million at 1981 exchange rates) in damage. In explaining this behavior, Jacques Paltz, a member of the regional coordinating body, said that peaceful resistance had failed in previous cases (as in Plogoff), leaving violence as the only option (*Le Monde,* 8 October 1981). Subsequently, the EDF offered Golfech 1.2 billion francs' worth (approximately $135 million at 1984 exchange rates) of contracts to local companies, with 10 million francs (approximately $1.1 million) a year in subsidies during construction, followed by 6 million francs (about $670,000) for the year after completion (*Financial Times,* 6 June 1984). Such compensation offered to host communities may sway the views of local elected and government officials more than those of average citizens, however (Boy 1999, 240). Newspapers report that pressure from local businesses made municipal council members far more interested in subsidies than the overall population was (*Libération,* 26 November 1981).

Additional EDF incentives in the early 1980s included reduced prices on electricity for communities within a 10 kilometer radius of the plant (*Financial Times,* 6 June 1984; Office of Technology Assessment 1984, 198): host communities benefited from "preferential electricity tariffs, 17 percent reductions for private consumers and 12 percent for industry" (OECD 1984, 34). EDF and state bureaucrats agreed in interviews that the discount eased the burden for communities, which consumed only a small fraction of the electricity produced at the nearby nuclear plant. But even though the tariff reduction was largely symbolic, given the low cost of electricity, the Conseil d'Etat blocked the move as violating the principle of standardized rates.[23]

In May 1975, EDF announced a new public relations campaign to combat strong anti-nuclear protests. Promising to make a "special effort" to keep potential host communities informed, the EDF created several new outreach and public relations departments to diffuse information (*Libération,* 3 May 1975). In the same year, EDF created a new compensation and subsidy system,

---

23. Although some continue to report that France offers this discount (see, Lesbirel 1998, 38), that is no longer accurate. In France, unlike Japan, the ministry worked against the EDF to limit the ways communities could be compensated and rewarded for cooperation in the siting procedure.

known as the "large construction sites" (*grands chantiers*) system, to smooth over the economic and social problems caused by construction (Payen 2003). In many early siting cases, communities had complained about the economic and social costs of construction, such as large but short-term demand for new schools, roads, and other infrastructure for temporary workers on the site (Frigola 1985, 19–20). EDF responded with the *grands chantiers* and *après-chantier* systems, providing money to help construct temporary schools and other facilities in communities struggling with an enormous influx of migrant workers. These programs also funded professional training to help local workers reach the standards necessary for employment in the construction of a nuclear power plant. EDF updated this system of subsidies and loans twice, in 1980 and 1982.

Even though EDF responded to local demands—unlike the French state itself—siting was not always smooth. A typical case is Flamanville, a poor mining community hit hard when its mine shut down in 1963. EDF promised that a nuclear plant would bring in 2,000 jobs for at least six years, along with 4 million francs (approximately $720,000 at 1970 exchange rates) from the *patente*. New political cleavages appeared, with workers and merchants supporting the plant, and wealthy landowners and teachers opposing it, concerned about expropriation. Because of local resistance, EDF declared its willingness to expropriate the necessary land. Caught between pro- and anti-nuclear sides, Flamanville's mayor experimented with a referendum. Although anti-nuclear groups published booklets and provided information to the people, EDF representatives also visited the village, offering information and tours of nearby plants.[24] Approximately half the residents voted, the majority supporting the siting (*Le Monde,* 12 March 1975; Vergne 1975). Similarly, the municipal council, in an extraordinary session, voted 10-to-2 in favor of the plant (Gatignol 1992, 298).

Both state bureaucrats and EDF leaders used various hard social tools to control public opinion and the way anti-nuclear activists were portrayed. EDF leaders, for example, painted as leftists those who resisted or even feared nuclear power plants (*Politique Hebdo* 1975). State authorities labeled opponents of nuclear power as reactionaries and incompetents (*Le Monde,* 22 November 1974). In one case, a bureaucrat in charge of nuclear safety argued that humanity faced a choice: to abandon progress and accept a return to the age

24. Interestingly, at the site in Saint-Laurent-des-Eaux the EDF believed that it had successfully overcome local opposition, but on completing the construction phase, it was forced to upgrade a variety of facilities to meet local demands—among them, 2 million francs (approximately $400,000) for a wall to reduce the noise of the facility (*Le Monde,* 28 November 1974).

of disease, or to continue progress through nuclear power; he concluded that those who opposed nuclear power were fooling themselves (*Le Monde,* 22 November 1974). When a lone EDF official published a book critical of nuclear energy, he apparently was asked to resign (Nelkin and Pollak 1981, 173). With official state scientists supporting nuclear power, public opposition was inevitably seen as "irrational" or the result of poor information (Boy 1999, 237–238). Originally, the government stressed that without nuclear power the country would face "chaos," or that the choice would be "nuclear or candlelight." More recently, the government has shifted to a different formula: nuclear power or catastrophic climate change (Laponche 2003, 5).

In addition to casting their opponents as irrational people who were holding back France's economic development, the state used hard social control to prevent alternative views from being heard. Claude Otzenberger's film *Les atomes nous veulent-ils du bien?* (Do atoms wish us good?) questioned the push into nuclear power. Otzenberger explained why he was motivated to make the film: the CEA and EDF constantly repeated the overly simplistic and paternalistic reassurances about their nuclear facilities (*France Nouvelle,* 18 November 1974)—and the state kept it from being shown on television. Similarly, the movie *Nucléaire, danger immédiat* (Nuclear energy, an immediate danger), put out in 1977 by Serge Poljinsky, was partially censored because of pressure from authorities (Colson 1977, 79).

The state made it hard to acquire information about the power plants, even for politicians. When the deputy of Isère, where the Superphoenix reactor was to be located, asked the Ministry of Industry about the progress of the project, he was told that "work has not yet started" (Colson 1977, 107) although construction was well under way. In June 1973 a member of Parliament submitted to the government a written questionnaire about nuclear power and nuclear waste. In response to question five, presumably written by the Ministry of Industry, the parliamentarian was told that the primary radioactive waste product of nuclear plants is cobalt-60, with a half-life of five years. As a side note, it added, "Certain waste products, however, have a longer half-life" (*EDF service de l'information* 1979). This understatement overlooks a key fact: the half-life of plutonium-239 (irradiated fuel) is 24,000 years, and for the product of its decay, uranium-235, the figure is closer to 700,000 years.

Anti-nuclear groups and mainstream media sources regularly report that bureaucrats use hard social control to suppress debate on the nuclear power state (*Comité STOP Nogent-sur-Seine* 93/94 [July–October 2002]: 4). Groundwater pollution at Grenoble from CEA radioactive waste was never discussed openly, and accidents were often covered up or the actual radioactivity release levels minimized in public reports (Colson 1977, 42–43). In 1975 the government suppressed a list of major nuclear incidents in the year 1973. One group sent a letter inquiring about a 1976 accident and pointing out that no public information had been released. In response, the local information commission (CLI), citing information obtained from authorities, acknowledged a minor escape of radioactive materials but did not respond to the inquiry about public information; observers assume that the accident was never reported (*La Gazette Nucléaire* 147/148 [February 1995]: 16).

In 1978 the state severed ties between committees on nuclear power and nuclear safety, arguing that they should not be mixed (*Le Monde,* 2 July 1987), perhaps for fear of increasing public concern about nuclear energy. In 1979 the Ministry of Industry commissioned a report from twenty-four experts, "expecting an endorsement of their program." When, instead, the Cremieux report "concluded that by 1990 the program would be an embarrassing economic and social white elephant," the ministry modified it for publication, removing the critical sections. Similarly, when Haroun Tazieff, a volcanologist, pointed out that La Hague and other nuclear facilities were located on geological faults, the state responded by erasing fault lines from published reports (*The Guardian,* 7 May 1981). When anti-nuclear activists set up a radio station in 1975 to protest the Superphoenix plant, it was quickly "banned as a violation of the French public radio monopoly legislation" (Nelkin and Pollak 1981, 72).

The year 1975 brought a "perfunctory debate" on nuclear power in the National Assembly, but no one "seriously challenged the government's heavy reliance on nuclear power to meet France's future needs" (Hatch 1986, 153–154). This virtual silence reflects a larger issue: national political representatives were failing to create and carry out policy. "Between 1968 and 1983, 80 percent of the bills which the parliament passed into law were of governmental origin, with the figure reaching 95 percent in 1981, the year the Socialist party arrived in power" (Baumgartner 1987, 36). Soon after the parliamentary "debate," the state mandated that parties seeking to site nuclear plants must carry out assessments. Article 1 of that legislation requires an environmental impact assessment, which should "systematically determine the effects of a nuclear facility on the environment, as well as the local population" (Christensen 1979, 348). This law brought the siting procedures closer to those of other nations (like Japan and America) and allowed the state to display its concerns about "ecological" issues. An environmental impact study can be released *after* the local public inquiry has ended, however, denying its potential ammunition to local anti-nuclear protesters (Marignac and Pavageau 1998, 17).

The municipality of Creys-Maville provided the stage for the most dramatic confrontations between anti-nuclear groups and the state. In 1972, when the government proposed construction of the 1,200-megawatt, sodium-cooled, fast breeder reactor known as the Superphoenix, its incredibly repressive response to protests underscored the state's continued reliance on coercion.[25] The Superphoenix involved untested technologies—fast breeders produce more fissile material than they consume—and posed greater risks of catastrophic accidents than typical reactors. As one article explained, residents did not want to be the "guinea pigs for the world's first operational breeder reactor. They feel that there are simply too many unknown factors, and no one knows exactly what will happen" (Christensen 1979, 351, citing *L'Express,* 8 August 1977).

Some argue that Creys-Malville initiated the first really wide-spread discussions of nuclear power in France (Colson 1977, 9). The importance of these events in raising national consciousness can be seen in figure 16, which shows the number of articles in *Le Monde* on anti-nuclear activities and

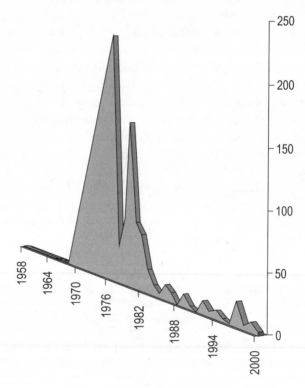

Figure 16.  *Le Monde* articles on antinuclear events
*Source:* Number of *Le Monde* articles on antinuclear events

25.  Despite wide-scale protests in the area, construction on the fast breeder reactor began in 1976 and was completed in 1985.

groups during the postwar period. Until the mid-1970s, coverage of anti-nuclear groups was essentially nil—whatever local resistance the state encountered, coverage was confined to the local media.[26] Beginning in 1977 with the Superphoenix, however, coverage jumped to more than 200 articles per year, then decreased rapidly in the 1980s as its salience diminished. Anti-nuclear activists explained that as time went on, and even the largest protests were shown to be ineffectual, many lost the spirit to keep fighting. Even the meltdown at Chernobyl in 1986, which caused panicked reactions across the rest of Europe, barely registered in the French media. Critics assert the pro-nuclear media and governmental officials were deliberately distorting and downplaying the news (Rucht 1994, 146). Creys-Malville disrupted the typical lack of media coverage of anti-nuclear events.

Citizens in Creys-Malville, the site targeted to host the Superphoenix, encountered the standard obstacles to citizen participation and procedural transparency. When the first public inquiry began, newspapers noted that no local groups were consulted and that almost no citizens participated. Angered at being shut out of the process, a local anti-nuclear group succeeded in reopening the public inquiry, but construction work on facilities had already begun (*Libération*, 29 January 1975; Colson 1977, 110). Local officials had approved the fast breeder reactor after visiting other EDF facilities and hearing of the enormous fiscal windfall of the *patente*. And, EDF ran a large, daily local public relations campaign with assurances from Nobel prize-winning physicist Louis Neel that the plant was safe.

With work under way, anti-nuclear opponents nevertheless gathered in 1976 and 1977 for the largest recorded anti-nuclear demonstrations in France. Estimates of their size vary from 20,000 to 100,000 (Goldschmidt 1980, 456; Treuthardt 1987, 1). With Friends of the Earth as a core organizer, additional participants came from Germany. Although anti-nuclear leaders stressed from the outset that rallies would be nonviolent, radical elements seized the opportunity to engage state security forces, and there were guerilla activities from smaller cells of more violent groups. On 9 July 1977, activists destroyed the apartment of Marcel Boiteux, the EDF's director general (Lamiral 1988, 220). Soon, state strategies for responding to protest moved solely toward coercion. The police used violence to suppress the protests, killing one demonstrator, Vital Michalon, and wounding 100 others (Dorget 1984, 134; de Marcellus 1992, 2) in what activists called a "cruel example of *électrofascisme*" (Colson 1977, 53).

26. *Le Monde*'s archives and indexes do not cover every year between 1958 and 1977, but interviews with anti-nuclear activists and state bureaucrats alike confirm this trend. As mentioned earlier, national papers tended to be less critical of nuclear power than local and independent ones.

One activist pointed out to me that participants expected the casualties to be a "focal point" for future protests in which even nonactivists in France would "wake up and say, 'Wow, they're killing us over nuclear power!'"

In fact, "rather than changing state policy, the violence at Creys-Malville had the effect of intimidating protesters" (Boyle 1998, 155). Furthermore, although locals first received the protesters gladly, the move toward violence forced many of them to reconsider. Some, "disgusted" by the actions of the radicals, asked the groups to leave (Lamiral 1988, 221–222). Others argued that because the public saw the anti-nuclear associations as at least partially responsible for the violence, "public credibility was lost to a great extent and . . . never fully recovered" (Rucht 1994, 145). For many activists, the police response provided additional evidence that "the use of force was the only official response" to anti-nuclear movements (Colson 1977, 87). Boyle notes that "Creys-Malville was the last significant antinuclear demonstration in France during the period," and the number of French nuclear cases argued before the Conseil d'Etat immediately dropped from a high of over 20 cases in 1977 to only 5 in 1980 (Boyle 1998, 156, fig. 2).

Along with extra-legislative methods, anti-nuclear opponents attempted to use the courts to stop state plans. Because "French courts had a tendency to dismiss cases" and took "a strict interpretation of standing," however, the state and EDF "never lost a significant case" (Boyle 1988, 155–156). Courts in France regularly support the state's drive for nuclear power and "energy independence"; to give one example, they ruled that it was legal to begin construction on a nuclear facility before receiving a license to do so (MacLachlan 1990, 7). Anti-nuclear lawsuits have "proved uniformly unsuccessful," in the words of one observer (Hatch 1986, 158). Even when the courts temporarily suspended construction permits in Flamanville and Belleville-sur-Loire because of irregularities, construction resumed within a few months. Boyle argues that the NGOs and other anti-nuclear groups continued to file cases against nuclear plants despite their lack of success in order to signal "the frustration of members of civil society with state policies" (1988, 156; on French law and nuclear power, see also Hébert 1980).

In 1977 an independent information commission was established in Fessenheim to provide a forum where locals could learn more about nuclear plant operations. In the same year the state moved to provide more information to the people through the Council for Information on Nuclear Energy (CIEN), whose eighteen members reported to the prime minister (Dorget 1984, 167). Critics attacked the council, which included representatives from the ministries of industry, health, culture, and the environment, for being too close to the government to be independent. They also said the government provided information too slowly; in most cases, local citizens did not learn about the particulars of a facility until the siting decision had been made (*Le Monde,* 10 November 1977). The CIEN was abandoned in 1981, less than four years after its inception (*Le Monde,* 2 July 1987). Fessenheim's local information commission served as the model for Nogent's local information commission (CLI); considered a success, it was adopted wholeheartedly in 1981. Here, the state took no initiative to provide additional information but merely copied an existing institution designed by local groups. The Ministry of Industry did provide some funds to the local CLIs, but these organizations were also funded through taxes (École nationale d'administration 2002b, 71).

In 1981 the prime minister outlined the local information commissions' tasks: "to disseminate information and organize a dialogue between the administration, experts, local elected representatives, associations, and other stakeholders." But because CLI members were chosen by the regional prefect, who was appointed by the central government, it was "impossible for them to open up on issues at hand and develop new knowledge." It was also "extremely difficult for them to take into account the various identities' involvement" (Chavot and Masseran 2003, 4). Among its other responsibilities, the CLI was to inform locals of evacuation in case of an accident (DGEMP 2000, 110).

Only two years later, the state passed a new law requiring greater "democratization" of public inquiries and formed the Parliamentary Office for the Evaluation of Scientific and Technical Options. OPECST was to "inform Parliament on scientific and technological consequences, particularly with a view to enlighten [*sic*] the decision making process" (Chavot and Masseran 2003, 2). Composed equally of senators and Parliament members, the OPECST published seventy-five studies; many focused on nuclear power and waste, and others on extending the life of existing reactors (OPECST 2003). Critics point out that the OPECST—unlike its American counterpart, the Congressional Office of Technological Assessment[27]—operated solely for the purposes of Parliament, and its materials were often unavailable to the public (Boy 1999, 232–233).

Anti-nuclear groups within civil society which sought allies among the political parties found themselves betrayed by brief alliances with politicians. François Mitterrand, the leader of the Socialists, promised in his presidential election platform to hold a national debate on nuclear energy, cancel the Superphoenix program, decentralize decision making, and end plans for the Plogoff reactor in Brittany; in a written letter to the Committee against

---

27. The OTA closed down in September 1995 after twenty-odd years of service.

Atomic Pollution he promised not to extend the treatment and processing facilities there (Dorget 1984, 118–199). In the end, however, in what many Green and Socialist Party members viewed as a duplicity, Mitterrand only canceled the Plogoff reactor in 1981, doing little else to slow the nuclear program (Reuters News, 1 December 1981), though he did refuse to endorse the official government "all nuclear" policy (*Libération,* 4 June 1981, 5). In 1981, 331 Parliament members voted to approve the national energy program, with only 67 opposing. Activists said that Mitterrand's about-face "completed the demoralization of the anti-nuclear movement" (Treuthardt 1987, 1).

Mitterrand's attention focused on the city of Plogoff because it was one of several municipalities in Brittany where civil society groups maintained strong anti-nuclear opposition and visibly impacted state plans.[28] These protests demonstrated the state's continued lack of flexibility and its reliance on expropriation and police coercion, while showcasing the EDF's flexibility and adaptability.[29] In 1974, Minister of Industry, Michel D'Ornano, announced three potential host communities along the banks of the Loire River: Le Carnet, Plogoff, and Pellerin. By 1976, Pellerin had been chosen as the top candidate, and on 9 October some 3,000 protesters rallied in the streets. The local town council voted 18 to 2 against the plan, but the Conseil d' Etat went on record in favor of it (*Libération,* 26 November 1981). In January 1977, local peasants formed a cooperative to purchase the land as a way to slow expropriation, much like the *hito-tsubo* strategy of Japanese movements. Twelve local mayors participated in the protest, making the overall feelings of opposition quite clear (Dorget 1984, 135). On 8 May 1977, 10,000 people attended an anti-nuclear festival held nearby; some protesters angrily burned the official DUPs. Unable to dissuade the central government, local farmers used tractors to block the town hall entrance and sprayed the subprefect, who coordinated the public inquiry procedure, with liquid manure. Five farmers were charged with violating the anti-riot law, and 2,000 people rallied in front of the courts at Nantes on 10 June to protest the holding of "five hostages to nuclear power." After thirteen days the farmers were released.

On 7 July 1977, residents set up barricades in the streets of Cheix-in-Reitz. Using helicopters, vans, and batons, anti-riot police units and state security forces smashed their way through. Despite all this, on 12 October 1978 the State Council approved the siting plan. This move resulted in the mass resignation of Pellerin's and Cheix's town councils, and 7,000 people marched in various

---

28. That is, plans for constructing nuclear power plants in these communities were either officially canceled or put on hold because of intense, long-term mobilization by local civil society.

29. The following section draws heavily on Brenon and Cozic (1997).

rallies. The prime minister signed off on the project on 10 January 1978, bringing out 10,000 demonstrators who marched in Nantes. Two days before the 1981 election, Mitterrand announced that Pellerin would not receive a nuclear power plant. With this freeze in place, the central government surveyed neighboring local officials for their opinions. Seven communes and ninety-eight officials went on record against the plant; five communes and eighty-three officials argued for it. On 14 April 1983, Pierre Mauroy, then prime minister under President Mitterrand, signed a decree ending the project.

As Pellerin was shut down, however, authorities were investigating potential site in nearby Le Carnet. From January through March 1982, local opponents faced off against the state security forces protecting the surveyors. In one case a landowner blocked authorities from entering his property and, when confronted by the police, threw a beehive at them (*Loire-Atlantique,* 20–21 February 1982); others threw Molotov cocktails (*Libération,* 22 February 1982). Initially, the EDF had been able to acquire 126 hectares for the plant without resorting to expropriation (*Presse Océan,* 22 March 1988). Local officials, including members of regional and municipal councils, argued for the "absolute necessity" of the project at Le Carnet. In January 1985 these governing bodies sent Mitterrand several telegrams insisting that the state locate the reactor in their community because of pressing energy needs (*Presse Océan,* 8 January 1985; *La Nouvelle République,* 8 January 1985); they expressed satisfaction with the potential accompanying economic benefits, and a referendum in nearby Paimbouef approved the plant. But protesters burned a bus and *Confédération Générale du Travail* trade union members occupied the site with students to express their opposition.

In 1987, after these strong showings from local civil society groups, the government slowed down the work at Le Carnet so that another survey could be taken. Of 320 entries in the official register of the public inquiry, only 60 were favorable—and then, despite a police guard, it was stolen. Local papers reported that police used excessive force against anti-nuclear demonstrations. Nevertheless, in 1988, President Jacques Chirac signed off on the DUP for 126 hectares (*Nucleonics Week,* 30 January 1997, 4). In 1993 the state mandated an interministerial decree that allowed for an extension of future expropriations after the original DUP expired. After 1993, the prefect reopened the public inquiry, bringing out more waves of protest: 16,000 citizens signed a petition along with 216 local elected officials, including the mayor of Nantes, and of 334 statements, in the project's register, only 7 were favorable. In early 1997, Prime Minister Alain Juppé endorsed the plan, and Ministry of Industry maps that spring showed Le Carnet as a renewed candidate for a power plant. Still, officials backpedaled, claiming that it could be either a thermal or nuclear plant (*Le Nouvel Economiste,* 25 April 1997, 15). Edouard Hamon, a farmer who held land at the proposed site, swore that he would not sell even if EDF offered him a million francs per hectare. Anti-nuclear activists destroyed a mobile laboratory that returned to continue surveys on the site and organized a 25-kilometer human chain around the area, with 12,000 to 25,000 people joining hands (*Libération,* 2 June 1997). In the autumn of 1997, Prime Minister Lionel Jospin asked EDF to drop its plans for Le Carnet (*Nucleonics Week,* 18 September 1997, 1). Soon thereafter, in December 1997, two municipalities and a nuclear workers' union filed suit against the government for canceling the power plant (*Nucleonics Week,* 8 January 1998, 7).

Nuclear reactor siting attempts at Plogoff, chosen in March 1976, also relied on strategies of coercion, including police intimidation, violence, and land expropriation. In January 1977, before the public inquiry officially began, local officials burned the stacks of documents—weighing almost four kilograms—that the state had assembled to justify the project; 3,000 protesters set up and manned barricades; and on 3 February, 20,000 people demonstrated. Local inhabitants impeded the arrival of trucks carrying materials for the public inquiry (*Le Monde,* 10 February 1980). The atmosphere in Plogoff, heavily strained by violence between the police and protesters, led to three-quarters of the population signing a petition requesting that state security forces depart (*Le Monde,* 12 February 1980, 40). Unable to secure the town hall because of the resistance, the government brought in "town hall annexes," large vans guarded by security forces (Dorget 1984, 135), to provide "secure" locations in which to conduct public inquiries (*Le Monde,* 22 February 1980). By April 1980, 542 residents had consulted the DUP documents.

The media reported that CRS forces regularly tear-gassed Plogoff protesters for no apparent reason and that police often scuffled with nearby demonstrators (*Le Monde,* 18 March 1980). After there were additional eyewitness reports of police brutality, a *Le Monde* political cartoon (8 March 1980, 20) showed the "EDF Information Booth" manned by a police officer. That year, Friends of the Earth and local anti-nuclear groups ran a series of advertisements showing CRS forces arrayed in armored personnel carriers with the caption "Why are armored tanks in Plogoff?"

Activists began cutting down trees as barricades to block roads and many locals faced court charges for their actions. In mid-March, 7,000 people demonstrated at Trogor, and police forces used eighty-five tear gas and stun grenades in battling them. Despite the show of strong local opposition, both the local inquiry commission (in the spring of 1980) and then Prime Minister Raymond Barre (in November 1980) signed the DUP for construction of a nuclear reactor in Plogoff. A contemporary political cartoon shows a member of the local public inquiry commission splattered with apples, tomatoes, and tin cans, guarded by two policemen similarly adorned with garbage, stating, "After consultation with the population, we have decided to construct a nuclear power plant" (*Le Monde,* 17 April 1980, 42).

Interestingly, although the state remained fixed on expropriation and police coercion during the siting process, with only a single brochure utilizing suasion, the EDF changed policies in midstream. Recognizing that a "softer" approach was necessary, the company began a marketing strategy aimed at local officials. EDF managers stressed the potential economic and financial benefits of the plant and carried out a habituation strategy of taking the officials on organized trips to nearby operating nuclear facilities (*Le Monde,* 7 February 1981). Only the election of Socialist Mitterrand brought the high drama to a close (*Libération,* 4 June 1981, 5). In 1996 the EDF officially released the thirty-eight hectares of land it had acquired through the DUP.

Frustration at closed procedures had driven French anti-nuclear groups toward violence and sabotage. After Three Mile Island, French activists bombed $15 million worth of equipment bound for Iraq at the La Seyne-sur-Mer plant (*WSJ,* 9 April 1979, 7). In December 1981, around 2,500 anti-nuclear activists clashed with police forces at the site of a proposed reactor near Valence d'Agen; with close to two dozen were injured, and Molotov cocktails thrown at the state security forces blinded one policeman (Reuters News, 1 December 1981). In 1982 a power station under construction near Lyons was attacked by rockets, and activists damaged the Superphoenix (Kyodo Newswire, 20 January 1982). One report pointed to the "isolation of the anti-nuclear movement and the absence of any legitimate political outlet" to "explain the steep increase in the number of criminal acts since 1979, in particular the attempts to blow up EDF office and pylons and the rocket attack on the Superphoenix reactor" (OECD 1984, 30). On 30 March 1982, anti-nuclear protesters organized a 1,000-person march from Creys-Malville to Paris. Authorities argued that the march, "mustering no more than 800 people [compared with 40,000 in 1977] showed how weakened the movement had become" (OECD 1984, 30).

### Slow Deterioration of Public Support: 1985 to the Present

Following the Chernobyl meltdown, the proportion of French people viewing nuclear power in terms of its advantages dropped below 50 percent. While citizens in neighboring countries destroyed their crops and took iodine pills as preventive measures against the radioactivity spreading across Europe, French state scientists insisted that there was nothing to worry about, thus undermining the

government's credibility. Service Central de Protection Contre les Rayonne-
ments Ionisants, the "mouthpiece" for government information on radiation,
"initially denied that the radioactive cloud had passed over France" (Coles
1987, 475). Although American anti-nuclear groups were visible after Chernobyl, in France "only government spokespersons appeared, to reassure the
public" (Jasper 1995, 60). Government documents admit that the public felt
misinformed about the dangers of Chernobyl (DGEMP 2000, 148).

By 2001, despite the state's prevarication about Chernobyl, 70 percent of
the French people surveyed held a positive opinion about nuclear power, and
63 percent said they wanted France to continue its nuclear program, although
70 percent wanted no new plants built (Nuclear Canada 2001, 1; Klein 2002,
94). Figure 17 reflects one set of CEA opinion polls, from mid-1975 through
late 1996. Public opinion toward nuclear power dropped again after the
Creys-Malville violence in 1977, rose after Mitterrand's 1981 election, and
dropped again after Chernobyl. The percentage of favorable opinions remains
at 50 percent or less. Support for nuclear power is faltering.

Figure 17.  Percentage of French respondents in favor of nuclear power
*Source: La Croix,* 23 April 1997, 12, from CEA data

During the late 1980s the central government took small steps to improve public acceptance through new communication techniques. In 1988 one state organization, the Central Service for Nuclear Installations Safety (SCSIN) "hired a public relations consultant and created a logo for its reports" to improve public relations; it also began a videotex magazine (MacLachlan 1988; 10).[30] While the state perhaps moved too late to change its harsh image, the EDF continued to demonstrate flexibility and adaptability in handling local civil society groups. Much like Japanese bureaucrats, the EDF worked diligently to identify "target groups" in society who were "opinion leaders." As one manager told colleagues at an international conference:

> We have identified a number of target groups who are opinion leaders, and provide them with information and material appropriate to the group. Doctors, for instance, are basically in favor and are important opinion leaders, but they are often asked questions by their patients about radiation and so on. We make sure that they have the necessary information to answer such questions competently and on the basis of the latest scientific knowledge. Farmers are basically favorable to nuclear power but are sometimes worried about the effect it may have on the food they produce and the consumer's confidence in it. We have just started a program to provide them with appropriate information. Teachers on the other hand are not always favorably disposed towards nuclear power. A special information kit has been prepared for them in conjunction with the Ministry of Energy. (Vigna 1989, 5)

EDF also engaged social scientists to carry out network analyses of host communities and was thus able to identify village opinion leaders and move to engage them by assigning them a "contact" from the nuclear plant. This targeting parallels the course taken by Japanese bureaucrats handling nuclear siting; however, in France, the semipublic EDF took the lead over the Ministry of Industry and other state agencies.

In the early 1990s, EDF began a series of strong pro-nuclear advertising campaigns, spending $4 million for spots in seventeen national newspapers and magazines plus forty-second television commercials. Stressing "nuclear power's contribution to energy independence and the French economy in general," the campaigns "targeted different groups, including women and young people" (MacLachlan 1997, 10). Using surveys, authorities identified

30. In 1993 the state transformed the SCSIN into the Direction de la Sûreté des Installations Nucléaires (DSIN), the new safety agency for nuclear industries (ASN 2003, 135). Even more recently, the regulatory framework for nuclear safety (but not for siting per se) was reorganized under the L'Autorité de Sûreté (Nucléaire Nuclear Safety Authority, ASN).

women as more hesitant then man to support nuclear power (*Figaro,* 14 December 1978). EDF, like Japanese bureaucrats, also worked to provide documents for classroom use in host communities, aiming the materials at primary school students aged eight to ten and at older students aged sixteen to eighteen, noting that 40 percent of visitors to nuclear power plant information centers and to nuclear plants were children, often on school tours (Chaussade 1992, 368).

In 1994 the state attempted to "consolidate the national consensus" on economic and energy concerns through twenty regional debates and six major conferences (*Ecole nationale d'administration* 2002b, 24). It also introduced legislation to broaden the public discussion of nuclear power. In February 1995, Environment Minister Michel Barnier set up a law that required public debate on all large new public projects. In May 1996 the government passed a decree creating the National Commission for Public Debate (CNDP), a permanent coordinating body on issues of interest to the public. In June 1996 the government announced its intention to use the Internet and other communications media to "broaden public input into public inquiry proceedings for licensing of nuclear and other facilities" (MacLachlan 1996). The CNDP has held four debates since its inception, including one on an EDF-proposed high-tension-wire siting.

The new laws have yet to be applied to nuclear facilities, however. For example, struggles in the 1990s to locate three nuclear-waste-storage laboratories did not lead to public debate, as state authorities decided such debate would be inappropriate. If the next generation of nuclear power plants, the European Pressurized Water Reactors (EPRs), goes forward as planned, the CNDP might see its first real application. As one EDF official pointed out, though, the CNDP is really about informing the public—not debating the choice of sites or nuclear power in general—and as such is redundant to the locally held public inquiry, which also informs the populace and allows feedback in the form of written comments. One report stated that the CNDP "tends to give more import to its information mission, at the expense of its two other missions, namely consultation and dialogue" (Chavot and Masseran 2003, 3). Despite the promise of strengthened national and local commissions, and belief that the CNDP is a portent of real democratic change within the siting system (Boy 1999, 241), observers point out a "lack of local political will in many places to constitute commissions to scrutinize the work of what may be the region's best employer and taxpayer, such as an *Électricité de France* nuclear power plant" (MacLachlan 1996).

In 2001 the state created Energy Days (Les Journées de Energie) as a pilot program run by the DGEMP within the Ministry of Industry to provide additional information to citizens. In reviews, however, researchers argued that the program lacked funds and did not garner enough publicity (*École nationale d'administration* 2002a, 49). In 2002 the administration put forward a law to increase local democracy, connecting siting to the CNDP (ASN 2003, 93).

Despite these attempts to involve more citizens in a "democratic" process, the state has admitted that it faces a "slow deterioration of public acceptance" (*Ministère de l'économie* 2004, 7). While support for nuclear power has remained constant at around 50 percent of respondents, the percentage viewing it in terms of its disadvantages has increased.[31] Significantly, among those viewing it negatively are individuals who previously had no opinion on the subject; that is, people who previously did not commit to either side are becoming increasingly anti-nuclear.

Although the state has initiated strategies that seem to indicate a new transparency and openness in siting, police coercion and intimidation are not simply relics of nuclear power's early years. In 2000, security forces used tear gas to disrupt a peaceful demonstration of GSIEN and other groups at the Blayais plant (*La Gazette Nucléaire,* 183/184 [July 2000]: 2). In 2004 the state surveyed and intimidated groups it deemed harmful to nuclear power. When Greenpeace activists, for example, began to ask difficult questions about the transport of nuclear materials in 2003 and 2004, authorities responded by placing police in front of their offices. "We would leave our building and see them, sitting in cars near our building, sometimes taking pictures," one activist explained to me. With the development of EPRs, both the state and EDF could face renewed protest. In January 2004, anti-nuclear activists embarked on a hunger strike against the EPR (*Le Monde,* 17 July 2004) after a large anti-nuclear rally staged by 6,000 people.

Facing weak groups within civil society which do not sustain widespread opposition over time, the French state remained wedded to coercion and hard social control without seeking to expand its toolkit of responses. The most successful of French anti-nuclear civil society groups were able to sustain seven years of broad protest; others lasted less than five years. Compared to the decades of resistance in Japan, anti-nuclear dissent in France has been short-lived and fragmented. Analysts point out that with only a few exceptions, "the government implemented its initial plans" for siting reactors (Rucht 1994, 153), an accomplishment far surpassing Japan's record, where close to half the sitings failed. Recent innovations in the nuclear plant siting process, such

31. In this survey, approximately 2,000 people were asked this question: In what terms do you think of the production of 75 percent of France's electricity from nuclear power: benefits or drawbacks?

as the Committee for National Debate, can in fact be seen as extensions of information-diffusion tools because these forums are not open to the public in any serious way.

Without long-term, high-level opposition from civil society, states will not be forced to move beyond the standard operating procedures of coercion and hard social control. The French government constructed a full-scale national program based on expropriation, surveillance, and repression, policy instruments quite unlike those employed by Japanese authorities. State officials controlled the flow of information to the public and censored movies, data, and knowledge that could negatively influence public opinion. Through these instruments, the "French state successfully marginalized antinuclear legal activity" (Boyle 1998, 153). That is, in France, the protest movement "was unable to gain any permanent access to policymaking, and its supporters were ignored and actively suppressed until organized antinuclear sentiment all but disappeared" (Jasper 1995, 59). As one newspaper article explained the process, if a local council refused to accept a nuclear power plant, the state would shift to the regional council. If the regional council also voted against the plant, the decision would be taken up by Parliament (*Le Monde,* 25 October 1981). Frustrated at their inability to penetrate the walls surrounding decision making, anti-nuclear activists often resorted to violence, which further damaged their credibility with a mostly pro-nuclear public.

In 1986, Lord Walter Marshall, then chairman of the Central Electricity Governing Board in England, cited four reasons for France's nuclear success: "France has no coal, France has no oil, France has no gas, France has no choice" (Bacher, Panossian, and Riollet 1989, 159). Interestingly, Japan also lacks natural energy resources and places a high priority on "energy security," but Japanese authorities did not phrase their choice as irreversible or unavoidable. The director of the CEA's Nuclear Reactor Division argued that "within Europe at large, one often speaks of a 'French exception' where nuclear power is concerned" because of the supposedly low levels of opposition to nuclear power (NGSK 43/6 [1999]: 25). France is not exceptional in its steady use of coercive policy instruments (expropriation, police suppression, informational control, blocked institutional access) and its hard social control tactics, such as the public inquiry system and the state's ability to censor or suppress alternative viewpoints. All these create powerful disincentives for would-be protesters. Where Japanese bureaucrats faced similarly low-level resistance from civil society, as in airport siting and dam siting, they too relied on such tools.

Central government officials regularly assert that the French nuclear power industry is an open and democratic one. To the claim that the issue of nuclear power itself was never debated, one CEA director responded that it was nonsensical; if it were true, that "would mean that nine successive prime ministers under four different presidents of the Republic had succeeded in forcefully imposing the nuclear program we have on the entire French nation, including the political parties, the press, the trade unions, and the mayors" (Errera 1988, 42). Yet the French state does use force—legal, administrative, and coercive—to control the nuclear arena. One study concluded that although "public opposition has been expressed in anti-nuclear demonstrations, in demonstrations at particular sites, and in the formation of ecology parties which have challenged candidates in local and regional elections," none of these "has had any substantial impact on the French nuclear program" (OTA 1984, 191).

The central government "consults" with local elected officials and assemblies only to confirm selected sites. Mitterrand himself stated in a televised presidential debate in 1974 that local populations and officials, even if such bodies vehemently protest the plans, hold no right to veto a siting (Turpin 1983, 26). Environmental impact studies can be published *after* the conclusion of the local inquiry. With citizens unable to express their opinions at public inquiries except in written comments, and with courts and procedural institutions also closed to them, the anti-nuclear movement in France sought to express its frustration through violence (attacks on plants, companies, and state security forces) and "expressive" lawsuits. In a vicious cycle, however, the use of violence further alienated the anti-nuclear movement from French citizens who had come to accept the government's framing of activists as leftist radicals and criminals. Thus, even as active supporters dwindle, overall public opinion remains more pro-nuclear than in America.

State reliance on coercion and hard social control in France does contrast with the EDF, which studied the responses of local groups and developed targeted strategies; thus doctors, farmers, mayors, and schoolchildren received different information from this quasi-private utility. The EDF also worked to upgrade and improve the subsidies provided to local communities during and after construction. Its ad campaigns focused on specific demographic subgroups, such as women and young people, much as Japanese nuclear bureaucrats did. Furthermore, the EDF showed flexibility during its attempt to site at Plogoff, where it adopted new habituation and suasion strategies, whereas the state, rather than help the EDF to win over local communities, stalled the utility company's attempt to provide additional benefits. As one study pointed out, the Ministry of Industry is not known for its openness in discussing the nuclear program; it released very few materials to the public (Ecole nationale d'administration 2002b, 68).

The French case shows that without sustainable and dynamic civil society to challenge their policies, state agencies have little incentive to create new instruments for handling contestation. Perhaps as a result of the coercion employed by state authorities, the anti-nuclear movement in France has been marginalized, and public opinion there, though wavering, remains more supportive of nuclear power than in other advanced industrialized nations. In Japan, on the other hand, broadly mobilized civil society forced the state away from expropriation and other coercive policy instruments toward soft social controls and incentives.

# Conclusion

## Areas for Future Investigation

THIS BOOK PROVIDES EVIDENCE that civil society alters state policies in advanced industrial democracies in at least two important ways. First, dense local networks and voluntary associations with greater capacity push siting authorities to choose localities with diminished social capital as host communities for public bads. By avoiding areas with greater potential for resistance—even before any protests begin—bureaucrats and developers hope to avoid delays or cancellations. Second, stronger civil society forces authorities to move away from standard coercive policy instruments in handling conflict and to create new policies and tools for dealing with current and future contention. And although it is certainly accurate that transnational advocacy coalitions can improve the chances for groups within domestic civil society to stall or end state plans (Khagram 2004), international pressure is not necessary to cause changes in state policies and strategies.

Casual observers have argued that when siting controversial facilities such as nuclear power plants, France and Japan "never gave much leeway to pesky locals" (*The Economist,* 23 November 2006), but that is a serious mischaracterization. Rather, domestic networks of voluntary groups, even in supposedly "strong" nations, hold some leverage over state policy. Quantitative evidence from Japan and anecdotal evidence from France demonstrate that the strength of networks in local communities strongly determines the placement of controversial facilities.

This chapter builds on these arguments to explore three important themes that flow from the ways states handle conflict with civil society over public bads. The Machiavellian behavior of states, the role of competition in state toolkit development, and the future of the siting of public bads around the globe are vital issues that should be of concern to social scientists and can help guide future research into state–civil society interaction.

## The Machiavellian State

Several strong suppositions guide research on states and bureaucracies, especially concerning the responsiveness of states to their citizens and the roles played by nonelected state agencies in the policy process. Many social scientists hold fast to the normative assumption that the ways in which states interact with their citizens are tied to the times. Kent Calder (1988a) made this explicit argument in linking Japanese state response to certain historical periods when challengers pushed the dominant ruling party to alter its policies and expand its programs to new constituencies. John Noakes (2001) and others make a more teleological argument about the development of "softer" ways of handling contention over time, pointing out that police departments within the United States have moved from explicit coercion to management of protests. An obvious example is that whereas police departments may have used barking dogs, fire hoses, truncheons, and tear gas to handle protest marches in mid-twentieth-century America, demonstrations in the twenty-first century at annual political party conventions and international conferences have been handled by means of prearranged "arrest zones" and roped-off "protest areas." Similarly, analysts often believe that modern states in the early twenty-first century face more pressure to develop policies that reflect the interests of their constituents than in the past, as average citizens can better punish legislators and governments who fail to meet their needs. Also, better educated citizens have more access to information about the actions of their representatives; accordingly, researchers assume that they have greater sway over national and local policy.

At the same time, political scientists regularly view bureaucracy relative to its capacity to create or enforce legislation (see Huber and McCarty 2004). In this sense, bureaucracies are often compared to politicians who follow cues from voters to determine their course of action, with a common reading of bureaucracies as agents for their politician principals (Ramseyer and Rosenbluth 1993). Bureaucracies can do more than merely monitor and enforce laws, however. Some analysts have distinguished between mere politicians, who enact policies they imagine will allow them to retain their electoral seats, and statesmen, who seek to guide their people toward a new future. Franklin D. Roosevelt stands out as a paradigmatic statesman who utilized a variety of techniques, such as "fireside chats" and other innovative pulpits, to push both Congress and the American people toward new social agendas, ranging from a radically altered role for the government in promoting employment and the arts to lending programs for America's European "neighbors" (Kernell 1997). Bureaucrats too can do more than simply enact popular policies; they can also act as statesmen, guiding the nation on a new path (Johnson 1982).

Unelected civil servants within powerful ministries—the Ministry of International Trade and Industry (now METI) in Japan, the Ministry of Industry in France, or the Atomic Energy Commission (now Nuclear Regulatory Commission) in the United States—can seek to lead the country in a new direction, whether it is one in which nuclear power is the dominant source of electricity or one in which dams block the flow of every river. Thus, although pluralists and normative democratic theorists believe that democratic states initiate policies demanded by constituents and that the ties between citizen interests and state policy should only be tightening over time, this study illustrates the opposite. I stand with previous scholarship in not seeing "any clear trend towards citizen inclusion in governmental decision making" (Flam 1994b, 330). Even in the early twenty-first century, states—especially their bureaucratic agencies responsible for siting controversial facilities—are not influenced by public opinion to the degree that democratic and pluralist theorists would claim; often, authorities either ignore public opinion or attempt to shape it. And government bureaus, seeking to implement their often independent agendas smoothly, ignore or manipulate public opinion to meet their goals.

The Japanese state, for example, employed a broad variety of policy instruments: it wrote school curricula, tested opinions through focus groups, provided side payments, and used public relations campaigns to lower resistance to the siting of nuclear power plants. Joseph Morone and Edward Woodhouse (1989, 148), in a discussion of nuclear energy, argue that Japan is "actively shap[ing] technology to serve social purposes": that is, adopting programs and policies involving the peaceful use of the atom which meet the interests of Japanese citizens. Their argument should be reversed: Japanese officials, along with authorities in other advanced industrial democracies, seek to shape social purposes and preferences to serve technology. Once states set themselves on certain development and technological trajectories, future policies, even if they become unpopular, rarely deviate from these initial choices.

Most important, states display remarkably Machiavellian behavior in responding to societal opposition to their policies. When their plans activate only small portions of contentious civil society, state agencies remain wedded to tools and strategies based firmly in coercion and hard social control. Even under pressure, many governments do not alter their core goals of "energy independence" and remain committed to taking land from uncooperative citizens or using police force and intimidation to increase the costs of resistance for citizens' and residents' movements. As Eric Nordlinger (1981) pointed out long ago, states and bureaucracies often envision citizen preferences as malleable rather than fixed; that is, they believe the preferences of individuals within civil society can be molded to match those of the state. Only when pushed strongly by contentious politics do state agencies move toward softer social control strategies and incentives to manage restive populations.

The willingness of the state to seek to change citizen preferences has been supported by quantitative research on public opinion regarding nuclear power. James Jasper traced public opinion in France, Sweden, and the United States starting in the mid-1970s, when it was more or less the same in all three countries before diverging strongly. He concluded, "Public opinion was influenced by state policies more than it influenced them." In France he found that "public opinion grew steadily more pro-nuclear in the years after 1978, while American opinion grew more anti-nuclear. Sweden, where the direction of nuclear policy remained uncertain, retained a roughly even split of opinion" (Jasper 1995, 95). He argues that public opinion is most heavily a function of state handling of the issue. Because French bureaucrats and authorities supported nuclear power and marginalized those who opposed it, many citizens were swayed to support the state's position, despite misgivings about nuclear power. The converse was true in the United States, where official support for nuclear power declined rapidly—as state organizations' internal unity fragmented—and hence anti-nuclear forces could more easily mobilize opinion on the issue (Baumgartner and Jones 1991).

Perhaps more pernicious for normative views of the relationships between civil society and the state, the ministries and government agencies analyzed in this study regularly developed superficially more "democratic" procedures that seemed to take citizen interests into account in response to rising expectations about public involvement in decision making. Trying to convince citizens of their goodwill and acquiescence to public participation, state ministries simultaneously ratcheted up tools such as eminent domain so that they could more quickly expropriate property from unwilling owners. While calls for a more "democratic" process caused the Japanese Ministry of Construction to adopt, among other policies, environmental assessment plans, local deliberation boards, and review councils to consider the necessity of proposed projects, the MOC simultaneously moved to close the loopholes and procedures that citizens were exploiting to delay projects. The Ministry of Transportation in Japan apologized to anti-Narita protesters for its use of expropriation, which had resulted in widespread violence, but then it immediately demolished several of their buildings. The French government displayed a dazzling array of new institutions designed to increase citizen participation in siting procedures but fell back on expropriation and force whenever those procedures were held up. In short, governments endeavored to provide a more democratic and equitable image of their siting procedures but meanwhile reinforced their core siting tools.

Expropriation procedures became almost impossible to overcome once bureaucrats learned from their interaction how to handle citizens who entangle siting procedures with resistance tactics, such as the purchase and division of the land necessary for the project: bureaucrats can defeat such citizen tools by increasing the strength of their powers of eminent domain. As many Japanese researchers studying siting procedures have pointed out, it is essentially impossible for large-scale construction projects like dams to reflect the opinions and viewpoints of Japanese citizens (Hagiwara 1996; Shimizu 1991,19; Shimouke Matsubara 1972, 464). In most cases, the only actual two-way interaction between central government officials and citizens affected by dams involves bargaining over how much money citizens will receive and the location of their new homes. Observers who viewed Japanese ministries as becoming more open or altering core approaches to dam siting were perhaps too hasty in their conclusions. Citizens' frustration with their lack of involvement in the process of facility siting continues; in early 2007 a landowner whose property lay within an area earmarked for the construction of the Shizuoka Airport immolated himself in protest, believing that perhaps through death he would be able to make his voice heard (*Mainichi Shinbun,* 6 February 2007).

While the rhetoric of states has changed to reflect changing demands for transparency and accountability, the actions of states continue to expose their true nature. Landowners who resist state siting plans in the coming year are just as likely as earlier ones, if not more, to find their land confiscated by the state. In Japan the use of the coercive tool of land expropriation has not diminished over time, even after notorious cases such as the Matsubara and Shimouke Dam attempts and the decades-long struggle over the expropriation of land for the Narita Airport. In North America, airport expansion in several urban cities required the uprooting of hundreds, in some cases thousands, of families: "St. Louis's plan, for example, required the taking of more than 2,000 homes; Atlanta's, 650; and Chicago's 600" (Altshuler and Luberoff 2003, 172). The U.S. Supreme Court has ruled that even private developers working solely for profit can expropriate the land of homeowners and businesses if local town councils or governments judge the project appropriate (*New York Times,* 24 June 2005). A survey of eight states' responses to anti-nuclear movements across Western Europe confirmed that half of these states relied on their monopoly over force and used coercion—often police suppression—in responding to contention (Flam 1994c, 302). Figure 18 shows that between 1953 and 2001, the overall number of approved applications for land expropriation has increased, not decreased, in Japan, despite common expectations about diminishing numbers of such takings. The government has allowed the taking of private property in greater numbers of cases over time.

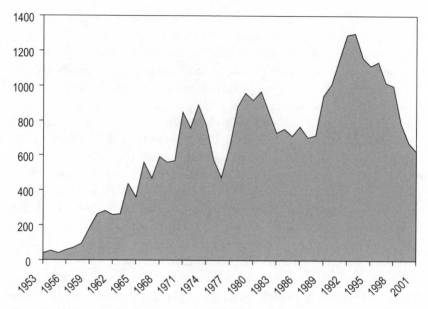

Figure 18. Total approved expropriation applications per year in Japan
*Source: Yōchi Janaru* (Land Use Journal), November 2001, 49

Scholars should closely investigate the tools that democratic states use in handling conflict in other highly contentious areas, such as anti-war, anti-police, or anti-globalization movements within civil society, to see whether similar secular trends toward coercive policy instruments exist. Both scholars and citizens need to take the toolkits of states seriously.

### Competition and the Development of State Toolkits

The Machiavellian behavior of states in handling contention has led to mixed opinions about the ability of civil society to influence state policies. Some researchers conclude that citizens' movements have strongly impacted policies in fields such as nuclear arms control and disarmament (Wittner 2003). Yet statistical analyses of anti-nuclear, ecology, and peace movements in the United States, Italy, and Switzerland lead others to conclude that these movements "have not been very successful" in altering national public policy (Giugni 2004, 219). This book moves beyond those debates to show how competition between civil society and the state drives the coevolution of both actors. Political scientists could learn much from the literature in organizational theory that recognizes the importance of the competitive environment around the organization

(Hannan and Freeman 1989; Barnett and Hansen 1996; Levitt and March 1988; H. Aldrich 1999). Such approaches underscore the need for conflict in a democracy as an important mechanism in moving the state forward. Although many have worried about the dangers of "excessive" contestation and struggle between state and civil society (Crozier, Huntington, and Watanuki 1975), this research hints that such confrontation, though unpleasant, may be necessary to improve states' tools and to upgrade the social movements' tactics.

Democracies are not staid constellations of interest representing institutions; rather, despite scholarship that has downplayed the role of competition in domestic politics, this book shows at least some of them as evolving through competition and conflict (Pierson 2004). In industrialized societies with strong and organized civil society, democracy involves a coevolutionary process, molding the forms of both state and citizenry. Research has shown how new structures and systems arose from state-society interaction, especially from long-term contestation. Studies of Japan, for example, often dwell on the weakness of nongovernmental organizations and citizens' groups: not only is the political culture supposedly passive, but in the overall environment, NGOs and other nonstate actors find it difficult to move and lobby freely. But the analysis employed here shows that the concentration of civil society has strongly affected state siting policies. In reacting to strong anti-nuclear contention, for example, the Japanese state created a series of policy tools to manage opposition from these groups. The Japanese Ministry of International Trade and Industry spawned a number of new institutions solely for the purpose of distributing incentives to potential and actual host communities for nuclear power plants. Current conflicts within American society over "activist judges," the teaching of evolution or creationism in schools, and recent elections show that coevolutionary metamorphoses of civil society and the state will continue.

The tools available to states in their toolkits, such as the complex Japanese *Dengen Sanpō,* which distributes hundreds of millions of dollars a year in incentives to host communities, do not spring into being automatically. Nor are the tools used by one ministry merely replicated by its counterparts in other policy areas. At its core, the primeval state is a merely a coercive apparatus, a way of extracting resources from the population and accomplishing the purely self-interested goals of power holders, such as boundary preservation or expansion (war) or their enrichment (taxes) (Tilly 1985, 1990). Ghosts of this minimum state can be viewed in early nineteenth-century European nations and even today in predatory states such as Haiti, Belize, and Democratic Republic of the Congo. These predatory states have not developed welfare programs to compensate for the problems of capitalism, or expanded educational programs to unify the populace or increase economic efficiency.

Many undeveloped nations do not experience a "double push" of economic, free-market liberalism counterbalanced by calls for social protection (Polanyi 1944). Developing a sophisticated toolkit that holds anything more than the most basic of tools is a long-term process requiring an active civil society. Because most Western, industrialized states developed more conscious and demanding citizenries over the nineteenth and twentieth centuries, authorities were forced to move beyond absolutist or predatory states. Thus we see the development of public-order policing as a result of the expansion of suffrage, especially in England, where authorities recognized that they could no longer treat citizens like subjects but rather had to develop new approaches and tactics for handling confrontation (Tarrow 1998, 64).

Hannah Arendt (1969) argued that when civil society threatens or challenges state authority, the state responds with force or coercion; however, acute contestation may in fact push states to develop a broader array of more refined, and often more subtle, tools.[1] Perhaps no development has spurred the sophistication of the modern state more than the spread of democracy. States undergoing acute and sustained challenges from civil society are more likely to innovate and adapt their strategies than states that are not. Unperturbed states remain slumbering lions, content to rely on their considerable, if unimaginative, tools. Alternatively, states with dominant strategies may undercut efforts to diversify, expand, or enhance their capacity to manage society. The impetus for state innovation is often a strong, sustained challenge from civil society.

Japanese, French, and North American ministries encountering only low-level or sporadic resistance to their policies have been most likely to rely on coercive tools such as police force and land expropriation. Thus, dam siting in the United States and Japan, airport siting in Japan, and nuclear power plant siting in France regularly rely on eminent domain and hard social control techniques. Agencies encountering longer-term, acute resistance, such as the Japanese MITI, moved away from such tools to develop new incentives and soft social controls. These tools were not copied across ministries, despite assumptions about national bureaucratic cultures; instead, competition was solely responsible for the evolutionary development of states' toolkits. In this sense, civil society fits better with neo-Gramscian visions than with neo-Tocquevillean ones, since it serves as a counterweight to the state, not necessarily as a force enhancing or enabling state capacity (Alagappa 2004, 28, 468).

---

1. This is similar to the point that all police organizations have and are legally authorized to use force-based, coercive tools such as batons, handcuffs, and firearms. More important is that most police actions *never involve force;* officers have developed techniques and strategies of cajoling, implicit or explicit threats, legal constraints, and suasion to carry out their goal of public order (Bayley 1982; Noakes 2001).

Competition is not a one-shot interaction between the state and contentious civil society. State–civil society interactions are processes and cannot be captured in models or analyses that evaluate a single moment in time. Investigations of short periods in time—such as one year in the early 1960s, or several months in the early 2000s—would yield conclusions about the responses of relevant ministries that are far from reality. In the late 1950s, for example, many agencies had little reason to move beyond the standard core tactics of land expropriation in siting nuclear power plants, dams, and airports. At that time, Japanese planners in the field of nuclear power were beginning to alter their practices, as individual projects met with resistance, but had not yet created more advanced incentives and soft social control tools because they had not yet met with broadly organized opposition. A superficial view of formal policies in the early twenty-first century would misleadingly appear to show institutional mimesis, as bureaucracies such as construction and transportation ministries developed common but superficial language about "citizen involvement" and "public acceptance." This empirical study underscores the need to look closely at the long-term historical events involving organizations.

Certain state tools, such as the use of preference-altering techniques, may take years to become effective. Students in middle school immersed in the pro-nuclear curricula created by nuclear agencies may not become relevant actors as voters or demonstrators for years to come, and studies that take state tools seriously would need to follow the long-term effects, if any, of such educational tools. Similarly, the process of coevolution, by which the techniques and strategies of state agencies evolve through interaction, underscores the need to follow politics over time. Looking at any single encounter would provide no evidence of the agility demonstrated by the Agency of Natural Resources and Energy over the course of thirty years. Paul Pierson (2004) has challenged scholars to move away from typical "snapshot" models of institutional and policy development and toward longer-term studies that better capture subtle alterations over time. The field of American political development has taken this challenge seriously in its studies of Congress (Schickler 2001) and bureaucracy (Carpenter 2001), as have comparativists (e.g., Thelen 2004). By focusing on institutional development, scholars shift from functionalist, snapshot studies of institutions where they represent the Panglossian "best of all possible worlds" to in-depth process-tracing that highlights the processes of institutional change under a variety of pressures.[2]

2. Some have seen institutions such as the United States Congress as vehicles for solving cycling problems in decision making (Shepsle 1979), while others have seen them as the best form of assembly for maximizing reelection probabilities (Mayhew 1974, 81–82).

## The Future of Siting Public Bads

In the future, conflict over facility siting will only intensify as the amount of available land decreases, citizen expectations and activism increase, and pressures build for new energy sources, transportation networks, and water supplies. As of early 2008, governments around the world envision constructing close to thirty new nuclear power plants in the next decades, despite domestic and international opposition. In a period labeled by some as the "nuclear renaissance," Canada, Britain, France, Iran, China, and Japan hope to further increase their nuclear capacity. Developing nations such as Vietnam and Indonesia also hope to construct nuclear reactors in the next decade.

Although the U.S. nuclear industry has been paralyzed by opposition and uncertainty since the late 1970s, the early twenty-first century brings utilities pushing for new sites near Port Gibson, Mississippi; Columbia, South Carolina; and Scottsboro, Alabama. In late 2005 the U.S. Nuclear Regulatory Commission (NRC) approved a new 1,000-megawatt Westinghouse reactor type (*Physics Today,* February 2006). Constellation Energy, a utility holding company, planned to apply for a reactor-operating license in late 2007 (Wald 2006). Although one Japanese utility formally canceled long-contested plans to construct a nuclear plant in Kumihama in Kyoto prefecture (*Yomiuri Shinbun,* 6 March 2006), ANRE is advocating a new type of fast breeder reactor to replace the failed Monju model. The Japanese state continues to push for a closed fuel cycle, involving fuel recycling and reprocessing, at its Rokkasho facility, which is under construction, along with plans to build additional nuclear plants over the next fifty years (Katsuta 2006). Further, Japanese nuclear firms see new markets both in China and in the United States and have moved aggressively to increase their international presence. Japan's Toshiba Corporation, for example, purchased Westinghouse Electric Company in late January 2006 in the kind of merger that may become commonplace as joint ventures and international projects flourish.

Such optimism from both firms and the state may be premature. Given that politics, "rather than economic, engineering, environmental, or philosophical concerns," most often determines the outcome of controversial facilities (Simpson 2005, 162), and that labels of "regulatory risk" are actually "a euphemism for fears that politicians, planning officials, and protesters will hold up or entirely derail the construction of new plants" (*The Economist,* 11 November 2006, 71), the future of public bads siting remains a book to be written primarily by citizen-state interaction. Technological advances in energy production, such as the development of the pebble-bed nuclear reactor and cleaner-burning coal facilities, will succeed only if authorities can find

locations for them. Authorities and scholars working on issues of energy production plants and other large-scale facilities too often forget that without
host communities, their plans are useless. Although ongoing conflict with civil
society has not deterred states from making long-term plans for energy independence, the success or failure of those plans lies in the hands of local residents
around the globe.

Regular admissions from utility companies in Japan, such as TEPCO, that
they falsified hundreds of inspection reports for nuclear facilities will certainly
not increase citizen confidence in either the state or the private sector (*Asahi
Shinbun,* 1 February 2007). More shocking to observers were admissions from
several utilities that they had covered up earlier emergency shutdowns of nuclear reactors (*Asahi Shinbun,* 2 March 2007; *Japan Times,* 13 March 2007).
Mirroring conflict over nuclear power plants, anti-facility sentiment in North
America has created an environment in which only the city of Denver has
"managed to build a new passenger airport since the early 1970s." More the
norm were failures in Morris County, New Jersey, and Dade County, Flor-
ida, as well as Los Angeles, Chicago, Minneapolis/St. Paul, and St. Louis to
site airports due to local civil society (Altshuler and Luberoff 2003, 136–137,
279). French plans for a new Paris-area international airport that would require expropriation of local land have sparked protest among both residents
and environmental groups (*Aviation Week and Space Technology,* 6 November
2000). States control many aspects of the siting process, and agencies serious
about long-term relationships with residents now understand that true citizen
involvement is key.

State agencies must navigate a treacherous path between the Scylla of coercion, which can result in backlash, and the Charybdis of soft social control
tools, which may not guarantee success. Too often, when government agencies faced diffuse or diminished groups within civil society, they made decisions which, as was said of the Tennessee Valley Authority, "solve short-range
problems but in the long run, prove injurious" (Wheeler and McDonald 1986,
14). When the Japanese state used coercion and expropriation, it achieved an
80 percent completion rate for dams and a 95 percent rate for airport siting
attempts. But these policy instruments will be less effective in the future as
citizen groups mobilize and organize more efficiently. Just as Japanese bureaucrats felt that expropriation would short-circuit any goodwill in future
attempts at nuclear plant siting, so too agencies around the world in advanced
democracies will soon discover the dangers of coercing more and more vigorous civil societies.

At the same time, soft social control tools and incentives rarely result in immediate or even long-term success, as has been seen in both North America

and Japan. Japanese efforts at nuclear plant siting have most often been stalled or stymied but have also seen the greatest development of incentives and soft social control techniques by the state. Thus state authorities may hesitate to move toward incentives and soft social control because research has shown that attitudes toward issues such as nuclear power are not easily changed by public information or educational campaigns (Slovic et al. 2000, 98). Even offering money to communities in exchange for hosting facilities has often had a perverse effect, driving out voluntarism and lowering support for the projects (Frey, Oberholzer-Gee, and Eichenberger 1996; Frey and Oberholzer-Gee 1997). In fact, "economic strategies, including those that emphasize generous compensation packages as the ultimate balm of siting tensions, almost invariably fail" (Rabe 1994, xiv).

Democratic states need to look beyond short-term solutions toward long-range approaches that incorporate citizen feedback, true voluntarism, and a recognition of local residents' nonmonetary concerns. Increasing contention from civil society has produced at least partially successful, softer solutions to siting conflicts. More than changing policy tool types to offer incentives, educational curricula, and the like, agencies could work to actually involve local residents in plans for controversial facilities. Research has demonstrated that government agencies involving citizens directly in the decision-making process often create better policies for controversial facilities than top-down, state-directed ones (McAvoy 1999). As voluntary associations around the world continue to mobilize and counterbalance state plans, conflict between state and society will create more sustainable, if not necessarily always successful, strategies for responding to citizen concerns. States must recognize the degree to which national plans rest on the reactions of local communities and work to involve them in decision making.

# Appendix 1: Data Sources

## Political Data

Steven Reed, *Shūgiin Giin Sōsenkyo Kōhoshabetsu Tokuhyō Kekka, 1947–1995*
[Japan election data, House of Representatives, 1947–1995]; Takayoshi Miya-
gawa, *Shō senkyoku Handobukku* (Handbook of Single Member Constituencies)
(Tokyo: Seiji Kōhō Sentā [Center for Political Public Relations], 1996); and
direct surveys of mayoral offices, gubernatorial offices, and fishing cooperatives carried out by the author, June 2002–September 2003.

## Facility Data

Direct surveys of local ministerial offices and controversial facility-siting
authorities by the author, June 2001–September 2001 and June 2002–
September 2003; *Genshiryoku shiryō jōhō shitsu* [Citizens' Nuclear Informa-
tion Center, CNIC]; *Genshiryoku shimin nenkan 2002* [Citizens' yearbook on
nuclear energy] (Tokyo: CNIC, 2002); *Hangenpatsu Undō Zenkoku Renraku kai*
[National Anti-Nuclear Liaison Group]; *Hangenpatsu Shinbun* [Anti-Nuclear
Newspaper] (Tokyo: Hangenpatsu Undō Zenkoku Renraku kai, 1978–1998);
*Asahi Shinbun* [Asahi Newspaper]; *Asahi Shinbun Sengo Midashi Sakuin* [Asahi
Newspaper Headline Database 1945–1995] (Tokyo: Asahi Shinbun); *Nihon
Damu Kyōkai* [Japan Dam Federation]; *Damu Nenkan* [Dam Yearbook] (Tokyo:
Nihon Damu Kyōkai); and http://www.mlit.go.jp/koku/04_outline/01_kuko/
01_haichi/index.html.

## Demographic Data

*Tōyō Keizai Shinpōsha, Jinkō tōkei sōran: kokusei chōsa shūtaisei* [Population statistics of Japan: Summary of national censuses and other surveys, 1872–1984]

(Tokyo: Tōyō Keizai Shinpōsha, *1985*); Sōmuchō Tōkeikyoku [Statistics Bureau, Home Affairs Ministry], *Nihon no Jinkō: Heisei Ninen Kokuseichōsa Saishūhōkokusho* [Population of Japan: Final report of the 1990 population census] *(Tokyo:* Sōmuchō Tōkeikyoku, 1995); Sōmuchō Tōkeikyoku [Statistics Bureau, Home Affairs Ministry], *Nihon no Jinkō: Heisei Nananen Kokuseichōsa Saishūhōkokusho* [Population of Japan: Final report of the 1995 population census] (Tokyo: Sōmuchō Tōkeikyoku, 2000); Sōmuchō Tōkeikyoku [Statistics Bureau, Ministry of Home Affairs], *Heisei Jūninen Kokuseichōsa Saishūhōkokusho Jinkōsōsū, Dai ichi maki* [Total population: 2000 population census of Japan, vol. 1] (Tokyo: Sōmuchō Tōkeikyoku 2002).

## Geologic and Geographic Data

Nihon Daiyonki Gakkai hen [Japan Association for Quaternary Research], ed., *Nihon Daiyonki chizu* [Quarternary maps of Japan] (Tokyo: Tōkyō Daigaku Shuppankai, 1987); International Society for Educational Information, *Atlas of Japan: Physical, Economic, and Social* (Tokyo: International Society for Educational Information, 1970); and electronic GIS databases available at http://www.cast.uark.edu/jpgis.

# Appendix 2: Methodological Details

## Data Set Creation Methodology

Analysts who build observational data sets without ensuring that their cases involve "apples and apples," as opposed to dissimilar subject samples, do so at their peril (see Rosenbaum and Rubin 1985; Reiter 2000). Taking this warning to heart, I used an *equal-shares, choice-based* sampling method to create a data set with cases where the Japanese state attempted to site a controversial facility alongside cases where it did not. I captured the entire universe of attempted sitings of nuclear power plants and airports where the state was either entrepreneur or founder of the project, and half of the state-led dam cases (cases selected at random). The balance of observations where $Y = 0$ (where no siting was attempted) and $Y = 1$ (where the government sought to create a facility) within the data set was approximately .5 ($\hat{Y} = .494$).

I matched the set of cases where authorities attempted siting against those where no siting had occurred—temporally, geographically, and geologically. In matching the observations where $Y = 0$ to those where $Y = 1$, I followed the explicit decision heuristics of siting authorities according to both interviews and archival records. I relied upon both geographic information systems (GIS) data and extensively detailed geological and geographical maps of Japan. Accordingly, areas where nuclear power plants could potentially be sited met four geologic, geographic, and demographic criteria: (1) solid bedrock (and not alluvial plain) to ensure aseismicity, (2) distance from large population centers such as Osaka and Tokyo, (3) proximity to water so that cooling towers could draw in seawater to dissipate heat from the nuclear reactors, and (4) relatively low population density to ensure that evacuation plans would be feasible. I excluded a number of landlocked prefectures from the nuclear power plant potential sample subgroup of the $Y = 0$ set because of their lack of access to seawater (including Tochigi, Gunma, Saitama, Yamanashi, Nagano, Gifu, and Nara). I excluded Toyama prefecture because of ground quality and Tokyo because of the need for feasible evacuation plans. Potential host communities for dams and similar water projects (river gates, rerouting, etc.) required, obviously, bodies of water and, when possible, bodies of water that extended across prefectures (as the central government is most likely to build dams on "first grade" rivers that do so). Thus I excluded Fukuoka and Nagasaki prefectures from possible dam locations. Airports required proximity to large urban centers that would generate demand for such facilities, along with suitable geographic conditions (no whole prefectures were excluded from the possible airport siting location subset). These balancing cases also matched the $Y = 1$ cases in terms of time; hence, observations match on both spatial and temporal axes (i.e., each case of an actual siting attempt in 19XX is balanced by a non-event in 19XX which has the same suitability for that type of controversial facility).

## Variable Proxies

I measure the presence of party legislators through data on the number and percentage of such representatives in the Upper House of Parliament. I measured over-time support for the Liberal Democratic Party by compiling a yearly, prefectural index of votes for LDP candidates in the Upper House (House of Councilors) and averaged each area's "score" between 1956 and 1989.[1] I used Upper House election data as opposed to Lower House (House of Representatives) election data for three main reasons. First, Upper House elections take place at regularly scheduled intervals, and their outcomes are not endogenous with election timing, as is often a problem with Lower House elections. Second, unlike the Lower House electoral processes, Upper House elections are nonpersonalistic and are seen to reflect party interest, not personal voting patterns (Curtis 1971, 1999). Third, Upper House election data map well onto prefectures, thanks to the single, non transferable vote (SNTV) districting procedures. To analyze the effect of powerful hegemonic politicians, I tracked the number of LDP politicians serving six terms or longer in the Lower House; these are often referred to as *daijin,* or cabinet-level politicians, because long-tenure candidates regularly gain seats within the cabinet. I separately measured the presence or absence of prime ministers from these localities.

I measured civil society capacity as the change in employment in the percentage of workers employed in the primary sector from 1980 through 1995.

---

1. Thanks to Rob Weiner and Ross Schaap for their assistance and suggestions with this measure.

Fishermen and farmers constitute the bulk of employment in this sector (more than 98 percent), and their membership rates in associations and unions that regularly participate in siting procedures are close to 100 percent. Changes in this percentage over time reflect the strength of fishermen and farmers vis-à-vis their community and other potential competitors. Seventy percent of the nuclear power plant siting attempts took place during this time period, the remainder occurring in the 1960s and 1970s; even for earlier attempts, this variable still measures the long-term viability of first sector strength. For analysts concerned that this proxy measure obfuscates the exactly opposite causal relationship—that instead of serving as an independent variable which affects exclusion of localities, the health of the primary sector should instead be a dependent variable which is effected by the siting of public bads—I carried out a test using propensity-matching scores and average treatment effects to ensure that this was not the case.

Propensity-score matching of concomitants to produce balance between control and treatment groups provides an alternative to standard analysis techniques even in observational studies (Rosenbaum and Rubin 1983, 1985; Angrist and Krueger 1999, 1314–1315). Propensity score matching, the attempt to match observations in the treatment group (e.g., those that receive nuclear power plants) with those in the untreated group (those that do not), brings with it a number of benefits. Creating treated and control groups that are as similar as possible theoretically reduces the bias in estimators by controlling for confounding factors (Becker and Ichino 2002). We estimate average treatment effects on the treated units "by averaging within match differences in the outcome variable between the treated and untreated units" (Abadie and Imbens 2002, 1).

Using nearest-neighbor matching, the standard average treatment effect of siting a public bad on the percentage change in primary workers over the 1980 to 1995 period was −.0665, a figure statistically significant at the .003 level. That is, the placement of a nuclear power plant, dam, or airport in a locality is responsible, on average, for a decrease of less than seven percent in the employment rates of farmers and fishermen there. There is a feedback effect on local fishermen and farmers from siting, but it is a minor one. For example, all other factors being equal, a seven percent decrease in the concentration of workers in the primary sector has little effect on the probability of selection as host community; the threshold effect for locational inclusion for nuclear power plants, for example, is closer to 30 percent. Given that the average locality in this data set saw a decrease of 30 *percent* in its primary employment over that time period, I believe that concern about reverse-causality is misplaced. Public-bad siting is primarily a function of the health of the primary sector, not vice versa.

## Weighting Correction

There are two main methods for correcting estimates when one selects on the dependent variables: (1) prior correction and (2) weighting. Such additional techniques must be employed to "compensate for differences in the sample ($\hat{y}$) and population ($\tau$) fraction of ones induced by choice based sampling" (King and Zeng 2001a, 144). While the data set contained a ratio of $Y = 1$ to $Y = 0$ of 1:1, the actual population of cases is closer in nuclear power plants, for example, to 1:600, in dams closer to 1:888, and 1:144 in airports. That is to say, when a nuclear power plant was sited in year 19XX, there were 600 other localities with the same suitable geographic and geologic criteria which were not selected. I calculated the population of ones to zeros in the actual population (i.e., the fraction of localities in Japan which met the geographic and geologic requirement), using GIS data and existing geographic and geological maps, for each type of facility. Those estimations allowed me to reweight the data set to create a population roughly equivalent to that found in the field. Because prior correction requires proper model specification, it is slightly disadvantageous compared with weighting (Xie and Manski 1989).

## Coefficient Tables

Full details on the estimated coefficients, standard errors, and significance of the variables under study are available on the author's website.

# APPENDIX 3: INTERVIEWEES

### JAPAN (80 individual interviews)

NONGOVERNMENTAL ORGANIZATIONS
  Citizens' Nuclear Information Center
  Committee for Reconsidering the Hosogōchi Dam
  Committee for Reconsidering the Yanba Dam
  Committee for Symbiosis between the Local Community and Narita
    Airport
  Group for the Protection of Life and Land from Narita Airport
  Group for the Protection of Nature in Nagashima
  Gunma Prefectural Nature Protection Group
  Kaminoseki Antinuclear Power Movement
  Opposition to Nuclear Power in Futaba Union

CENTRAL GOVERNMENT
  Narita Airport Authority
  Ministry of Economy, Trade, and Industry: Agency for Natural Resources
    and Energy
  Ministry of Economy, Trade, and Industry: Global Environmental Affairs
    Office
  Ministry of Land, Infrastructure, and Transport: Civil Aviation Bureau
  Ministry of Land, Infrastructure, and Transport: Water Resources, Dam
    Section

LOCAL GOVERNMENT
  Kaminoseki City
  Kitō Village
  Ōkuma Village
  Shibayama Town Council

## QUASI-GOVERNMENTAL ORGANIZATIONS
Japan Atomic Energy Relations Organization
Japan Industrial Siting Center

## POLITICIANS
Akira Amari, Liberal Democratic Party
Nakamura Atsuo, Green Party Japan
Satō Kenichiro, Democratic Party
Sasaki Kensho, Communist Party
Harada Shozo, Liberal Democratic Party
Kanō Tokio, Liberal Democratic Party

## MASS MEDIA
*Asahi Shinbun*

## THINK TANKS
Central Research Institute of Electric Power Industry
Energy Forum
Institute of Energy Economics
Institute for Sustainable Energy Policies

## CORPORATIONS AND INDUSTRY ORGANIZATIONS
Chubu Electric Power Company
Chugoku Electric Power Company
Federation of Electric Power Companies
FracMan Technology Group
Japan Atomic Energy Relations Organization
Japan Atomic Energy Research Institute
Japan Dam Foundation
Tokyo Electric Power Company

## LAWYERS, ACADEMICS, AND ANALYSTS
Kodama Fumio, University of Tokyo
Kaneko Kumao, Tokai University
Robert Ricketts, Wako University
Paul Scalise, Dresdner Kleinwort Wasserstein
Wilhelm Vosse, International Christian University
Kaido Yuichi, Lawyer

## CONTROVERSIAL-FACILITY VISITS AND INTERVIEWS
Anti-Hosogōchi Dam movement, Tokushima prefecture
Anti-Kawabegawa Dam citizens' movement meeting, Tokyo

Anti-nuclear demonstration, Hibiya Park, Tokyo
Fukushima Dai-Ichi nuclear power complex, Fukushima prefecture
Kaminoseki nuclear plant site, Yamaguchi prefecture
Kominono Dam and Shabo Dam, Tokushima prefecture
Miyagase Dam, Kanagawa prefecture
Narita Airport, Chiba prefecture
Yanba Dam and Shinagi Dam, Gunma prefecture

## FRANCE (24 interviews)

### NONGOVERNMENTAL ORGANIZATIONS
Greenpeace France
Organization of Scientists for Information about Nuclear Energy (Groupement de Scientifiques pour l'Information sur l'Energie Nucléaire)
World Information Service on Energy, Paris

### CENTRAL GOVERNMENT
Commission on Atomic Energy (Commissariat à l'Energie Atomique)
Foreign Ministry
Ministry of Economy, Finance, and Industry Nuclear Safety Authority (Autorité de Sûreté Nucléaire)
Parliamentary Office for Scientific and Technological Assessment

### LOCAL GOVERNMENT
Nogent sur Seine

### POLITICIANS
Christian Bataille, Socialist Party
Claude Birraux, Union pour un Mouvement Populaire (UMP)

### MASS MEDIA
*Nucleonics Week*

### CORPORATIONS AND INDUSTRY ORGANIZATIONS
AREVA
Électricité de France

### ACADEMIA
Centre de Recherche sur le Politique, l'Administration, la Ville et le Territoire

Centre de Recherches Politiques de Sciences Po
Ecole Nationale Supérieure des Mines

## CONTROVERSIAL-FACILITY VISITS AND INTERVIEWS
Nogent-sur-Seine nuclear power plant

# Periodicals and News Services

*Airport, International*
*AS (Asahi Shinbun)*
AP News
AP Wire
*AS* News Service
*CNIC Monthly*
*Comite STOP Nugent-sur-Seine*
*Damu Nenkan* (Dam Yearbook)
*Denki Shinbun*
*Economist, The*
*Figaro*
*Financial Times*
*France Nouvelle*
*GDN* (Dam Digest Monthly)
*Guardian, The*
*Ise Shinbun*
Interpress Service
*Japan Times*
*Journal Officiel*
Jiji Press Ticker
*Kakugi Kettei*
*Kumamoto Nichinichi*
*Kumamoto Shinbun*
Kyodo Newswire
*La Croix*
*La Gazette Nucleaire*
*La Nouvelle Republique*

*La Tribune de l'Expansion*
*L'Aube*
*Le Monde*
*Le Nouvel*
*Economiste*
*Le Peuple Breton*
*Les Echos*
*Liberation*
*Loire Atlantique*
*Mainichi Shinbun*
*New York Times*
NGSK (Japan Atomic
    Industrial Forum)
*Nikkei*
*Nikkei Bijinesu*
*Nikkei Weekly*
*Nouvel Observateur*
*Nucleonics Week*
*Physics Today*
*Presse Ocean*
Reuters News Service
*SOFRES*
TBS, Japan News Network
*WSJ (Wall Street Journal)*
*Washington Post*
*Yomiuri Daily*
*Yomiuri Shinbun*

# References

Abadie, Alberto, David Drukker, Jane Leber Herr, and Guido Imbens. 2002. Implementing Matching Estimators for Average Treatment Effects in STATA. Working paper. Available at http://elsa.berkeley.edu/~imbens/statamatch_02oct17.pdf.

Abadie, Alberto, and Guido Imbens. 2002. Simple and Bias-Corrected Matching Estimators for Average Treatment Effects. Working paper. Available at http://elsa.berkeley.edu/~imbens/sme_02oct14.pdf.

Abel, Troy. 2001. Community Involvement in Environmental Justice Decision Making. Paper prepared for the annual meeting of the Midwest Political Science Association, Palmer House Hilton, Chicago.

Acemoglu, Daron, and James Robinson. 2001. Inefficient Redistribution. *American Political Science Review* 95 (3): 649–661.

Adachi, Tadao. 1991. *Tochi shūyō Seido no Mondaiten* (Problems with the land expropriation system). Tokyo: Nihon Hyoron Sha.

Adachi, Takeo. 1977. Kōyō Shūyō to Sonshitsu Hoshō (Compensating loss and expropriation for public use). In *Damu Kensetsu to Suibotsu Hoshō* (Compensation for submersion and dam construction), 58–78. Tokyo: Nihon damu Kyōkai.

Aida, Masato. 1977. Suigen chiiki taisaku tokubetsu sochi hō sono ato no unyō to kongo no Kadai (The establishment of the special law for measures for water resource areas, the employment of its funds and current problems). In *Hoshō Jitsumu kōshūkai tekisuto* (The text of a practical course on the problems of compensation), 51–65. Tokyo: Nihon Damu Kyōkai.

Alagappa, Muthiah, ed. 2004. *Civil Society and Political Change in Asia: Expanding and Contracting Democratic Space.* Stanford: Stanford University Press.

Aldrich, Daniel P. 2005a. The Limits of Flexible and Adaptive Institutions: The Japanese Government's Role in Nuclear Power Plant Siting over the Postwar Period. In *Managing Conflict in Facility Siting,* ed. S. Hayden Lesbirel and Daigee Shaw, 111–136. Northampton, Mass.: Edward Elgar.

———. 2005b. Controversial Facility Siting: State Policy Instruments and Flexibility. *Journal of Comparative Politics* 38 (1): 103–123.

———. 2005c. "Japan's Nuclear Power Plant Siting: Quelling Resistance," *Japan Focus,* June.

Aldrich, Howard. 1999. *Organizations Evolving.* London: Sage.

Allen, Arthur. 1987. Report from Brittany: Village "Betrayed" by N-Plant Closing. *Newsday,* 23 August.

Alsop, Ronald. 1983. Widespread Fear of Hazardous Waste Sites Thwarts State and Industry Plans. *Wall Street Journal,* 10 March.

Altshuler, Alan, and David Luberoff. 2003. *Mega-Projects: The Changing Politics of Urban Public Investment*. Washington, D.C.: Brookings Institution Press.

Amano, Reiko. 2000. Construction Dams in Japan with a Special Focus on the Nagara River. Paper prepared for the Fourth Regional Consultation of the World Commission on Dams, Hanoi, Vietnam, February 26–27.

———. 2001. *Damu to Nihon* (Dams and Japan). Tokyo: Iwanami Shoten.

Ambroise-Rendu, Marc. 1975. Les Français devant le choice nucléaire (The French in front of the nuclear choice). *Le Monde* (12–13 January), 7.

Angrist, Joshua, and Alan Krueger. 1999. Empirical Strategies in Labor Economics. In *Handbook of Labor Economics*, 3:1277–1357. New York: Elsevier Science Publishers.

Apter, David, and Nagayo Sawa. 1984. *Against the State: Politics and Social Protest in Japan*. Cambridge: Harvard University Press.

Arai, Yōichi. 1995. *Kyodai jinkōshima no sōzō* (The creation of an enormous manmade island). Tokyo: Shokokusha.

Aranson, Peter, and Peter Ordeshook. 1985. Public Interest, Private Interest, and the Democratic Polity. In *The Democratic State,* ed. Roger Benjamin and Stephen Elkin, 87–177. Lawrence: University Press of Kansas.

Arendt, Hannah. 1969. A Special Supplement: Reflections on Violence. *New York Review of Books* 12 (4).

Argote, Linda, and Ron Ophir. 2002. Intraorganizational Learning. In *Companion to Organizations,* ed. Joel Baum, Boston: Blackwell.

Argyris, Chris, and Donald Schon. 1978. *Organizational Learning: A Theory of Action Perspective*. Reading, Mass.: Addison-Wesley.

Asahi Shinbun Yamaguchi Shikyoku. 2001. *Kokusaku no Yukue: Kaminoseki Genpatsu Keikaku no Nijū nen* (The direction of national policy: Twenty years of planning for a nuclear power station at Kaminoseki). Kagoshima: Nanbo Shinsha.

Ashford, Norman, H. P. Stanton, and Clifton Moore. 1997. *Airport Operations*. New York: McGraw-Hill.

ASN (Autorité de Sûreté Nucléaire: Nuclear Safety Authority). 2003. *La sûreté nucléaire et la radioprotection en France en 2002* (Nuclear safety and radiation protection in France in 2002). Paris: Directorate General for Nuclear Safety and Radiation Protection.

———. 2004. *La sûreté nucléaire et la radioprotection en France en 2003* (Nuclear safety and radiation protection in France in 2003). Paris: Directorate General for Nuclear Safety and Radiation Protection.

Astolfi, Jean-François, Patrice Brunet, and Jean-Claude Ithier. 1998. Choix des sites de centrales nucléaires (The selection of sites for nuclear power plants). Techniques de l'Ingénieur BN 3-255.1

Atlas, Mark. 2001. Testing for Environmental Racism Again: An Empirical Analysis of Hazardous Waste Management Capacity Expansion Decisions. Paper prepared for 2001 APSA annual conference in San Francisco, CA.

Austin, R., and M. Schill. 1991. Black, Brown, Poor, and Poisoned: Minority Grassroots Environmentalism and the Quest for Eco-Justice. *Kansas Journal of Law and Public Policy* 1:69–82.

Axelrod, Robert. 1984. *The Evolution of Cooperation*. Basic Books.

Baba, Yoshio. 2002. The Problems Facing Nuclear Power in Japan Emphasizing Law and Regulations. *Nuclear Law Bulletin* (69): 16–28.

Bacher, Pierre, Jacques Panossian, and G. Riollet.: 1989. Ingredients of Success in the Design and Construction of the French Nuclear Power Plants. In *Good Performance in Nuclear Projects: Proceedings of an International Symposium April,* 158–172. Tokyo: Nuclear Energy Agency, OECD.

Baiocchi, Gianpaolo. 2002. Synergizing Civil Society: State-Civil Society Regimes in Porto Alegre, Brazil. *Political Power and Social Theory* 15.

Barnett, William, and Robert Burgelman. 1996. Evolutionary Perspectives on Strategy. *Strategic Management Journal* 17:5–19.

Barnett, William, and Morten Hansen. 1996. The Red Queen in Organizational Evolution. *Strategic Management Journal* 17:139–157.

Barnett, William, and Olav Sorenson. 1998. The Red Queen in Organizational Creation and Development. Draft manuscript.

Bataille, Christian. 1990. *Rapport sur la gestion des déchets nucléaires à haute activité* (Report on the management of high-level nuclear waste). Paris: Office Parlementaire d'Evaluation des Choix Scientifiques et Technologiques. December.

Baumgartner, Frank. 1987. Parliament's Capacity to Expand Political Controversy in France. *Legislative Studies Quarterly* 12 (1): 33–44.

Baumgartner, Frank, and Bryan Jones. 1991. Agenda Dynamics and Policy Subsystems. *Journal of Politics* 53 (4): 1044–1074.

———. 1993. *Agendas and Instability in American Politics.* Chicago: University of Chicago Press.

Bayley, David. 1982. *Patterns of Policing: A Comparative International Analysis.* New Brunswick: Rutgers University Press.

Becker, Gary. 1983. A Theory of Competition among Pressure Groups for Political Influence. *Quarterly Journal of Economics* 98 (3): 371–400.

Becker, Sascha, and Andrea Ichino. 2002. Estimation of Average Treatment Effects Based on Propensity Scores. *Stata Journal* 2 (4): 358–377.

Beierle, Thomas, and Jerry Cayford. 2002. *Democracy in Practice: Public Participation in Environmental Decisions.* Washington D.C.: Resources for the Future.

Belbéoc, Bella, and Roger Belbéoc. 1998. *Sortir du nucléaire* (Leaving nuclear power). Paris: L'Esprit Frappeur.

Beltran, Alain, and Patrice Carré. 1991. *La fée et la servante* (The fairy and the maidservant). Paris: Belin.

Bennett, Andrew. 2000. *Causal Inference in Case Studies: From Mill's Methods to Causal Mechanisms.* Atlanta: American Political Science Association Conference.

Berman, Sheri. 1997. Civil Society and the Collapse of the Weimar Republic. *World Politics* 49 (3): 401–429.

Bermeo, Nancy. 2002. A New Look at Federalism: The Import of Institutions. *Journal of Democracy* 13 (2): 96–110.

Berry, Jeffrey, Kent Portney, and Ken Thomson. 1993. *Rebirth of Urban Democracy.* Washington, D.C.: Brookings Institution.

Berry, William D. 1990. The Confusing Case of Budgetary Incrementalism: Too Many Meanings for a Single Concept. *Journal of Politics* 52 (1): 167–196.

Blechinger, Verena. 2000. Corruption through Political Contributions in Japan. Paper prepared for Transparency International workshop on corruption and political party funding, La Pietra, Italy.

Block, Jacques. 1971. *Airports and Environment.* Paris: Aeroport de Paris.

Blustein, Paul. 1994. Japan's Sky High Airport. *Washington Post Foreign Service,* 22 August.

Bodon, Virginie. 2002. *La modernité au village: Tignes, Savines, Ubaye...La submersion de communes rurales au nom de l'intérêt général, 1920–1970* (Modernity in the village: Tignes, Savines, Ubaye...The Immersion of rural communes in the name of the public interest). Grenoble: Presses Universitaires de Grenoble.

Bowen, Roger. 1975. The Narita Conflict. *Asian Survey* 15 ( July): 598–615.

Boy, Daniel. 1999. *Le progrès en procès* (Progress on trial). Paris: Presses de la Renaissance.

Boyle, Elizabeth H. (1998). Political Frames and Legal Activity: The Case of Nuclear Power in Four Countries. *Law and Society Review* 32 (1): 141–174.

Brenon, Michel, and Jean-Charles Cozic. 1997. *Du Pellerin au Carnet: Vingt ans de contestation nucléaire en Basse-Loire* (From Pellerin to Carnet: Twenty years of nuclear contestation in the lower Loire area). Nantes: Journal Presse-Océan, 19 September.

Brewer, John, Adrian Guelke, Iane Hume, Edward Moxon-Browne, and Rick Wilford. 1996. *The Police, Public Order, and the State: Policing in Great Britain, Northern Ireland, the Irish Republic, the USA, Israel, South Africa, and China.* New York: St. Martin's Press.

Brion, Dennis. 1991. *Essential Industry and the NIMBY Phenomenon.* New York: Quorum Books.

Broadbent, Jeffrey. 2002. "Japan's Environmental Regime: The Political Dynamics of Change." In *Environmental Politics and Policy in the Industrialized Countries,* ed. Uday Desai. Cambridge: MIT Press.

Broderick, Mick, ed. 1996. *Hibakusha Cinema: Hiroshima, Nagasaki, and the Nuclear Image in Japanese Film.* New York: Kegan Paul International.

Bullard, Robert. 1994. Overcoming Racism in Environmental Decision-making. *Environment* 36:10–17.

——. 2000. *Dumping in Dixie: Race, Class, and Environmental Quality.* Boulder Colo.: Westview Press.

Calder, Kent. 1988a. *Crisis and Compensation.* Princeton: Princeton University Press.

——. 1988b. Japanese Foreign Economic Policy Formation: Explaining the Reactive State. *World Politics* 40 (4): 517–541.

Cameron, David. 1988. "Distributional Coalitions and Other Sources of Economic Stagnation." *International Organization* 42:561–604.

Campbell, John C. 1977. *Contemporary Japanese Budget Politics.* Berkeley: University of California Press.

Campbell, John L. 1988. *Collapse of an Industry.* Ithaca: Cornell University Press.

Carpenter, Daniel. 2001. *The Forging of Bureaucratic Autonomy: Reputations, Networks, and Policy Innovation in Executive Agencies, 1862–1928.* Princeton: Princeton University Press.

Castle, Geoffrey, and Don Munton. 1996. Voluntary Siting of Hazardous Waste Facilities in Western Canada. In *Hazardous Waste Siting and Democratic Choice,* ed. Don Munton, 57–83. Washington, D.C.: Georgetown University Press.

CFGB (Comité Francais des Grands Barrages). 2003. *Barrages et Developpement Durable en France* (Dams and sustainable development in France). Paris: CFGB.

Cha, Yong-Jin. 1997. Environmental Risk Analysis: Factors influencing Nuclear Risk Perception and Policy Implications. Ph.D. dissertation, University of Albany, State University of New York.

Chambolle, Thierry. 1980. *L'information dans le procédures électronucléaires* (Information on nuclear power plant procedures). Paris: Editions Olivier Lesourd.

Chan-Tiberghien, Jennifer. 2004. *Gender and Human Rights Politics in Japan: Global Norms and Domestic Networks.* Stanford: Stanford University Press.

Chaussade, Jean-Pierre. 1992. Pour une meilleure acceptation du nucléaire par le public: Une information large, honnête, sans complexe (For a better public acceptance of nuclear power: vast, honest, uncomplicated information). In *Public Participation in Nuclear Decision Making,* OECD Nuclear Energy Agency, 367–373. Paris: OECD.

Chavagne, Yves. 1975. EDF vous "informe"... A sa maniere (EDF "informs" you... in its own manner). *Témoignage Chrétien* (17 April), 9.

Chavot, Philippe, and Anne Masseran. 2003. Public Consultation and Foresight Exercises in France: In Search for Hybrid Flora. In *Optimizing Public Understanding of Science and Technology,* ed. Ulrike Felt. Available at http://www.univie.ac.at/Wissenschaftstheorie/OPUSReport.

Chipello, Christopher. 1991. Mr. Ogawa's Tale: How Sweet Potatoes Grounded an Airport. *Wall Street Journal Europe* (16 April).

Choy, Jon. 2000. Japan Rethinks Public Works Policy. *Japan Economic Institute Report,* no. 34 (1 September).

Christensen, Steven. 1979. Nuclear Power Plant Siting: A Comparative Analysis of Public Interaction in the Siting Process in France and the United States. *Denver Journal of International Law and Policy* 8 (1): 266–343.

Chūbu Kūkou Chōsa kai (Research committee on the Central Japan Airport) 1991. *Chūbu Shin kokusai kūkō Chōsa Hōkokusho* (Research report on the New Central Japan International Airport). Nagoya: Zaidan Hōjin Chūbu Kūkou Chōsa kai.

CNIC (*Citizens' Nuclear Information Center Monthly*). *Nuke Info Tokyo.* Tokyo: CNIC.

Clemens, Elisabeth. 1997. *The People's Lobby.* Chicago: University of Chicago Press.

Clingermayer, James. 1994. Electoral Representation, Zoning Politics, and the Exclusion of Group Homes. *Political Research Quarterly* 47 (4): 969–984.

Cohen, David. 1998. Amateur Government. *Journal of Public Administration, Research and Theory* 8, no. 4:450–497.

Cohen, Linda, Mathew McCubbins, and Frances Rosenbluth. 1995. The Politics of Nuclear Power in Japan and the United States, in *Structure and Policy in Japan and the United States,* ed. Peter Cowhey and Mathew McCubbins, 177–202. Cambridge: Cambridge University Press.

Cole, Luke W, and Sheila R. Foster. 2001. *From the Ground Up: Environmental Racism and the Rise of the Environmental Justice Movement.* New York: New York University Press.

Coles, Peter. 1987. French Suspect Information on Radiation Levels. *Nature* 329 (8 October).

Colignon, Richard, and Chikako Usui. 2003. *Amakudari: The Hidden Fabric of Japan's Economy.* Ithaca: ILR Press.

Collier, David, and Henry Brady. 2001. *Rethinking Social Inquiry: Diverse Tools, Shared Standards.* Berkeley: Public Policy Press, University of California.

Colson, Jean-Philippe. 1977. *Le nucléaire sans les Français: Qui décide, qui profite?* (Nuclear power without the French: Who decides, who benefits?) Paris: François Maspero.

Conan, Eric. 1988. Laissez le long fleuve tranquille (Leave the long, quiet river alone). *L'Express* (11 November).

CNFC. Council for Nuclear Fuel Cycle. Plutonium. Accessible at http://www.cnfc. or.jp/e/journal/index.html.

Crie, Hélène. 1989. Les ecologistes font barrage au nom de la Loire. *Libération,* 29 April.

Crozier, Michael, Samuel Huntington, and Joji Watanuki. 1975. *The Crisis of Democracy: Report on the Governability of Democracies to the Trilateral Commission.* New York: New York University Press.

Curtis, Gerald. 1971. *Election Campaigning, Japanese Style.* New York: Columbia University Press.

———. 1999. *The Logic of Japanese Politics: Leaders, Institutions, and the Limits of Change.* New York: Columbia University Press.

Dahl, Robert, and Charles Lindblom. 1953. *Politics, Economics, and Welfare.* Chicago: University of Chicago Press.

Dauvergne, Peter. 1993. Nuclear Power Development in Japan: "Outside Forces" and the Politics of Reciprocal Consent. *Asian Survey* 33 (6): 576–591.

Deaton, Brady J., Larry C. Morgan, and Kurt R. Anschel. 1982. The Influence of Psychic Costs on Rural-Urban Migration. *American Journal of Agricultural Economics* 64 (2): 177–187.

Debeir, Jean-Claude, Jean-Paul Deléage, and Daniel Hémery. 1986. *Les servitudes de la puissance* (In the servitude of power). Paris: Flammarion.

Debrest, Patrick. 1990. Faire barrage au barrage (Making dams with dams). *Rouge* (19 July).

Delegation generale a l'information. 1975. *L'énergie nucléaire: Données techniques économiques écologiques* (Nuclear energy: technical, economic, ecological data). Paris.

Della Porta, Donatella, 1995. *Social Movements, Political Violence, and the State.* New York: Cambridge University Press.

Della Porta, Donatella, and Herbert Reiter. 1997. *The Policing of Protest in Contemporary Democracies.* Florence, Italy: European University Institute Working Papers.

———. eds. 1998. *Policing Protest: The Control of Mass Demonstrations in Western Democracies.* Minneapolis: University of Minnesota Press.

Delmas, Magali, and Bruce Heiman. 2001. Government Credible Commitment to the French and American Nuclear Power Industries. *Journal of Policy Analysis and Management* 20 (3): 433–456.

de Marcellus, Olivier. 1992. Breeding Disaster: France's Nuclear Program. *Multinational Monitor* 14 (4).

Dempsey, Paul, Andrew Goetz, and Joseph Szyliowicz. 1997. *Denver International Airport.* New York: McGraw-Hill.

Dengen Chiiki Shinkō Sentā (Center for development of power supply regions). 1997. *Jigyō no goannai* (Outline of Operations Booklet). Tokyo, Japan: Dengen Chiiki Shinkō Sentā.

———. 2000. *10 nen no ayumi* (A record of the past 10 years). Tokyo: Dengen Chiiki Shinkō Sentā.

———. 2002. Jigyō no goannai (Outline of Operations Booklet). Tokyo, Japan.

Denki jigyō kōza henshū iinkai (Editorial committee of the Electric Enterprise Program). 1997. *Genshiryoku hatsuden* (Nuclear power plants). Tokyo: Denryoku Shinpōsha.

DGEMP (Direction Générale de L'Énergie et des Matières Premières). 2000. *L'énergie nucléaire en 100 questions* (Nuclear energy in 100 questions). Paris: Ministère de l'Economie des Finances et de l'Industrie.

DiMaggio, Paul, and Walter Powell. 1983. The Iron Cage Revisited: Institutional Isomorphism and Collective Rationality in Organizational Fields. *American Sociological Review* 48:147–160.

Doi, Takeo. 1974. *Amae no Kōzō* (The structure of dependence.) Tokyo: Kobundo.

Dorget, François. 1984. *Le choix nucleaire Français* (The French nuclear choice). Paris: Economica.

Dryzek, John. 1992. Good Society versus the State: Freedom and Necessity in Political Innovation. *Journal of Politics* 54 (2): 835–850

Dupuy, Herve. 1989. Vers un nouveau larzarc? (Toward a new Larzac?) *Rouge,* 13 April.

Eckstein, Rick. 1997. *Nuclear Power and Social Power.* Philadelphia: Temple University Press.

Ecole nationale d'administration, Groupe 14. 2002a. *Pour la France: Evolution du rôle de l'Etat dans la définition et la mise en œuvre d'une politique de l'énergie* (For France: the evolution of the role of the State in the definition and implementation of an energy policy). Paris: ENA.

——, Groupe 18. 2002b. *L'Information et le debate dans le domaine de l'energie* (Information and debate in the energy domain). Paris: ENA.

*Economist, The.* 2003a. Darkness Falls on Tokyo (17 July).

*Economist, The.* 2003b. Damming Evidence: The Pros and Cons of Big Earthworks (19 July), 9–16.

EDF service de l'information et des Relations Publiques, Division des Relations exterieures. 1979. *Dossier sur le Nucléaire au Parlement 1952–1973* (The parliamentary file on nuclear energy, 1952–1973). Paris: EDF.

Edwards, Rob. 2002. Japan's Nuclear Safety "Dangerously Weak." *NewScientist.Com* (2 October).

Ehrman, Richard. 1990. *NIMBYism: The Disease and the Cure.* London: Centre for Policy Studies.

Ekiert, Grzegorz, and Jan Kubik. 1999. *Rebellious Civil Society: Popular Protest and Democratic Consolidation in Poland, 1989–1993.* Ann Arbor: University of Michigan Press.

Elazar, Daniel. 1966. *American Federalism: A View from the States.* New York: Thomas Crowell.

Eldredge, Niles. 1985. *Time Frames: The Evolution of Punctuated Equilibria.* Princeton: Princeton University Press.

Eldredge, Niles, and Stephen J. Gould. 1972. Punctuated Equilibria: An Alternative to Phyletic Gradualism. In *Models In Paleobiology,* ed. T. J. M. Schopf. San Francisco: Freeman Cooper.

Ellis, Joseph. 2001. *Founding Brothers: The Revolutionary Generation.* New York: Knopf.

Enerpresse. 1997. La nouvelle campagne d'EDF sur l'energie nucleaire (The new EDF campaign for nuclear energy). No. 6963 (1 December): 1.

Enerugi sōgō suishin iinkai (Committee for the comprehensive promotion of energy). 2002. Enerugi shisetu ni taisuru shakaiteki juyō (Social responses toward energy facilities [report]). Tokyo, Japan. March.

*Engineering News Record* (ENR). 2000. Japan Slows Plant Building. 244 (13): 14+.

Epstein, Richard. 1985. *Takings: Private Property and the Power of Eminent Domain.* Cambridge: Harvard University Press.

——. 1993. *Bargaining with the State.* Princeton: Princeton University Press.

Errera, Gérard. 1988. CEA Information Policy. *RGN International Edition* A (July): 41–42.

Evans, Peter, Dietrich Rueschemeyer, and Theda Skocpol, eds. 1985. *Bringing the State Back In.* New York: Cambridge University Press.

Fagnani, François, and Alexandre Nicolon. 1979. *Nucleopolis matériaux pour l'analyse d'une société nucléaire* (Nucleopolis: Materials for analyzing a nuclear society). Grenoble: Presses Universitaires de Grenoble.

Faid, Yacine. 2001. French Nuclear Industry Licensing Procedure. Internal memo from WISE-Paris (World Information Service on Energy). 7 November.

Falk, Jim. 1982. *Global Fission: The Battle over Nuclear Power.* New York: Oxford University Press.

Farkas, Andrew. 1998. *State Learning and International Change.* Ann Arbor: University of Michigan Press.

Feldman, Elliot. 1985. *Concorde and Dissent: Explaining High Technology Project Failures in Britain and France.* Cambridge: Cambridge University Press.

Feldman, Elliot, and Jerome Milch. 1982. *Technocracy versus Democracy: The Comparative Politics of International Airports.* Boston: Auburn House.

Ferejohn, John. 1974. *Pork Barrel Politics: Rivers and Harbor Legislation, 1947–1968.* Stanford: Stanford University Press.

*Financial Times.* 1991. "Electricity Industry (3): Energy Policy Divided" (25 April), 37.

Fischer, Gregory, and Mark Kamlet. 1984. Explaining Presidential Priorities. *American Political Science Review* 78:356–371.

Flam, Helena, ed. 1994a. *States and Anti-Nuclear Movements.* Edinburgh: Edinburgh University Press.

———. 1994b. Political Responses to the Anti-Nuclear Challenge: Democratic Experiments and the Use of Force. In *States and Anti-Nuclear Movements,* ed. Helena Flam, 329–354. Edinburgh: Edinburgh University Press.

———. 1994c. Political Responses to the Anti-nuclear Challenge: Standard Deliberative and Decision-making Settings. In *States and Anti-Nuclear Movements,* ed. Helena Flam, 299–328. Edinburgh: Edinburgh University Press.

Flanagan, Scott. 1978. The Genesis of Variant Political Cultures. In *The Citizen and Politics,* ed. Sidney Verba and Lucian Pye, 129–163. Stamford, Conn.: Greylock.

Flyvbjerg, Bent. 1998. *Rationality and Power: Democracy in Practice.* Trans. Steven Sampson. Chicago: University of Chicago Press.

Fox, Robert. 2000. Review of *Histoire du service de la production thermique d'eléctricité en France. Technology and Culture* 41 (1): 154–156.

Francisco, Ronald. 1996. Coercion and Protest: An Empirical Test in Two Democratic States. *American Journal of Political Science* 40 (4): 1179–1204.

Frank-Keyes, John. 2002. The Pierre Chassigneux Interview. *Communique: Airport Business* (March/April): 7–9.

Frappat, Bruno. 1974. Les projets de construction d'une centrale dans le Morbihan (Construction projects for a nuclear power plant in the department of Morbihan). *La Croix.*

French, Howard. 2002. Safety Problems at Japanese Reactors Begin to Erode Public's Faith in Nuclear Power. *New York Times* (16 September), A8.

Freudenburg, William R. 1984. Boomtown's Youth: The Differential Impacts of Rapid Community Growth on Adolescents and Adults. *American Sociological Review* 49 (5): 697–705.

Frey, Bruno, and Felix Oberholzer-Gee. 1997. The Cost of Price Incentives: An Empirical Analysis of Motivation Crowding Out. *American Economic Review* 87 (4): 746–755.

Frey, Bruno, Felix Oberholzer-Gee, and Reiner Eichenberger. 1996. The Old Lady Visits Your Backyard: A Tale of Morals and Markets. *Journal of Political Economy* 104 (6): 1297–1313.

Friedrich, Carl. 1963. *Man and His Government.* New York: McGraw-Hill.

Frigola, Pierre. 1985. *L'industrie nucleaire Francaise, 1979–1983: Bilan et perspectives* (The French nuclear industry, 1979–1983: Overview and perspectives). Paris: Ministere du Redeploiement Industriel et du Commerce Exterieur.

Fujita, Megumi. 1999. *Yuzu no Sato: Sonchō Funsen Ki* (Village of the Yuzu: Record of a yillage mayor`s hard fight). Tokyo: Yuhisha.

Fukui, Haruhiro, and Shigeko Fukai. 1996. Pork Barrel Politics, Networks, and Local Economic Development in Contemporary Japan. *Asian Survey* 36 (March): 268–286.

Fung, Archon. 2004. *Empowered Participation: Reinventing Urban Democracy.* Princeton: Princeton University Press.

Galbraith, John Kenneth. 1985. *The Anatomy of Power.* Boston: Houghton Mifflin.

Gale, Roger. 1978. Nuclear Power and Japan's Proliferation Option. *Asian Survey* 18 (11): 1117–1133.

Gamson, William. 1968. *Power and Discontent.* Homewood, Ill.: Dorsey Press.

Garcia-Gorena, Velma. 1999. *Mothers and the Mexican Antinuclear Power Movement.* Tucson: University of Arizona Press.

Garon, Sheldon. 1997. *Molding Japanese Minds: The State in Everyday Life.* Princeton: Princeton University Press.

Garran, Robert. 1997. Japan's Nuclear Meltdown. *The Australian* (29 April): 25.

Gatignol, Claude. 1992. Le nucléaire en cotentin: Une aventure industrielle réussie? (Nuclear energy in Cotentin: A successful industrial adventure?) In *Public Participation in Nuclear Decision Making,* OECD Nuclear Energy Agency. 297–301. Paris: OECD.

Gaventa, John. 1980. *Power and Powerlessness: Quiescence and Rebellion in an Appalachian Valley.* Chicago: University of Illinois Press.

Gellner, Ernest. 1983. *Nations and Nationalism.* Ithaca: Cornell University Press.

George, Alexander, and Timothy McKeown. 1985. Case Studies and Theories of Organizational Decision Making. *Advances in Information Processing in Organizations* 2:21–58.

George, Timothy. 2001. *Minamata: Pollution and the Struggle for Democracy in Postwar Japan.* Cambridge: Harvard University Press.

Georges, Michele. 1975. Le débat nucléaire: L'exemple d'Avoine (The nuclear debate: The example of Avoine). *L'Express* (31 March): 88–89.

Gill, Tom. 2002. Government Responses to Homelessness: The View from the Ground Level. *Social Science Japan* (April): 24–28.

Giugni, Marco. 2004. *Social Protest and Policy Change: Ecology, Antinuclear, and Peace Movements in Comparative Perspective.* New York: Rowman and Littlefield.

Gogatsusha (May committee). 1982. *Hangenpatsu Rōdōundō—Densan Chūgoku no Tatakai* (Labor movements against nuclear power—The battle of the Chugoku branch of the Japan Electrical Workers' Union). Tokyo: Gogatsusha.

Goldschmidt, Bertrand. 1980. *Le Complexe Atomique* (The atomic complex). Paris: Fayard.

Gorton, Michael. 1997. Damming the Agatsuma River. Master's thesis, University of Montana.

Gould, Jay. 1986. *Quality of Life in American Neighborhoods: Levels of Affluence, Toxic Waste, and Cancer Mortality in Residential Zip Code Areas.* Boulder, Colo.: Westview Press.

Gould, Stephen, and Niles Eldredge. 1977. Punctuated Equilibria: The Tempo and Mode of Evolution Reconsidered. *Paleobiology* 3:115–151.

Grant, Ruth. 2006. Ethics and Incentives: A Political Approach. *American Political Science Review* 100 (1): 29–39.

Gresser, Julian, Koichiro Fujikura, and Akio Morishima. 1981. *Environmental Law in Japan.* Cambridge: MIT Press.

Greve, Henrich. 1995. Jumping Ship: The Diffusion of Strategy of Abandonment. *Administrative Science Quarterly* 40:444–473.

Groth, David. 1987. Biting the Bullet: The Politics of Grass-Roots Protest. Ph.D. dissertation, Stanford University.

*The Guardian.* 1981. Power to the People (7 May).

Guedeney, Collete, and Gérard Mendel. 1973. *L'angoisse atomique et les centrales nucléaires* (Atomic anxiety and nuclear power plants). Paris: Parot.

Guisnel, Jean. 1981. Plogoff: Après la bataille antinucléaire, la guerre des moutons (Plogoff: After the antinuclear battle, the war of the sheep). Mimeograph, February.

Gurafu shiki (The four seasons displayed). 2002. Nihon Ricchi Sentā (Japan Industrial Location Center).

Gusterson, Hugh. 2000. How Not to Construct a Radioactive Waste Incinerator. *Science, Technology, and Human Values* 25 (3).

Gutmann, Amy and Dennis Thompson. 2004. *Why Deliberative Democracy?* Princeton: Princeton University Press.

Habermas, Jürgen. 1996. *Between Facts and Norms: Contributions to a Discourse Theory on Law and Democracy.* Cambridge: MIT Press.

Hacker, Jacob. 2000. Boundary Wars: The Political Struggle over Public and Private Social Benefits in the United States. Ph.D. dissertation, Yale University.

Hagiwara, Yoshio. 1996. *Yanba Dam no Tatakai* (The struggle over Yanba Dam). Tokyo: Iwanami Shoten.

Hahn, Jinyong. 1998. On the Role of the Propensity Score in the Efficient Estimation of Average Treatment Effects. *Econometrica* 66:315–332.

Hall, Peter. 1993. Policy Paradigms, Social Learning, and the State: The Case of Economic Policymaking in Britain. *Comparative Politics* 25 (3): 275–296.

Halperin, Morton, Jerry J. Berman, Robert L. Borosage, and Christine M. Marwick. 1976. *The Lawless State: The Crimes of the U.S. Intelligence Agencies.* New York: Penguin.

Hamilton, David, and Masayoshi Kanabayashi. 1994. Belief Grows That Japans Environment Has Been Sacrificed for the Economy. *Wall Street Journal* (13 May): 6.

Hamilton, James. 1993. Politics and Social Costs: Estimating the Impact of Collective Action on Hazardous Waste Facilities. *RAND Journal of Economics* 24 (1): 101–125.

Hamilton, James, and Kip Viscusi. 1999. *Calculating Risks? The Spatial and Political Dimensions of Hazardous Waste Policy.* Cambridge: MIT Press.

Hamilton, Scott. 1991. "Planning for Noise Compatibility," in *Airport Regulation, Law, and Public Policy,* ed. Robert Hardaway, 85–86. New York: Quorum Books.

Hammel, E. A. 1990. Demographic Constraints on the Formation of Traditional Balkan Households (in Symposium on the Byzantine Family and Household). *Dumbarton Oaks Papers* 44:173–186.

*Hangenpatsu Shinbun* (Antinuclear newspaper). 1978–1998. Issues 1–240. Tokyo: Hangenpatsu Undō Zenkoku Renraku kai (National liaison conference of the antinuclear movement).

Hangenpatsu Undō Zenkoku Renraku kai (National liaison conference of the anti-nuclear movement). 1997. *Han Genpatsu Undō Mappu* (An outline of the antinuclear movements). Tokyo: Ryokuhu Shuppan.

Hannan, Michael, and John Freeman. 1989. *Organizational Ecology.* Cambridge: Harvard University Press.

Hase, Toshio. 1978. Genshiryoku Hatsudensho to Jūmin Undō (Nuclear power plants and citizens' movements). *Toshi Mondai* (Urban problems) 69 (4): 79–87.

Hasegawa, Kōichi. 1998. Kakunenryō saikuru mondai no keika to gaiyō (A summary of the development of problems in the nuclear fuel cycle). In *Kyodai Chiiki Kaihatsu no kōsō to kiketsu* (Vision versus results in a large-scale industrial development project in the Mutsu-Ogawara district), ed. Harutoshi Funabashi, Kōichi Hasegawa, and Nobuko Ijima, 43–72. Tōkyō: Tōkyō Daigaku Shuppansha.

—— 2002. The Organization and Activation of the Civil Sector: Rapid Development during the "Lost Decade." *Social Science Japan* (April): 5–7.

—— 2004. *Constructing Civil Society in Japan: Voices of Environmental Movements.* Melbourne Australia: Trans Pacific Press.

Hatakenaka, Kengo. (1972). Genshiryoku hatsudensho kensetsu hantai undō (Opposition to the construction of nuclear power plants). *Jurisuto* 508 (1 July): 44–48.

Hatch, Michael. 1986. *Politics and Nuclear Power: Energy Policy in Western Europe.* Lexington: University of Kentucky Press.

Hayes, Graeme. 2002. *Environmental Protest and the State in France.* New York: Palgrave Macmillan.

Hayes, Michael. 1992. *Incrementalism and Public Policy.* New York: Longman.

Hébert, Jean. 1980. French Case Law and the Use of Nuclear Energy. *OECD Nuclear Law Bulletin* 25: 57–69.

Hecht, Gabrielle. 1997. Enacting Cultural Identity: Risk and Ritual in the French Nuclear Workplace. *Journal of Contemporary History* 32 (4): 483–507.

——. 1998. *The Radiance of France: Nuclear Power and National Identity after World War II.* Cambridge: MIT Press.

Heckman, James, Hidehiko Ichimura, and Petra Todd. 1997. Matching as an Economic Evaluation Estimator: Evidence from Evaluating a Job Training Program. *Review of Economic Studies* 64 (4): 605–654.

Heclo, Hugh. 1974. *Modern Social Politics in Britain and Sweden: From Relief to Income Maintenance.* New Haven: Yale University Press.

Hiraiwa, Takeo. 1979. *Dokyumento: Kansai Shinkūkō* (Documents: The new Kansai airport). Tokyo: Aki Shobō.

Hiraki, Kunio. 1983. *Haneda Kūkō no Rekishi* (The history of Haneda airport). Tokyo: Asahi Shinbunsha.

Hirano, Shigeo. 2002. Electoral Systems and Threshold Effects: Quantitative Evidence from the Japanese Experience in the 1990s. Unpublished Working Paper, 27 September.

Hirose, Toshio. 1977. Kensetushō ni okeru Suigen chiiki taisaku ni tsuite (About the measures for water resource areas at the Ministry of Construction). In *Hoshō Jitsumu kōshūkai tekisuto* (The text of a practical course on the problems of compensation), 1–21. Tokyo: Nihon Damu Kyōkai.

Hirschman, Albert. 1970. *Exit, Voice, Loyalty.* Cambridge: Harvard University Press.

Hoffman, George. 1957. The Role of Nuclear Power in Europe's Future Energy Balance. *Annals of the Association of American Geographers* 47 (1): 15–40.

Horie, Kō. 2000. Genshiryoku hatsudensho kensetu ni tomonau Dengen Sanpō seido tekiyō ni kansuru kenkyū (A study of the application of the Dengen Sanpō system to nuclear power plant construction). *Nihon Toshi Keikakugakkai gakujutu kennkyu-uron bunshū* 35:259–264.

Horonjeff, Robert. 1983. *Planning and Design of Airports.* New York: McGraw-Hill.

Howard, Christopher. 1997. *The Hidden Welfare State: Tax Expenditures and Social Policy in the United States.* Princeton: Princeton University Press.

Hoyman, Michele. 2001. Prisons in North Carolina: Are They a Viable Strategy for Rural Communities? *International Journal of Economic Development,* SPAE, special issue: "Community Economic Development."

Hoyman, Michele, and Micah Weinberg. 2006. The Process of Policy Innovation: Prisons as Rural Economic Development. *Policy Studies Journal* 34 (1).

Huber, John, and Nolan McCarty. 2004. Bureaucratic Capacity, Delegation, and Political Reform. *American Political Science Review* 98 (3): 481–494.

Hurley, Andrew. 1995. *Environmental Inequalities: Class, Race, and Industrial Pollution in Gary Indiana, 1945–1980.* Chapel Hill: University of North Carolina Press.

Hyōgo ken Keikakubu (Hyogo prefectural planning office). 1973. *Ōsaka Kokusai Mondai no Tebiki* (A guide to the problems of Ōsaka international airport). Osaka, Japan.

IAEA (International Atomic Energy Agency). 1998. *Country Nuclear Power Profiles.* Vienna, Austria: IAEA.

Igarashi, Takayoshi. 1999. Public Works at a Crossroads. *Social Science Japan* (December): 3–5.

Ijima, Nobuko. 1998. Josei no kankyō undō to Aomoriken no Hankaihatsu–Hankakunen undō (Women's roles in environmental movements and in Aomori prefecture's antidevelopment / antinuclear fuel movements). In *Kyodai Chiiki Kaihatsu no Kōsō to Kiketsu* (Vision versus results in a large-scale industrial development project in the Mutsu-Ogawara district), ed. Harutoshi Funabashi, Kōichi Hasegawa, and Nobuko Ijima, 271–300. Tōkyō: Tōkyō Daigaku Shuppansha.

Ikenberry, G. John. 1986. The Irony of State Strength: Comparative Responses to the Oil Shocks in the 1970s. *International Organization* 40 (1): 105–137.

Inamura, Shigekatsu. 1990. Sōgōteki na Suigen chiiki taisaku no Suishin (The promotion of the general measures for water resource areas). *Damu Nenkan,* 11–16.

Inglehart, Ronald. 1998. The Renaissance of Political Culture. *American Political Science Review* (December): 1203–1230.

Inhaber, Herbert. 1998. *Slaying the NIMBY Dragon.* New Brunswick, N.J.: Transaction.

——. 2001. NIMBY and LULU. *Cato Review of Business and Government.*

Inoue, Shigeru. 2002. Patonashippukei chiiki tsukuri no susume (Toward creating regions using a partnership model). *Gekkan Nihon Damu* 10 (696): 7–12.

Isa, Chihiro. 1988. *Shōtotsu: Narita Kūkō Higashimine Jūjiro Jiken* (Collision: The events at the crossroads between Narita airport and Higashimine). Tokyo: Bungeishujū.

Ishihara, Kosaku. 1974. Narita Kūkō yōchi mondai no kunren ni tuite Omō (Thinking about lessons from the land problems with Narita airport). In *Hoshō Jitsumu kōshūkai tekisuto* (The text of a practical course on the problems of compensation), 43–47. Tokyo: Nihon Damu Kyōkai.

Ito, Reiji. 1954. Entei Gairon (An introduction to dams). In *Damu no Keikaku kara Sekkō Made* (From dam planning to completion), 1–26. Tokyo: Nihon Kasen Kyōkai.

Jacobs, Lawrence, and Robert Shapiro. 2000. *Politicians Don't Pander.* Chicago: University of Chicago Press.

JAERO (Japan Atomic Energy Relations Organization, Zaidan Hōjin Nihon Genshiryoku). 2002. Activities Report.

Jasper, James. 1990. *Nuclear Politics.* Princeton: Princeton University Press.

———. 1995. Nuclear Policy as Projection: How Policy Choices Can Create Their Own Justification. In *Governing the Atom: The Politics of Risk,* ed. John Bryne and Steven Hoffman, New Brunswick, N.J.: Transaction.

Jenkins, J. Craig, and Charles Perrow. 1977. Insurgency of the Powerless: Farmworkers Movements (1946, 1972). *American Sociological Review* 42.

Jenkins-Smith, Howard, and Gilbert Bassett 1994. Perceived Risk and Uncertainty of Nuclear Waste. *Risk Analysis* 14 (5): 851–856.

Jinno, Naohiko. 1999. Public Works Projects and Japan's Public Finances. *Social Science Japan* (December): 6–9.

Jiyūminshutō (Liberal Democratic Party). 1964. *Genshiryoku sensuikan kikō ni tuite* (On the docking of a nuclear submarine). Tokyo: LDP.

———. 2001. *Proposal for Seven Approaches for Comprehensive Energy Policy.* Tokyo: LDP.

Johnson, Chalmers. 1982. *MITI and the Japanese Miracle.* Stanford: Stanford University Press.

———. 1989. MITI, NPT, and the Telecom Wars: How Japan Makes Policy for High Technology. In *Politics and Productivity,* ed. Chalmers Johnson. Boston: Ballinger.

Jones, Bryan, Frank Baumgartner, and James True. 1998. Policy Punctuations: US Budget Authority 1947–1995. *Journal of Politics* 60 (1): 1–33.

Jones, Bryan, Tracy Sulkin, and Heather Larsen. 2003. Policy Punctuations in American Political Institutions. *American Political Science Review* 97 (February): 151–169.

Joppke, Christian. 1993. *Mobilizing against Nuclear Energy: A Comparison of Germany and the United States.* Los Angeles: University of California Press.

Jōtatsu, Toshio. 1990. Waga Damu ni Okeru Damu jigyō no PR (Public relations for dam construction can be done at our dams). *Gekkan Nihon Damu* no. 12, 554:22–29.

Jūmin sanka yūshikisha kaigi (Expert commission on citizen participation). 2001. *Chihō bunken to Jūmin sanka wo kangaeru* (Thinking about citizen participation and decentralization of power). Tokyo: Shakai keizai seisanseihonbu (Japan Productivity Center for Socioeconomic Development).

Kafka, Franz. 1925. *The Trial (Der Prozess).*

Kaido, Yūichi. 1999. Enerugi Genshiryoku Mondai to Kankyō (Nuclear and energy problems and the environment). In *Kankyō Hō Nyūmon* (An introduction to environmental law), ed. Ryoichi Yoshimura and Takeo Mizuno. Tokyo: Hōritsu Bunkasha.

Kakuchi, Suvendrini. 2000. "No" Vote Fails to Detract Tokyo from Dam Plan. *Interpress Service* (1 February).

Kakugi Kettei (Cabinet decision). 1966. Shin Tōkyō kokusaikūkō Ichi kettei ni Tomonau shisaku ni tuite (Measures accompanying the decision to locate the New Tokyo International Airport). 4 July.

Kamata, Satoshi. 1991. *Kamata Satoshi no Kiroku 3: Shōsūha no Koe* (The third diary of Kamata Satoshi: Minority voices). Tokyo: Iwanami Shoten.

Kamimura, Naoki. 2001. Japanese Civil Society, Local Government, and U.S-Japan Security Relations in the 1990s: A Preliminary Survey. Japan Center for Area Studies Occasional Paper 11.

Kase, Tsutomu. 2003. Sanrizuka Tōsō Zenshi (The prehistory of the battle over Sanri-zuka). *Tsubute* 37 (Winter): 129–137.

Kashima, Shoji. 1964. Shimouke Damu (Hachi no sujou) Yawa (A tale about the Shimouke Dam, also known as the Bees' Nest). In *Damu Nenkan,* 244–245. Tokyo: Nihon Damu Kyōkai.

Kasza, Gregory. 2002. War and Welfare Policy in Japan. *Journal of Asian Studies* 61, no. 2 (May): 417–435

Katayama, Kazuhiro. 2002. Unyu daijin kara kūkō hantai ha nōmin he shazaibun (A letter of apology to the anti-airport farmers from the Minister of Transporta-tion). *Yomiuri Weekly* (22 December): 33–35.

Katei, Hideo. 2001. *Datsu damu Sanka: Shimosuwa Damu Hantai Undō no kiseki* (In praise of removing dams: The miracle of the anti-Shimosuwa Dam movement). Nagano: Kawabe Shorin.

Katsuta, Tadahiro. 2006. Postpone the Full Operation of Rokkasho. *Japan Times* (23 De-cember).

Kawabegawa Risui Soshō Genkoku dan (Plaintiff group in the lawsuit against water use on the Kawabe River). 2000. *Damu wa iranai* (The dam is not necessary). Tokyo: Kadensha.

Kawagoe, Tetsuo. 1981. Dai 5 kai Mizu no Shuukan wo Mukaeru ni atatte (Welcoming the fifth Water Week). *Gekkan Damu Nihon* 7 (441): 1–4.

Kawai Kikaku ka (Kawai village planning department). 2001. Kōhō Kawai (Public relations for Kawai [brochure]). 9 (494).

Kearney, Richard, and Chandan Sinha. 1988. Professionalism and Bureaucratic Respon-sivness: Conflict or Compatability. *Public Administration Review* 48 (1): 571–579.

Keehn, Edward. 1990. Managing Interests in the Japanese Bureaucracy: Informality and Discretion. *Asian Survey* 30 (11): 1021–1037.

Keizai Sangyōshō (Ministry of Economy, Trade, and Industry, METI). 2002. Dai 28 kai Sōgō Enerugi Taisaku Suishin Kakuryō Kaigi Shiryō (Materials for the 28th meet-ing of the Ministerial Council for Promoting a Comprehensive Energy Policy). Tokyo (19 March).

Keizai Sangyōshō shigen enerugi chō (Agency for Natural Resources and Energy, ANRE), in METI. 2001. Heisei 13 nendo Dengen ricchi sokushin kōrōsha hyōshō ni Tuite (About the 2001 citation ceremony for electric power sources siting promoters).

———. 2002a. *Genshiryoku 2002* (Nuclear power in 2002). Tokyo: Nihon Genshiryoku Bunka Shinkō Zaidan.

———. 2002b. Dengen ricchi no Gaiyō (A summary of power supply siting).

Kelly, Tim. 2002. Tokyo Electric Cover-Ups May Thwart Japan's Nuclear Power Plans. *Bloomberg News* (30 September).

Kensetsushō Kasenkyoku (Ministry of Construction River Bureau). 1980. *Nihon no Tamokuteki Damu* (Japan's multipurpose dams). Tokyo: Sankaidō.

Kensetsushō Kasenkyoku Kaihatsuka (Ministry of Construction River Bureau, Development Group). 1985. *Damu no Kanri* (The management of dams). Tokyo: Sankaidō.

Kensetushō Tōhoku Chihō Kensetsukyoku Shichikadamu Kōji Jimusho (Northeastern Japan Area Branch Office of the Ministry of Construction, Shichika Dam Con-struction Office). 1988. *Shichika Damu Kōjishi* (Records of the construction work on the Shichika Dam). Tokyo: Sankaidō.

Kenshokuso Nyūsu (Ministry of Construction Union News). 2000. Yotō, chūshi kentō 233 jigyō wo kettei (The Ruling Party decides on investigations to cancel 233 public works projects). No. 482 (6 September).

KHCKODKJ (Kensetsushō Hokuriku Chihō Kensetsukyoku Ōmachi Damu Kōji Jimusho). Western Japan Area Branch Office of the Ministry of Construction, Ōmachi Dam Construction Office). 1986. Ōmachi Damu Kōjishi (Records of the construction work on the Ōmachi Dam). Nagano Prefecture: Fujiwara Insatsu.

KKCKCDTKJ (Kensetushō Kyūshū Chihō Kensetsukyoku Chikugogawa Damu Tōgō Kanri Jimusho). (Kyūshū Area Branch Office of the Ministry of Construction, Chikugo River Integrated Management Office). (1992). Matsubara Shimouke Damu no Kiroku (A record of the Matsubara and Shimouke Dams). Tokyo: Kensetsu Kōhō Kenkyūjo.

KTCKGDKJ (Kensetushō Tōhoku Chihō Kensetsukyoku Gosho Damu Kōji Jimusho). (Northeastern Japan Area Branch Office of the Ministry of Construction, Gosho Dam Construction Office). 1982. Gosho Damu Kōjishi (Records of the construction work on the Gosho Dam). Tokyo: Dai Nippon Insatsu.

KKCKYDKJ (Kensetsushō Kantō Chihō Kensetsukyoku Yanba Dam Koji Jimusho. (Kantō Area Branch Office of the Ministry of Construction, Yanba Dam Construction Office). 1989. Yanda dam Shūraku Kankyō Keikaku Hōkoku sho (Yanba Dam area environmental report).

Kernell, Samuel. 1997. Going Public: New Strategies of Presidential Leadership. Washington, D.C.: CQ Press.

Kerr, Alex. 2001. Dogs and Demons: The Fall of Modern Japan. London: Penguin.

Khagram, Sanjeev. 2004. Dams and Development: Transnational Struggles for Water and Power. Ithaca: Cornell University Press.

Khong, Yuen Foong. 1992. Analogies at War: Korea, Munich, Dien Bien Phu, and the Vietnam Decisions of 1965. Princeton: Princeton University Press.

Kihara, Shigeya. 2000. Damu hantai undō no soshiki senryaku to seijiteki kikai kōzō: Kawabegawa Damu Hantaiundō wo jirei ni shite (Organizational structures of anti-dam movements and political opportunity structures: A case of the anti–Kawabe River Dam movements). In Go kōgyō kōtō senmongakkō kenkyū hōkoku (Research report of the High-Level Industrial Vocational School), 64.

Kimura, Hiromi. 1971. Saikin no tochi shūyō wo meguro funsō ni tuite (About the recent disputes over the Land Expropriation law). In Damu Kensetsu to Suibotsu Hoshō (Compensation for submersion and dam construction), 136–172. Tokyo: Nihon damu Kyōka.

Kindleberger, Charles P. 1951. Group Behavior and International Trade. Journal of Political Economy 59:30–46.

King, Gary, Robert Keohane, and Sidney Verba. 1994. Designing Social Inquiry: Scientific Inference in Qualitative Research. Princeton: Princeton University Press.

King, Gary, and Lanche Zeng. 2001a. Logistic Regression in Rare Events Data. Political Analysis.

———. 2001b. Explaining Rare Events in International Relations. International Organization 55 (3): 693–715.

King, Gary, Michael Tomz, and Jason Wittenberg. 2000. Making the Most of Statistical Analyses: Improving Interpretation and Presentation. American Journal of Political Science 44 (2): 347–361.

Kitahara, Kōji. 1996. *Daichi no ran: Narita Tōsō* (Battle for the ground: The struggle at Narita). Tokyo: Ochanomizu Shobō.

Kitano, Hirohisa, and Keiichiro Ichinose. 1992. *Narita Chianhō: Kenpō ga Abunai* (The Narita Public Order Law: The Constitution is in danger). Tokyo: Shakai hyōronsha.

Kitschelt, Herbert. 1986. Political Opportunity Structures and Political Protest: Anti-Nuclear Movements in Four Democracies. *British Journal of Political Science* 16:57–85.

——. 1991. Industrial Governance Structures, Innovation Strategies, and the Case of Japan: Sectoral or Cross-National Comparative Analysis? *International Organization* 45 (4): 453–493.

——. 1994. *The Transformation of European Social Democracy.* New York: Cambridge University Press.

Klass, Gary M. 1993. Review Article on Incrementalism and Public Policy. *The Journal of Politics* 55 (2): 523–526.

Klein, Patrick. 2002. Public Opinion and Nuclear Waste. *CLEFS CEA,* no. 47 (Spring): 93–94.

Kobayashi, Eichiro. 1995. Damu to Chiiki kasseika ni Tuite (Improving communities and dams). *Damu Nenkan,* 20–27.

Kobayashi, Shinchiro. 2003. *Japan New Map.* Tokyo: East Press.

Kobayashi, Tadao, ed. 1994. *Kōyō Yōchi no Shutoku ni Tomonau Sonshitsu hoshō kijun yōkō no kaisetsu* (An explanation of the general plan of standards for compensating losses related to the acquisition of land for public use). Tokyo: Kindai Tosho Kabushiki Gaisha.

Kodama, Fumio. 1995. *Emerging Patterns of Innovation.* Boston: Harvard Business School Press.

Kodama, Hideyasu. 1998. Nihon ni okeru Genshiryoku hatsudensho ricchi Ukeire no Seiji katei (The political process that comes with accepting nuclear power plant siting in Japan). *Seisaku Kagaku* (Policy Science) 5 (2): 29–49.

Koh, Byung. 1989. *Japan's Administrative Elite.* Berkeley: University of California Press.

Kōkū Kōgai Bōshi Kyōkai (Association to prevent airport pollution). 1973. Ōsaka Kokusai Kūkō Shūhen ni Okeru Seikatu Kankyō Chōsa Hōkokusho (Report on the surveys of life and environment for the areas near the International Osaka Airport).

Kokudo Kaihatsu Gijutsu Kenkyū Sentā (Center for Research on Techniques for Land Development). 1987. *Suigen chiiki taisaku no tehiki* (A guidebook on the measures for water resource areas). Tokyo: Kokudo Kaihatsu Gijutsu Kenkyū Sentā.

Kokudochō Suishigenbu Suigenchiiki taisakuka (National Land Ministry, Water Resources Division, Measures for Water Resources Area Section). 1989. Suigen Chiiki Taisaku to Kikin (Funds and measures for water resource areas). *Gekkan Damu Nihon,* no. 541 (November): 9–16.

Kokudokōtsūshō Kasenkyoku (Ministry of Land, Infrastructure, and Transportation, River Bureau). 2002. *Me de miru Damu jigyō* (Visual introduction to dam projects).

——. 2003. *Damu Jigyō ni Kansuru Puroguramu Hyōkasho* (An evaluation of programs relating to dam projects).

Kokudokōtsūshō Kōkūkyoku (Ministry of Land, Infrastructure, and Transport, Airport Division). 2002. *Kokunai kūkou seibi ni tuite, Shiryō 2-2* (Packet 2-2, on domestic airport facilities). Kasumigaseki.

——. 2003. *Ippan kūkō n genjō ni tuite* (On the present conditions of mainstream airports). Kasumigaseki.

Kokudokōtsūshō Ōsaka kōkūkyoku Matsuyama Kūkō Jimusho (Ministry of Land, Infrastructure, and Transport, Osaka Airport Branch, Matsuyama Airport Office). 2003. *Matsuyama Kūkō no Gaiyō* (An outline of the Matsuyama Airport). Ehime Prefecture.

Konda, Laura S. 2003. The Effects of Airport Siting Decisions on Property Values: Three Essays. Ph.D. dissertation, University of Texas at Austin.

Koshar, Rudy. 1986. *Social Life, Local Politics, and Nazism: Marburg, 1880–1935.* Chapel Hill: University of North Carolina Press.

Koshida, Minoru. 1989. Japanese Police Lay Siege to Narita Protesters' Fortress. Reuters Limited (5 December).

Kotaka, Tsuyoshi. 1996. *Kurashi no sōdanshitsu: Yōchi baishū to hoshō* (Life Advice Center [explanation of] land purchasing and compensation). Tokyo: Yuhihaku.

Krasner, Stephen. 1984. Review Article: Approaches to the State: Alternative Conceptions and Historical Dynamics. *Comparative Politics* 16 (2): 223–246.

Kriesi, Hanspeter, Ruud Koopmans, Jan Duyvendak, and Marco Giugni. 1995. *New Social Movements in Western Europe: A Comparative Analysis.* Minneapolis: University of Minnesota Press.

Kristof, Nicholas. 1998. Japan Voters Send Message: No Change. *New York Times* (5 July): 4.

Kryder, Daniel. 2000a. *Divided Arsenal: Race and the American State during World War II.* New York: Cambridge University Press.

———. 2000b. Black Police and Wartime. In Social Reform and Major War in the Twentieth Century US. Draft manuscript.

Kunreuther, Howard, and Paul Kleindorfer. 1986. A Sealed Bid Auction Mechanism for Siting Noxious Facilities. *American Economic Review* 76 (2): 295–299.

Kuroda, Yasumasa. 1972. Protest Movements in Japan: A New Politics. *Asian Survey* 12 (11): 947–952.

Kuwabara, Konosuke. 1988. Nuclear Protest Grows at Grass-Roots Level. *Nikkei Shinbun* (August 6): 28.

Lambeth, Benjamin. 1972. Deterrence in the MIRV Era. *World Politics* 24 (2): 221–242.

Lamiral, Georges. 1988. *Chronique de trente années d'équipement nucléaire à Electricité de France* (30-year chronicle of nuclear facilities at EDF). Paris: Association pour l'Histoire de l'Électricité en France.

Laponche, Bernard. 2003. Trente ans de discussions, d'oppositions et de non-debat sur l'energie (Thirty years of discussions, opposition, and non-debate over nuclear energy). 24 June.

———. 2004. *Maîtriser la consommation d'énergie* (Controlling energy consumption). Paris: Le Collège de la Cité.

LeBlanc, Robin. 1999. *Bicycle Citizens.* Berkeley: University of California Press.

Lebouef, Michel. 1991. *Penly un Grand chantier nucléaire* (A large nuclear construction site at Penly). Paris: EDF.

Lebra, Takie. 1976. *Japanese Patterns of Behavior.* Honolulu: University of Hawaii Press.

Lecourt, Arnaud. 2003. Les conflits d'amenagement: Analyse theorique et pratique a partir du cas breton (Development conflicts: A theoretical and practical analysis based on the case of Brittany). Ph.D. dissertation, Universite de Haute Bretagne–Rennes II.

Lee, Matthew, and John Bartkowski. 2004. Love Thy Neighbor? Moral Communities, Civic Engagement, and Juvenile Homicide in Rural Areas. *Social Forces* 82 (3): 1001–1035.

Lengronne, Fabrice. 1989. Les experts et les citoyens (Experts and citizens). *Reforme* (15 July).

*Le Peuple Breton.* 1981. Le débat confisqué (The confiscated debate). (215): 10–11.

*Le Point.* 1975. Pas d'angoisse peu de grogne (No anxiety, few complaints) (12 May).

Le Saux, Bernard. 1974. Centrales nucleaires: Elus locaux consultés (Nuclear power plants: local elected officials consulted). *Quotidien de Paris* (3 December).

Lesbirel, S. Hayden. 1998. *NIMBY Politics in Japan: Energy Siting and the Management of Environmental Conflict.* Ithaca: Cornell University Press.

Lesbirel, S. Hayden, and Daigee Shaw, eds. 2005. *Managing Conflict in Facility Siting: An International Comparison.* Northampton, Mass.: Edward Elgar.

Lester, Richard. 1983. Japan's Lead in Nuclear Power. *Wall Street Journal* (16 November): 30.

Levin, Mark. 1999. Japan: Kayano et al., V. Hokkaido Expropriation Committee (The Nibutani dam decision). *International Legal Materials* 38 (394).

Levine, Michael, and Jennifer Forrence. 1990. Regulatory Capture, Public Interest, and the Public Agenda. *Journal of Law, Economics, and Organization* 6:167–198.

Levitt, Barbara, and James March. 1988. Organizational Learning. *American Review of Sociology* 14:319–340.

Levy, Jack. 1994. Learning and Foreign Policy: Sweeping a Conceptual Minefield. *International Organization* 48 (2): 279–312.

Levy, Jonah. 1999. *Tocqueville's Revenge: State, Society, and Economy in Contemporary France.* Cambridge: Harvard University Press.

Lewino, Frédéric. 1988. Tirs de barrage (Shooting the dam). *Le Point* (10 October).

Lewis, Anthony. 1980. Power of the Market. *New York Times* (19 June): A23.

Lewis, Jonathan. 1997. Review Article: *Japan under Construction* and *Kōkyō jigyō wo dō suru ka. Social Science Japan* (August): 33–35.

*Libero International.* 1977. Sanrizuka. Online at http://home.rmci.net/cwmorse/number3.htm#Sanrizuka.

Lichbach, Mark. 1995. *The Rebel's Dilemma.* Ann Arbor: University of Michigan Press.

Lieberman, Robert. 2002. Ideas, Institutions, and Political Order: Explaining Political Change. *American Political Science Review* 96 (4): 697–712.

Lieberthal, Kenneth, and Michel Oksenberg. 1988. *Policy Making in China: Leaders, Structures, and Processes.* Princeton: Princeton University Press.

Lindblom, Charles. 1959. The Science of Muddling Through. *Public Administration Review* 19:79–88.

——. 1965. *The Intelligence of Democracy.* New York: Free Press.

——. 1977. Authority Systems: Strong Thumbs, No Fingers, and the Limited Competence of Markets. In *Politics and Markets: The World's Political-Economic Systems,* ed. Charles Lindlom, 65–89. New York: Basic Books.

——. 1979. Still Muddling, Not Yet Through. *Public Administration Review* (November/December): 517–526.

Lindert, Peter. 1991. Historical Patterns of Agricultural Policy. In *Agriculture and the State,* ed. C. Peter Timmer, 29–83. Ithaca: Cornell University Press.

Linhardt, Dominique. 2004. La force de l'État en démocratie: La République Fédérale d'Allemagne à l'épreuve de la guérilla urbaine (The force of the State in democracy:

The Federal Republic of Germany at test by urban guerilla warfare). Ph.D. dissertation, l'Écoles des Mines de Paris.

Lobao, Linda, and Katherine Meyer. 2004. Farm Power without Farmers. *Contexts* 3 (4): 12–21.

Lukes, Steven. 1974. *Power: A Radical View.* London: Macmillan.

Machiavelli, Niccolo. 1532 (1999). *The Prince.* Trans. Quentin Skinner and Russell Price. Cambridge: Cambridge University Press.

MacLachlan, Ann. 1988. French Regulators Make Public Information Top Priority. *Inside N.R.C.* 10 (16). .

——. 1990. French Legislators Recommend Deep Changes in Nuclear Safety Oversight. *Inside N.R.C.* 12 (26).

——. 1996. France Hopes to Use Internet to Broaden Public's Input into Licensing. *Inside N.R.C.* 18 (12).

——. 1997. EDF Launches Sixth Ad Campaign Touting Nuclear Power Benefits. *Nucleonics Week* (20 November): 10.

——. 1998. Le Deaut Report Starts Process for Nuclear Regulatory Reform. *Nucleonics Week* 39 (28).

Maillard, Dominique. 1992. Le rôle du public en ce qui concerne l'implantation de centrales nucléaires et la délivrance des autorisations en france (The role of the public in nuclear plant siting and the granting of authorizations in France). In *Public Participation in Nuclear Decision Making,* OECD Nuclear Energy Agency, 215–221. Paris: OECD.

Malcolm, Andrew. 1978. Japanese Postpone Opening of Airport in Face of Protests. *New York Times* (28 March): 77.

Mansfield, Carol, George Van Houtven, and Joel Huber. 2001. The Efficiency of Political Mechanisms for Siting Nuisance Facilities: Are Opponents More Likely to Participate than Supporters? *Journal of Real Estate Finance and Economics* 22 (2/3): 141–161.

March, James, and Johan Olsen. 1976. Organizational Choice under Ambiguity. In James March and Johan Olsen, eds., *Ambiguity and Choice in Organizations,* 10–23. Bergen, Norway: Universitetsforlaget.

Marignac, Yves, and Mathieu Pavageau. 1998. *Procédures d'autorisation des installations nucléaires en France: Permis garanti* (Authorization procedures for nuclear installations in France: Permit guaranteed). Paris: WISE-Paris.

Marshall, Jonathan. 2003. Leveraging Accountability: How Freedom of Information Brought Courts into Governance in Japan. Ph.D. dissertation, University of California at Berkeley.

Maruyama, Masazumi. 2000. Suigen chiiki taisaku no genjō to kadai (Problems and conditions of the measures for water resource areas). In *Suigenchi mondai Jitsumu kōshūkai tekisuto* (The text of a practical course on the problems of river land acquisition), 1–35. Tokyo: Nihon Damu Kyōkai.

Matsukuma, Noriaki. 1990. Damu kensetsu kigyō no yori yoi Rikai wo Motomeru (Seeking clarity on dam construction projects). In *Gekkan Damu Nihon* 12 (554): 15–21.

Matsura, Motoyuki. 1974. Yōchi baishō, shūyō, hoshō (Land purchase, expropriation, and compensation). In *Hoshō Jitsumu kōshūkai tekisuto* (The text of a practical course on the problems of compensation), 121–131. Tokyo: Nihon Damu Kyōkai.

Matsuzawa, Yoshikatsu. 1969. Tochi Shūyō wo Meguru Shomondai ni tuite (About the various problems involved in land expropriation). In *Hoshō Jitsumu kōshūkai tekisuto* (The text of a practical course on the problems of compensation), 21–33. Tokyo: Nihon Damu Kyōkai.

Mayhew, David. 1974. *Congress: The Electoral Connection.* New Haven: Yale University Press.

Mazmanian, Daniel, and David Morell. 1994. The NIMBY Syndrome. In *Environmental Policy in the 1990s,* ed. Norman Vig and Michael Kraft, 233–242. Washington, D.C.: CQ Press.

McAdam, Doug. 1982. *Political Process and the Development of Black Insurgency, 1930–1970.* Chicago: University of Chicago Press.

McAdam, Doug, Sidney Tarrow, and Charles Tilly. 2001. *The Dynamics of Contention.* New York: Cambridge University Press.

McAvoy, Gregory. 1999. *Controlling Technocracy: Citizen Rationality and the NIMBY Syndrome.* Washington, D.C.: Georgetown University Press.

McColl, Greg. 1980. Comments on Tony Grey's Paper. In *Australia and Japan: Nuclear Energy Issues in the Pacific,* ed. Stuart Harris and Keichi Oshima, 52–57. Canberra: Australia-Japan Economic Relations Project.

McCormack, Gavan. 1996. *The Emptiness of Japanese Affluence.* New York: M. E. Sharpe.

———. 1997. "Village vs. State." *The Ecologist,* November/December.

———. 2002. Breaking Japan's Iron Triangle. *New Left Review* (January–February): 5–23.

McCubbins, Mathew, and Thomas Schwartz. 1984. Congressional Oversight Overlooked: Police Patrols versus Fire Alarms. *American Journal of Political Science* 28 (1): 165–179.

McGillivray, Fiona. 1997. Party Discipline as a Determinant of the Endogeneous Formation of Tariffs. *American Journal of Political Science* 41 (2): 584–607.

McKean, Margaret. 1981. *Environmental Protest and Citizen Politics in Japan.* Berkeley: University of California Press.

Mény, Yves. 1989. The National and International Context of French Policy Communities. *Political Studies* 37 (3): 387–399.

Mertens, Brian, and Sam Jameson. 1999. Sinking in Cement. *Asian Business* 35 (3): 20–26.

Migdal, Joel. 1988. *Strong Societies and Weak States: State-Society Relations and State Capabilities in the Third World.* Princeton: Princeton University Press.

Miller, Benjamin. 2000. *Fat of the Land.* New York: Four Walls Eight Windows.

Ministère de l'économie des finances et de l'industrie (Ministry of Economy, Finance, and Industry). 2004. *French Energy Prospective and Policy.* Paris: General Directorate for Energy and Raw Materials.

Mitchell, Robert, and Richard Carson. 1986. Property Rights, Protest, and the Siting of Hazardous Waste Facilities. *American Economic Review* 76 (2): 285–290.

Mitchell, William, and Michael Munger. 1991. Economic Theories of Interest Groups: An Introductory Survey. *American Journal of Political Science* 35:512–546.

Miyamoto, Tadao. (1978). Damu suibotsu hoshō no mondaiten to sono hansei ni tuite (A Reflection on the problem points with compensation for submersion due to dam construction). In *Damu Kensetsu to Suibotsu Hoshō* (Compensation for submersion and dam construction), 35–43. Tokyo: Nihon Damu Kyōkai.

Miyano, Yūichi. 2000. Suigen chiiki taisaku ni yoru kasen–suishigen kaihatsu no kōkyō jigyō no juyō to suigen chiiki–chihō zaisei (The local finances and the acceptance of public works projects for river and water resource development under the measures for water resource areas). In *Seisaku Kagaku* (Policy science) 7 (3): 163–195.

Mohai, Paul, and Bunyan Brant. 1992. Environmental Racism: Reviewing the Evidence. In *Race and the Incidence of Environmental Hazards: A Time for Discourse*, ed. Bunyan Brant and Paul Mohai, 163–176. Boulder, Colo.: Westview Press.

Monier, Françoise. 1989. La Nouvelle Guerre des camisards (The new war of the camisards). *L'Express* (11 August).

Morone, Joseph, and Edward Woodhouse. 1989. *The Demise of Nuclear Energy? Lessons for Democratic Control of Technology.* New Haven: Yale University Press.

Mulgan, Aurelia George. 2005. *Japan's Interventionist State: MAFF and the Agricultural Policy Regime.* London: RoutledgeCurzon.

Munton, Don. 1996. Siting Hazardous Waste Facilities, Japanese Style. In *Hazardous Waste Siting and Democratic Choice*, ed. Don Munton, 181–229. Washington D.C.: Georgetown University Press.

Murakami, Yoshio. 1983. Kūkō hantai tōsō ha rakunichi wo mukaeta no ka (Has the anti-airport war entered its twilight?). *Asahi Janaru* 25 (15): 94–97.

Murohara, Tomoyuki. 1971. Shimouke Dam to Watashi no Hantai Tōsō (My battle against the Shimouke Dam). In *Damu Kensetsu to Suibotsu Hoshō* (Compensation for submersion and dam construction), 79–91. Tokyo: Nihon Damu Kyōkai.

Musankaikyū Henshūbu (Editorial Department of the Proletariat). 1992. Sanrizuka Tataki wo Saseru hitobito (Those who helped the fight at Sanrizuka). In *Sanrizuka Ansorogi* (Sanziruka anthology), ed. Uzawa Hirofumi, Tokyo: Iwanami Shoten.

Naganohara, Shigetaro. 1954. Hoshō Mondai (The problems with compensation). In *Damu no Keikaku kara Sekkō Made* (From dam planning to completion), 54–64. Tokyo: Nihon Kasen Kyōkai.

Nagoya Kūkō Birudingu Kabushiki Gaisha (Nagoya Airport Construction Company) 1999. *Shin Hishō: Nagoya Kūkō no Hanseiki* (New flight: A half-century history of the Nagoya Airport). Aichi Prefecture: Nagoya Kūkō Birudingu Kabushiki Gaisha.

Naikaku Sōridaijin Kanbō Kōhōshitsu (Public relations division, prime minister's government secretariat). 1988. *Shin Tōkyō kokusai kūkō ni kansuru seronchōsa* (Public opinion polls on the New Tokyo International Airport). Tokyo.

Naito, Yoko. 2000. Nuclear Power in Mie Prefecture. *Chubu Weekly* 6 (4): 1.

Nakagawa, Masami, Masazaku Honda, Yoshinori Hirako, and Shinjiro Sadamatsu. 2004. Bikini: 50 Years of Nuclear Power, *Asahi Shinbun* 26, 27, 28 January; trans. Kyoko Selden in *Japan Focus* (23 January).

Nakagome, Michio. 1978. Suishigen Shūdatu ni kōsuru: Tanaka Shōzō no Matsuei (Resisting the robbery carried out by the Water Resources Act: The descendents of Tanaka Shōzō). *Asahi Janaru* (2 June): 103–106.

Nakai, Tomi. 1981. Sanrizuka Shibayama rengō kūkō hantaidōmei Ishibashi Shimasaji san ni kiku (Listening to Shimasahi Ishibashi of the Sanrizuka Shibayama Anti-Airport Movement Alliance). *Gekkan Sōhyō* (General Council of Trade Unions of Japan Monthly) 281 (5): 70–76.

Nakamura, Karen. 2002. Resistance and Co-optation: The Japanese Federation of the Deaf and Its Relations with State Power. *Social Science Japan Journal* 5 (1): 17–35.

Nakamura, Kikuo, ed. 1975. *Gendai Nihon no Seiji Bunka* (Contemporary Japanese political culture). Kyoto: Mineruba.

Nakane, Chie. 1978. *Tateshakai no rikigaku* (The workings of vertical society). Tokyo: Kodansha.

Narita Kūkō Chiiki kyōsei iinkai, Rekishi Tenjō bukai (History Division, Committee for Symbiosis between the local community and Narita Airport). 2001. *Kaitaku tte, Shittemasu ka* (Do you know about the settlements?). Sanrizuka Japan.

Narita Kūkō Mondai Entakukaigi no gōi jikō (Memorandum of understanding from the Narita Airport Problem Round table). 1994. 10 December.

Narita Kūkō no Santei Kassoro no Kyōyō Chūshi wo Uttaemasu (Committee appealing for an end to the temporary joint runway at Narita Airport). 2002. *Chakuriku Fuka* (The runway is unnecessary). Tokyo: Nanatsumori.

NDK (Nihon Damu Kyōkai), Japan Dam Federation. 1989. *Nihon damu Kyōkai 15 Nen shi* (The 15-year history of the Japan Dam Federation). Tokyo: Nihon Damu Kyōkai.

Nectoux, François. 1991. *Crisis in the French Nuclear Industry.* Amsterdam: Greenpeace Publications.

Nelkin, Dorothy, ed. 1979. Nuclear Power and Its Critics: A Siting Dispute. In *Controversy: Politics of Technical Decisions,* ed. Dorothy Nelkin. Beverly Hills, Calif.: Sage.

Nelkin, Dorothy, and Michael Pollak. 1981. *The Atom Besieged.* Cambridge: MIT Press.

Nelson, Jon. 2004. Meta-Analysis of Airport Noise and Hedonic Property Values: Problems and Prospects. *Journal of Transport Economics and Policy* 38 (1): 1–27.

Nemoto, Kazuyasu. 1981. Nuclear Power Controversy in Japan. *Nihon Genshiryoku Sangyō Kaigi* (August): 21–24.

New Tokyo International Airport Authority. 2002. *Environmental Report* 7 (December).

Nihon Bengoshi Rengōkai (Japan Federation of Bar Assocations). 1995. *Kawa to Kaihatsu wo Kangaeru* (Thinking about rivers and development). Tokyo: Jikkyo Shuppan.

NGSK (Nihon Genshiryoku Sangyō Kaigi, Japan Atomic Industrial Forum). 1970. *Genshiryoku hatsudensho to chiikishakai* (Nuclear power plants and their regional community). Tokyo: Nihon Genshiryoku Sangyō Kaigi.

Nihon Ricchi Sentā (Japan industrial location center). 2002a. *Hatsudensho Onsui Riyō Yōgyo no Seika* (The results of power plant warm water aquaculture). Tokyo: Nihon Ricchi Sentā (Japan Industrial Location Center) and Onsui Yōgyo kaikatsu Kyōkai (Assocation for the Development of Warm Water Aquaculture). October.

———. 2002b. *Nihon Ricchi Sentā no Enerugi Kōhō Katsudō* (The Japan Industrial Location Center's energy-related public relations activities). Tokyo: Nihon Ricchi Sentā (Japan Industrial Location Center).

———. 2002c. Yume (Dream). *Nihon Ricchi Sentā* 6-6 (64).

Niikura, Toshiko. 1999. Campaigns against Dams in Japan and the Nagara River Estuary Dam. *Organization and Environment* 12 (1): 99–104.

Nishiyama, Misako. 1971. Damu kensetsu ga jimoto zyūmin ni oyobosu eikyō (The impact on local citizens of dam construction). In *Damu Kensetsu to Suibotsu Hoshō* (Compensation for submersion and dam construction), 20–40. Tokyo: Nihon damu Kyōkai.

NKOGG (Nihon Kyosantō Ōsaka hu gikai giindan, Japan Communist Party group of the Osaka Metropolitan Council). 1980. *Kansai Shinkūkō Mondai tokushūgō* (Special series on the problems of the new Kansai Airport). Ōsaka.

Noakes, John. 2001. From Water Cannons to Rubber Bullets: How the Policing of Protest Has Changed and What It Means. *Long Term View* 5 (2): 85–94.

Nordlinger, Eric. 1981. *On the Autonomy of the Democratic State.* Cambridge: Harvard University Press.

Noru, Shigeo. 1971. Kai to Mura to Daisan no ka (Village, sea, and the third fire). *Shimin* 5 (November): 54–66.

Nuclear Canada. 2001. *Canadian Nuclear Association Electronic Newsletter* 2 (21).

Nye, Joseph. 2004. *Soft Power: The Means to Success in World Politics.* New York: Public Affairs.

Odagiri, Takashi. 1997. Koku ya ken ni tayorazu, jiritsu shita (Not relying upon the state or the prefecture, they achieved independence). *Daisan Bunmei* (October): 74–81.

OECD (Organization for Economic Cooperation and Development). 1984. *Nuclear Power and Public Opinion.* Paris: OECD.

———. 2001. *Nuclear Power in the OECD.* Paris: OECD/IEA.

Ogawa, Production. 1992. Nihon Kaihō Sensen (Japan's Liberation Front). In *Sanrizuka Ansorogi* (Sanziruka anthology), ed. Uzawa Hirofumi, 89–110. Tokyo: Iwanami Shoten.

Ōhashi, Tatsu. 1972. Kyōwa: Genshiryoku hatsudensho to hantaiundō (Cooperation: Nuclear power plants and opposition movements). *Shakaitō* (Socialist Party of Japan) 2 (180): 116–126.

Oikawa, Kiyoaki. 2002. Kankyō jōken ni yotte omomitukesareta kyori ni mototzuku meiwaku shisetsu no tekitō haichi mondai ni kansuru kenkyū (Research on the problem of the proper placement of controversial facilities based upon weighted distance of environmental conditions). Working Paper 12650610, University of Tokyo Graduate School of Frontier Sciences.

Oka, Takashi. 1970. Farmers Delay Tokyo's New Airport. *New York Times* (4 October): 14.

Ōkawara, Toru, and Kenshi Baba. 1998. Nuclear Power Plant Siting Issues in Japan: Relationships between Utilities and Host Communities. Central Research Institute of the Electric Power Industry, Report no. EY97003.

OKK (Ōsaka Kokusai Kūkō 50 Shūnen Kinen jigyō jikkō iinkai, Committee to commemorate the 50th anniversary of the Osaka International Airport). 1990. *Ōsaka Kokusai Kūkō 50 Shūnen* (50th anniversary of the Osaka International Airport). Osaka.

O'Looney, John. 1995. *Economic Development and Environmental Control.* Westport; CT: Quorum Books.

Olson, Mancur. 1965. *The Logic of Collective Action: Public Goods and the Theory of Groups.* Cambridge: Harvard University Press.

Onnée, Jean-François. 2004. A Critique of the Development of France's First Airport. MIT Class paper (December 9).

OPECST (Office Parlementaire d'Evaluation des Choix Scientifiques et Technologiques). 2003. *La durée de vie des centrales nucléaires et les nouveaux types de réacteurs* (The lifespan of nuclear power plants and the new types of reactors). Paris: Assemblée Nationale.

Ostrom, Elinor. 1990. *Governing the Commons.* New York: Cambridge University Press.

OTA (Office of Technology Assessment). 1984. *Nuclear Power in an Age of Uncertainty.* Washington, D.C.: U.S. Congress.

Ōtake, Hideo, and Naoto Nonaka. 2000. *Seijikatei no hikakubunseki: Furansu to Nihon* (A comparative analysis of political processes: France and Japan). Tokyo: Hōsō Daigaku Kyōiku Shinkōkai.

Ozawa, Michigasu. 1987. *Chiku jō Kaisetsu Tochi Shūyō Hō* (The detailed articles of the Land Expropriation Law). Tokyo:Gyōsei.

Paehlke, Robert. 2003. *Democracy's Dilemma: Environment, Social Equity, and the Global Economy.* Cambridge: MIT Press.

Palfreman, Jon. 1997. Why the French Like Nuclear Energy. *Frontline* (22 April).

Pastor, Manuel, Jim, Sadd, and John Hipp. 2001. Which Came First? Toxic Facilities, Minority Move Up, and Environmental Justice. *Journal of Urban Affairs* 23 (1): 1–21.

Paumgarten, Nick. 2002. Department of Corrections: Here Comes the Neighborhood. *New Yorker* (8 July): 24–25.

Payen, Gérard. 2003. *Grands Chantiers—Apres Chantiers* (Large construction sites: After construction). Paris: EDF.

Pean, Pierre. 1978. L'état-EDF (The EDF State). *Le Nouvel Economist,* no. 128 (17 April): 58–63.

Pekkanen, Robert. 2000a. Japan's New Politics? The Case of the NPO Law. *Journal of Japanese Studies* 26 (1).

———. 2000b. Hō, kokka, shimin shakai (Law, the state, and civil society). *Leviathan* 27 (Autumn).

———. 2004. Japan: Social Capital without Advocacy. In *Civil Society and Political Change in Asia,* ed. Muthiah Alagappa, 223–258. Stanford: Stanford University Press.

———. 2006. *Japan's Dual Civil Society: Members without Advocates.* Stanford: Stanford University Press.

Peltzman, Sam. 1976. Toward a More General Theory of Regulation. *Journal of Law and Economics* 19:211–240.

Pempel, T. J. 1998. *Regime Shift: Comparative Dynamics of the Japanese Political Economy.* Ithaca: Cornell University Press.

Perrignon, Judith. 1992. Barrage et désespoir pour les écologistes (Dams and despair for the ecologists). *Libération* (16 October).

Perry, Christopher. 1991. Energy Policy Divided—Japan Is Torn Between Nuclear Commitment and Green Issues. *Financial Times* (25 April): 37.

Pfiffner, James. 1987. Political Appointees and Career Executives: The Democracy-Bureaucracy Nexus in the Third Century. *Public Administration Review* 47 (1): 57–65.

Pharr, Susan. 1990. *Losing Face: Status Politics in Japan.* Berkeley: University of California Press.

———. 2003. Targeting an Activist State: Japan as a Civil Society Model. In: *The State of Civil Society in Japan,* ed. Frank Schwartz and Susan Pharr, 316–336. Cambridge: Cambridge University Press.

Pickett, Susan. 2002. Japan's Nuclear Energy Policy. *Energy Policy* 30:1337–1355.

Pierson, Paul. 2000a. Not Just What, But When: Timing and Sequence in Political Processes. *Studies in American Political Development* 14:73–93.

———. 2000b. Incréasing Returns, Path Dependence, and the Study of Politics. *American Political Science Review* 94 (2): 251–267.

———. 2004. *Politics in Time: History, Institutions, and Social Analysis.* Princeton: Princeton University Press.

Pierson, Paul, and Theda Skocpol. 2000. Historical Institutionalism and Contemporary Political Science. Paper prepared for American Political Science Association meeting, Washington, D.C.

Piller, Charles. 1991. *The Fail Safe Society: Community Defiance and the End of American Technological Optimism.* New York: Basic Books.

Pipard, Dominique, and Jean-Pierre Gualezzi. 2002. *La lutte contre le bruit* (The fight against noise). Paris: Le Moniteur.

Polanyi, Karl. [1944] 2001. *The Great Transformation: The Political and Economic Origins of our Time.* Boston: Beacon Books.

*Politique Hebdo* (Politics Weekly). L'information selon EDF (Information according to EDF). 9 April.

Portney, Kent. 1991. *Siting Hazardous Waste Treatment Facilities: The NIMBY Syndrome.* New York: Auburn House.

Posner, Paul, Timothy Conlan, and David Beam. 2002. The Politics That Pathways Make: A Framework for Contemporary Federal Policy Making. Presented at the annual meeting of APSA, Boston, August 29–31.

Putnam, Robert. 1976. *The Comparative Study of Political Elites.* Englewood, NJ: Prentice-Hall.

———. 1993. *Making Democracy Work: Civic Traditions in Modern Italy.* Princeton: Princeton University Press.

———. 1995. Bowling Alone: America's Declining Social Capital. *Journal of Democracy* 6 (1): 65–78.

———. 2000. *Bowling Alone: The Collapse and Revival of American Community.* New York: Simon and Schuster.

Pye, Lucian. 1985. *Asian Power and Politics.* Cambridge: Belknap Press of Harvard University Press.

Quah, Euston, and K. C. Tan. 2002. *Siting Environmentally Unwanted Facilities: Risks, Trade-Offs, and Choices.* Northampton, Mass.: E. Elgar.

Rabe, Barry. 1994. *Beyond NIMBY.* Washington, D.C.: Brookings Institution.

Ramseyer, J. Mark, and Eric Rasmusen. 2001. Why Are Japanese Judges So Conservative in Politically Charged Cases? *American Political Science Review* 95 (2): 331–344.

Ramseyer, J. Mark, and Frances Rosenbluth. 1993. *Japan's Political Marketplace.* Cambridge: Harvard University Press.

Ray, Edward John. 1981. The Determinants of Tariff and Nontariff Trade Restrictions in the United States. *Journal of Political Economy* 89 (1): 105–121.

Reiter, Dan. 1994. Learning, Realism, and Alliances: The Weight of the Shadow of the Past. *World Politics* 46 (4): 490–526.

Reiter, Jerome. 2000. Using Statistics to Determine Causal Relationships. *American Mathematical Monthly* (January): 24–32.

Reuter, Peter, and Edwin Truman. 2004. *Chasing Dirty Money: The Fight against Money Laundering.* Washington, D.C.: Institute for International Economics.

Rosa, Eugene, and Riley Dunlap. 1994. Poll Trends: Nuclear Power: Three Decades of Opinions. *Public Opinion Quarterly* 58 (2): 295–324.

Rose, Richard, and Terence Karran. 1987. *Taxation by Political Inertia: Financing the Growth of Government in Britain.* London: Allen and Unwin.

Rosenbaum, Paul, and Donald Rubin. 1983. The Central Role of the Propensity Score in Observational Studies for Causal Effects. *Biometrika* 70 (1): 41–55.

———. 1985. Constructing a Control Group Using Multivariate Matched Sampling Methods That Incorporate the Propensity Score. *American Statistician* 39 (1): 33–38.

Rothstein, Bo. 2004. Book Review of Comparative Historical Analysis in the Social Sciences. *Perspectives on Politics* 2 (3): 619–620.

Rucht, Dieter. 1994. The Anti-Nuclear Power Movement and the State in France. In *States and Anti-Nuclear Movements,* ed. Helena Flam, 129–162. Edinburgh: Edinburgh University Press.

Ruddle, Kenneth. 1987. Administration and Conflict Management in Japanese Coastal Fisheries. FAO Fish. Technical Paper 273.

Rüdig, Wolfgang. 1994. Maintaining a Low Profile: The Anti-Nuclear Movement and the British State. In *States and Anti-Nuclear Movements,* ed. Helena Flam, 70–100. Edinburgh: Edinburgh University Press.

Rueschemeyer, Dietrich, and Theda Skocpol, ed. 1996. *States, Social Knowledge, and the Origins of Modern Social Policies.* New York: Russell Sage Foundation.

Rule, James. 1988. *Theories of Civil Violence.* Berkeley: University of California Press.

Sabatier, P. A., and H. C. Jenkins-Smith, eds. 1993. *Policy Change and Learning: An Advocacy Coalition Approach.* Boulder, Colo.: Westview Press.

Sakurai, Yoshiko. 2000. *Nihon no kiki* (Japan's crisis). Tokyo: Shinchōsha.

Samuels, Richard. 1987. *The Business of the Japanese State.* Ithaca: Cornell University Press.

Sato, Ginji. 1977. Mizu no hi ni yosete (Approaching Water Day). *Gekkan Damu Nihon* 8 (394): 14–15.

Schattschneider, Elmer Eric. 1960. *The Semisovereign People.* New York: Holt, Rinehart and Winston.

Schelling, Thomas C. 1967. *Arms and Influence.* New Haven: Yale University Press.

Schickler, Eric. 2001. *Disjointed Pluralism: Institutional Innovation and the Development of the U.S. Congress.* Princeton: Princeton University Press.

Schlesinger, Jacob. 1997. *Shadow Shoguns: The Rise and Fall of Japan's Postwar Political Machine.* Stanford: Stanford University Press.

Schneider, Anne, and Helen Ingram. 1990. Behavioral Assumptions of Policy Tools. *The Journal of Politics* 52 (2): 510–529.

Schwartz, Herman. 2002. Down the Wrong Path: Path Dependence, Markets, and Increasing Returns. Draft manuscript presented at Harvard University.

Science and Technology Agency. 1996. *Nuclear Energy, Today and Tomorrow.* Tokyo: Japan Atomic Energy Relations Organization.

Scott, James C. 1998. *Seeing like a State: How Certain Schemes to Improve the Human Condition Have Failed.* New Haven: Yale University Press.

Scott-Stokes, Henry. 1978a. New Tokyo Airport Finally Opens with 13,000 Policemen on Hand. *New York Times* (20 May): 1.

———. 1978b. Tokyo Airport Showdown Is Quite Japanese. *New York Times,* 21 May, E3.

Seeliger, Robert. 1996. Siting Hazardous Waste Incinerators in Germany. In *Hazardous Waste Siting and Democratic Choice,* ed. Don Munton, 230–270. Washington, D.C.: Georgetown University Press.

Sené, Monique. 2002. Le lobby nucleaire: Mythe ou realite? (Nuclear Lobbying: Myth or reality?) *Gazette Nucléaire* (10): 9–10.

Senser, Robert. 1989. How Poland's Solidarity Won Freedom of Association. *Monthly Labor Review* (September): 34–38.

Sheingate, Adam. 2001. *The Rise of the Agricultural Welfare State: Institutions and Interest Group Power in the United States, France, and Japan.* Princeton: Princeton University Press.

Shepsle, Kenneth A. (1979). Institutional Arrangements and Equilibrium in Multi-dimensional Voting Models. *American Journal of Political Science* 23 (1): 27–59.

———. 1982. Review of *Politics of Regulation* by James Q. Wilson. *Journal of Political Economy* 90 (1): 216–221.

Shepsle, Kenneth A., and Bary R. Weingast. 1981. Structure-Induced Equilibrium and Legislative Choice. *Public Choice* 37:503–519.

Sherman, Daniel. 2006. Not Here, Not There, Not Anywhere: The Federal, State, and Local Politics of Low-level Radioactive Waste Disposal in the United States, 1979–1999. Paper presented at the 2006 Northeastern Political Science Association Conference, Boston.

Shibata, Tetsuji, and Hiroaki Tomokiyo. 1999. *Genpatsu Kokumin Seron—Seronchōsha ni miru Genshiryoku ishiki no hensen* (Citizens' public opinion on nuclear power: Changes in attitudes toward nuclear power seen through public opinion surveys). Tokyo: ERC.

Shimazaki, Hiroshi. 2001. Chūbu Kokusai kūkō kensetu hantai Hazu no Shizen wo Mamoritai Torasuto no Kai no Undō (The Hazu Environmental Trust Movement against the construction of the Chubu International Airport). *Gekkan Hodanren* 2 (693): 256–259.

Shimizu, Masatake. 1991. Nagaragawa Kakōzeki Shiron (Essay on the Nagara River gates). *Gekkan Damu Nihon* 4 (558): 11–20.

Shimizu, Shigeaki. 1978. Ohkawa Damu Kensetsu ni Tomounau Idō Hoshō ni tuite (About compensation for relocation related to the construction of the Ohkawa Dam). In *Damu Kensetsu to Suibotsu Hoshō* (Compensation for submersion and dam construction), 27–34. Tokyo: Nihon Damu Kyōkai.

Shimouke Matsubara Damu Mondai Kenkyūkai (Shimouke and Matsubara Dams Problem Study Group). 1972. *Kōkyō jigyō to kihonteki jinken* (Public works projects and basic human rights). Teikoku chihō gyōsei gakkai.

Shinharu Zadankai (New spring roundtable discussion group). 1975. Damu Kensetsu wo Meguru Shomondai (Various problems involved in dam construction). *Gekkan Damu Nihon* 1 (363): 30–46.

Shinoda, Takashi, and Tadaaki Takigawa. 1985. Suigen chiiki taisaku tokubetsu sochi hou shikō 10 nen wo furikaette (Looking back on 10 years since the implementation of the Measures for Water Resources areas). *Gekkan Damu Nihon* (491): 51–60.

Shin Tokyō kokusai kūkō shūhenseibi no tame no kuni no zaiseizyō no tokubetsuso-chi ni kansuru hōrei (Ordinances relating to the special measures for the central government's financing of maintanence for the areas near the new international airport at Tokyo). 1970. Tokyo.

*Shūkan Daiyamondo* (Weekly Diamond). 1996. Jimoto no mura ga danko hantai shite, utsute nashi no damu kaihatsu keikaku (With the villagers dead set against it, the dam development plan wouldn't go). (30 November): 30.

Siegel, Paul, and Jeffrey Alwang. 2005. Public Investments in Tourism in Northeast Brazil: Does a Poor Area Strategy Benefit the Poor? World Bank Latin America and Caribbean Region Sustainable Development Working Paper 22.

Silberman, Bernard. 1993. *Cages of Reason: The Rise of the Rational State in France, Japan, the United States, and Great Britain.* Chicago: University of Chicago Press.

Simon, Herbert. 1966. Thinking by Computers. In *Mind and Cosmos: Essays in Contemporary Science and Philosophy,* ed. Robert Colody, vol. 30. Pittsburgh: University of Pittsburgh Press.

———. 1997. *Administrative Behavior.* New York: Free Press.

Simonnot, Philippe. 1978. *Les Nucléocrates* (The Nucleocrats). Grenoble: Presses universitaires de Grenoble.

Simpson, John. 2005. *Dam! Water, Power, Politics, and Preservation in Hetch Hetchy and Yosemite National Park.* New York: Pantheon Books.

Sippel, Patricia. 2000. Controlling the Nagara: Changing Approaches to Water Management in Japan. *Water Policy* 2:283–297.

Skocpol, Theda. 1979. *States and Social Revolutions: A Comparative Analysis of France, Russia, and China.* Cambridge: Cambridge University Press.

———. 1996. Unraveling from Above. In *Ticking Time Bombs,* ed. Robert Kuttner. New York: New York University Press.

———. 1999. Advocates without Members. In *Civic Engagement in American Democracy,* ed. Theda Skocpol and Morris Fiorina. Washington, D.C.: Brookings Institution Press.

Skowronek, Stephen. 1994. *The Politics Presidents Make: Leadership from John Adams to George Bush.* Cambridge: Belknap Press of Harvard University Press.

Slovic, Paul, Baruch, Fischoff, and Lichtenstein, Saruch 1980. Facts and Fears: Understanding Perceived Risk. In *Societal Risk Assessment: How Safe Is Safe Enough,* ed. R. C. Schwing and W. A. Albers. New York: Plenum Press.

Slovic, Paul, James Flynn, C. K. Mertz, Marc Poumadere, and Claire Mays. 2000. Nuclear Power and the Public: A Comparative Study of Risk-Perception in France and the United States. In *Cross-Cultural Risk Perception: A Survey of Empirical Studies,* ed. Ortwin Renn and Bernd Rohrmann. Dordrecht, Neth.: Kluwer Academic.

Smith, Hank, and Howard Kunreuther. 2001. Mitigation and Benefits Measures as Policy Tools for Siting Potentially Hazardous Facilities: Determinants of Effectiveness and Appropriateness. *Risk Analysis* 21:371–382.

Smith, Sheila, ed. 2000. *Local Voices, National Issues: The Impact of Local Initiative in Japanese Policy-Making.* Ann Arbor: University of Michigan Press.

Snyder, Jack. 1991. *Myths of Empire: Domestic Politics and International Ambition.* Ithaca: Cornell University Press.

Soejima, Ken. 1969. Shimouke Dam—Matsubara damu kensetsu ni okeru yōchi shutoku kōshō no keiken to hanshō (Reflecting on experiences in the negoations over land acquisition in the Shimouke and Matsubara dam cases). In *Hoshō Jitsumu kōshūkai tekisuto* (The text of a practical course on the problems of compensation), 64–74. Tokyo: Nihon Damu Kyōkai.

Solingen, Etel. 1996. *Industrial Policy, Technology, and International Bargaining: Designing Nuclear Industries in Argentina and Brazil.* Stanford: Stanford University Press.

Spergel, Irving A. 1990. Youth Gangs: Continuity and Change. *Crime and Justice* 12: 171–275.

Sterngold, James. 1989. An Airport Is Being Strangled by Relentless Foes. *New York Times* (26 September): A4.

Stigler, George. 1981. The Theory of Economic Regulation. *Bell Journal of Economics and Management Science* 2:3–21.

Stone, Clarence. 1989. *Governing Atlanta '46–'88.* Lawrence: University Press of Kansas.

Stratford, Alan. 1974. *Airports and the Environment.* London: Macmillan.

Stroller, Gary. 2007. St. Louis' Airports Aren't Too Loud: They're Too Quiet. *USA Today* (January 9): 5A.

Sugitani, Takashi. 1998. Opposition Movement against Golf Course Development. *Geographical Review of Japan* 71 (1): 31–44.

———. 1999. Environmental Awareness of the Contributors to the National Trust. *Geographical Review of Japan* 72 (1): 48–62.

*Suisankai* (Fishing world). 2000. Genhatsu to Gyogyō no Kyōsan wa Kanō ka (Can fishing cooperatives and nuclear plants live together?). 2:64–67.

———. 2002. Genhatsu to Gyogyō no Kyōsan wa Kanō ka (Can fishing cooperatives and nuclear plants live together?). 2:62–65.

Suleiman, Ezra. 1974. *Politics, Power, and Bureaucracy in France: The Administrative Elite.* Princeton: Princeton University Press.

———. 2003. *Dismantling Democratic States.* Princeton: Princeton University Press.

Sumiya, Mikio. 1996. *Narita no Sora to Daichi* (Narita's skies and earth). Tokyo: Iwanami Shoten.

———, ed. 2000. *A History of Japanese Trade and Industry Policy.* Oxford University Press.

Sumner, Colin. 1997. Social Control: The History and Politics of a Central Concept in Anglo-American Sociology. In *Social Control and Political Order: European Perspectives at the End of the Century,* ed. Roberto Bergalli and Colin Sumner. London: Sage.

Suzuki, Atsushi. 1994. Suigen chiiki taisaku no gaiyō (An overview of the Measures for Water Resource areas). In *Suigenchi mondai Jitsumu kōshūkai tekisuto* (The text of a practical course on the problems of river land acquisition), 1–71. Tokyo: Nihon Damu Kyōkai.

Suzuki, Rokuya. 1964. Tochi shoyūken to shuyō ni yoru Enshō (Compensating landowner rights in government land acquisition). In *Damu Nenkan,* 241–243. Tokyo: Nihon Damu Kyōkai.

Suzuki, Tokuyuki. 1977. Damu yōchi hoshō ni tuite tsuiseki chōsa no jittai (The actual results of panel data on compensation for land used by a dam). In *Damu Kensetsu to Suibotsu Hoshō* (Compensation for submersion and dam construction), 192–232. Tokyo: Nihon damu Kyōkai.

Sylves, Richard. 1983. Review of *Global Fission: The Battle over Nuclear Power,* by Jim Falk. *American Political Science Review* 77 (3): 806–807.

Szarka, Joseph. 2002. *The Shaping of Environmental Policy in France.* New York: Berghahn Books.

Tabusa, Keiko. 1992. Nuclear Politics: Exploring the Nexus between Citizens' Movements and Public Policy in Japan. Ph.D. dissertation, Columbia University.

Tada, Yasuyuki. 2001. Hōshasen nado no kyōiku kinō kyōka he (Toward strengthening our capabilities for education about radioactivity and other issues). *Energy* (December): 105–109.

Takada, Akira. 1954. Chishitsu chōsa (geographic surveys). In *Damu no Keikaku kara Sekkō Made* (From dam planning to completion), 54–64. Tokyo: Nihon Kasen Kyōkai.

Takahashi, Lois. 1998. *Homelessness, AIDS, and Stigmatization: The NIMBY Syndrome in the United States at the End of the Twentieth Century.* Oxford: Clarendon Press.

Takahashi, Tsutomu, and Yasushige Seike. 1991. Ohmatsukawa Damu kōji no imeji appu (Improving the image of the Ohmatsukawa Dam). *Gekkan Damu Nihon,* no. 565 (November): 15–21.

Takahashi, Yuriko. 2000. *Dare no tame no kōkyō jigyō ka* (For whose benefit are public works projects?). Tokyo: Iwanami Shoten.

———. 2002. Kawabegawa Dam ni 'taigi' wa aru ka (In the Kawabegawa Dam, is there a Great Cause?) *Sekai* (March): 168–176.

Takase, Kiyoshi. 1971. Damu Kensetsu ni Okeru Suibotsusha no Seikatsu Saiken taisaku ni tuite (About measures at rebuilding the lifestyles of those relocated by dam construction-caused flooding). In *Damu Kensetsu to Suibotsu Hoshō* (Compensation for submersion and dam construction), 41–55. Tokyo: Nihon Damu Kyōkai.

Tamura, Yoshimi. 1998. Hosogōchi Damu Hantai Undō to Kitōmura no Mura tzukuri (The anti-Hosogōchi Dam movement and the rejuvenation of Kitō Village). *Gijutsu to Ningen* (Man and Technology) 27 (4): 17–20.

Tamura, Yoshiko, et al. 1990. Josei no Sanka wo Matsu (Awaiting women's participation in dams). *Gekkan Damu Nihon* 10 (552): 23–42.

Tanaka, Kakuei. 1972. *Building a New Japan: A Plan for Remodeling the Japanese Archipelago.* Tokyo: Simul Press.

Tanaka, Mitsuo. 1971. Genshiryoku hatsudensho secchi hantai tōsō no hōkō (The course of the struggle against the establishment of nuclear power plants). *Gekkan Jichiken* (monthly magazine of the All Japan Prefectural and Municipal Workers Union) 13 (1): 117–127.

Tanaka, Toyoho, Tsuneyoshi Takahashi, Masao Tsuda, Masahiko Nagaoka, and Tokihumi Mizusaki, eds. 1991. *Nagaragawa Sen Kakō zeki—Shizen Hakai ka Sessui Ka* (Are the Nagara River gates destroying nature or saving water?). Tokyo: Nagaragawa Kakōzeki ni Hantai Shimin no Kai.

Tanaka, Yoshiaki. 1977. Suigenchiiki taisaku kikin no gyoumu to kadai (The task and duties of the Measures for Water Resource Areas fund). In *Damu Kensetsu to Suibotsu Hoshō* (Compensation for submersion and dam construction), 48–57. Tokyo: Nihon damu Kyōkai.

Tanimura, Kiyoshi. 1982. Damu kensetsu ni Tomonau Hoshō no keikō to Mondaiten (Difficult points and trends in compensation accompanying dam siting). *Gekkan Damu Nihon* (455): 23–29.

———. 1989. Nagaragawa Kakōzeki to Seitai Hogo (The Nagara River gates project and ecological conservation). *Gekkan Damu Nihon* 7 (537): 10–24.

———. 1997. Damu kensetsu suishin no kinyōsei (The importance of promoting dam construction). *Gekkan Damu Nihon* 6 (632): 5–14.

Tarrow, Sidney. 1989. Struggle, Politics, and Reform: Collective Action, Social Movements, and Cycles of Protest. Cornell University: Western Societies Program Occasional Paper no. 21.

———. 1998. *Power in Movement: Social Movements and Contentious Politics.* New York: Cambridge University Press.

Tateishi, Tomoyoshi. 2003. Haneda Runway Row Must Be Settled Soon. *Yomiuri Shinbun* (13 August).

Taylor, R. H., S. D. Probert, and P. D. Carmo. 1998. French Energy Policy. *Applied Energy* 59 (1): 39–61.

Temeles, Ethan, and John Kress. 2003. Adaptation in a Plant-Hummingbird Association. *Science* 300 (25 April): 630–633.

Terazono, Emiko. 1996. Public Anxiety over Nuclear Power. *Financial Times* (19 July): 4.

Thaler, Richard H., Amos Tversky, Daniel Kahneman, and Alan Schwartz. 1997. The Effect of Myopia and Loss Aversion on Risk Taking: An Experimental Test. *Quarterly Journal of Economics* (special issue in memory of Amos Tversky, 1937–1996) 112 (2): 647–661.

Thelen, Kathleen. 2000. Timing and Temporality in the Analysis of Institutional Evolution and Change. *Studies in American Political Development* 14:102–109.

——. 2004. *How Institutions Evolve: The Political Economy of Skills in Germany, Britain, the United States, and Japan.* New York: Cambridge University Press.

Thomson, Robert. 1990. Between Tragic Nuclear Past and Unsure Energy Future. *Financial Times* (22 May): 8.

Tilly, Charles. 1964. *The Vendee.* Cambridge: Harvard University Press.

——. 1978. *From Mobilization to Revolution.* Reading, Mass.: Addison-Wesley.

——. 1985. War Making and State Making as Organized Crime. In *Bringing the State Back In,* ed. Peter Evans, Dietrich Rueschemeyer, and Theda Skocpol. New York: Cambridge University Press.

——. 1990. *Coercion, Capital, and European States A.D. 900–1900.* Oxford: Blackwell.

——. 1994. Social Movements as Historically Specific Clusters of Political Performances. *Berkeley Journal of Sociology* 38:1–30.

Tilly, Charles, Louise Tilly, and Richard Tilly. 1975. *The Rebellious Century: 1830–1930.* Cambridge: Harvard University Press.

Tōdai kōgakubu Joshukai (Tokyo University Engineering Department Support Club). 1973. Nihon no Genshiryoku hatsuden wo Kangaeru (Thinking about Japan's nuclear power plants). *Jishu kōza* (Independent lecture), no. 6, 25 September.

——. 1976a. Sōdensen wo kotowate (Refuse electricity transmission lines!). *Jishu kōza* (Independent lecture), no. 9, 16 February.

——. 1976b. Kashiwazaki Genpatsu Hantai Tōsō (The struggle against the nuclear reactors at Kashiwazaki). *Jishu kōza* (Independent lecture), no. 9, 12 July.

Todoroki, Tomoyuki. 2002. Meiwaku shisetsu no ricchi mondai: Narita Kūkō Mondai no Rei ni (The problems of siting controversial facilities: The Narita Airport problem as an example). Prepared for the 13th annual conference of Toshi ha Donna Mondai ni Chokumen shite iru ka (What problems confront cities?).

Tomkins, J., N. Topham, J. Twomey, and R. Ward. 1998. Noise Versus Access: The Impact of an Airport in an Urban Property Market. *Urban Studies* 35 (2): 243–259.

Tomlinson, Richard. 2004. The Queen of Nukes. *Fortune* 149, no. 10:122–129.

Tomura, Issaku. 1980. *Waga Sanrizuka: Kaze to Honō no Kioku* (My Sanrizuka: A record of wind and fire). Tokyo: Tabata Shoten.

Tomz, Michael, Jason Wittenberg, and Gary King. 2003. CLARIFY: Software for Interpreting and Presenting Statistical Results, Version 2.1. Stanford University, University of Wisconsin, and Harvard University. January 5. Available at http://gking.harvard.edu/.

Totman, Conrad. 1992. Preindustrial River Conservancy: Causes and Consequences. *Monumenta Nipponica* 47 (1): 59–76.

Touraine, Alaine, Zsuzsa Hegedus, François Dubet, and Michel Wieviroka. 1983. *Anti-Nuclear Protest: The Opposition to Nuclear Energy in France.* Trans. Peter Fawcett. Cambridge: Cambridge University Press.

Tracy, Michael. 1989. *Government and Agriculture in Western Europe*. New York: New York University Press.

Treat, John W. 1995. *Writing Ground Zero: Japanese Literature and the Atomic Bomb*. Chicago: University of Chicago Press.

Trenz, Hans-Jörg, and Erik Jentges. 2005. Beyond National Cleavages? The Case of Airport Protests in France and Germany. Paper prepared for The European Consortium for Political Research Conference, Budapest (8–10 September).

Treuthardt, Paul. 1987. Nuclear Power Encounters Little Protest in France. Associated Press (1 March).

Tsebelis, George. 2002. *Veto Players: How Political Institutions Work*. Princeton: Princeton University Press.

Tsugano, Yasuyuki. 1977. Mizu no Shūkan wo Mukaete (Welcoming Water Week). *Gekkan Damu Nihon* 8 (394): 14–15.

Tsunoda, Katsuya. 1999. Genshiryoku hatsuden ni Kan suru risuku ninchi no kitei'in ni kansuru kōsatsu (A study of determinants of risk perception concerning nuclear power generation). *Nihon Risuku Kenkyūgakkaishi* (Journal of the Japanese Society Risk Studies) 11 (1): 54–60.

———. 2001. Public Response to the Tokai Nuclear Accident. *Risk Analysis* 21 (6): 1039–1046.

Tsūshosangyōshō Shigen enerugi chō, (Agency for Natural Resources and Energy, ANRE, in MITI) 2000. *Dengen Sanpō katsuyō jireishū* (Listing of actual uses of the three laws relating to electricity production). Tokyo: MITI.

Tsuzaki, Takeshi. 1980. *Nihon no Kūkō* (Japan's airports). Tokyo: Rikuetsu.

Turpin, Dominique. 1983. Un Aspect du Débat: Le nucléaire est-il compatible avec la décentralisation? (An aspect of the debate: Is nuclear energy compatible with decentralization?) *Problemes Politiques et Sociaux* (468): 25–29.

Tversky, Amos, and Daniel Kahneman. 1992. Advances in Prospect Theory: Cumulative Representation of Uncertainty. *Journal of Risk and Uncertainty* 5:297–323.

Ueno, Kenichi. 1966. Tomisato Shinkokusai Kūkō Hantai Tōsō no Zenshin (Progress of the battle against the international airport at Tomisato). *Shakai Shugi* 175 (4): 45–53.

United Church of Christ. 1987. *Toxic Wastes and Race: A National Report on the Racial and Socioeconomic Characteristics of Communities with Hazardous Waste Sites*. New York: UCC Commission for Racial Justice.

Unyu Keizai Kenkyū Sentā (Transport Economics Research Center). 1976. *Kūkō Shūhen Ricchi Kisei ni Kan suru Hikakuhō seido* (Comparative laws and institutions concerning siting regulations for airport hosting communities). Tokyo: Unyu Keizai Kenkyū Sentā.

Unyushō (Ministry of Transportation, MOT). 1980. *Civil Aviation in Japan*. Tokyo.

———. 1983. Hakusho (white paper). Tokyo.

———. 1996. *Civil Aviation in Japan*. Tokyo.

Upham, Frank. 1976. Litigation and Moral Consciousness in Japan. *Law and Society* 10 (4): 579–619.

———. 1987. *Law and Social Change in Postwar Japan*. Cambridge: Harvard University Press.

Urashima, Etsuko. 1999. Haneji Ōkawa wa Shinda: Damu ni Shizumu furusato to hantai undō no kiseki (The Haneji River is dead: A focus on the movement against the dam that would submerge their hometown). *Shūkan Kinyōbi* 7 (265): 68–74.

Uzawa, Hirofumi. 1992. *Narita to wa Nani ka: Sengo Nihon no Higeki* (What is Narita? The tragedy of postwar Japan). Tokyo: Iwanami Shoten.

van Der Eyden, Ton. 2002. *Public Management of Society: Rediscovering French Institutional Engineering in the European Context.* Amsterdam: IOS Press.

Van Valen, Leigh. 1973. A New Evolutionary Law. *Evolutionary Theory* 1:1–30.

Van Wolferen, Karel. 1991. An Economic Pearl Harbor? *New York Times* (2 December): A17.

Vari, Anna, Patricia Reagan-Cirincione, and Jeryl Mumpower. 1994. *LLRW Disposal Facility Siting: Successes and Failures in Six Countries.* Boston: Kluwer Academic Publishers.

Verba, Sidney, Norman Nie, and Jae-On Kim. 1978. *Participation and Political Equality: A seven-nation comparison.* New York: Cambridge University Press.

Vergne, Anne. 1975. Flamanville: Le nucleaire aux urnes (Flamanville: nuclear power at the poll booths). *Liberation* (7 April).

Vif, Jean-Yves. 1991. Les ecologists se mobilisent contre le projet de barrage du Veudre (The ecologists mobilize against the dam at Veudre). *Le Monde* (12 March).

Vigna, Marie-Claude. 1989. Roundtable discussion at the JAIF (Japan Atomic Industrial Forum) on nuclear energy. January 26.

Vosse, Wilhelm. 2000. The Domestic Environmental Movement in Contemporary Japan. Ph.D. dissertation, University of Hannover, Germany.

———. 2003. Japanese Civil Society Reconsidered: Do NPOs and Referenda Make a Difference, or Are the 1990s a Lost Decade? Paper prepared for Asian Studies Conference, Japan, Sophia University, Tokyo (21–22 June).

Wald, Matthew. 2006. Slow Start for Revival of Nuclear Reactors. *New York Times* (22 August).

Walker, Jack L., Jr. 1977. Setting the Agenda in the U.S. Senate: A Theory of Problem Selection. *British Journal of Political Science* 7:423–445.

Wanat, John. 1974. Bases of Budgetary Incrementalism. *American Political Science Review* 68:1221–1228.

Watanabe, Masami. 2003. Ippan kūkō ni okeru arata na kūkō seibu purosesu ni tuite (About the new process for completing standard airports). *Gekkan Kensetsu* 47 (July): 27–29.

Watts, Jonathan. 2002. Cracks in Japan's Nuclear Sector. *Christian Science Monitor* (4 September).

Weaver, R. Kent. 1984. The Politics of Blame Avoidance. *Journal of Public Policy* 6:371–398.

Weaver, R. Kent, and Bert Rockman. 1993. *Do Institutions Matter? Government Capabilities in the United States and Abroad.* Washington, D.C.: Brookings.

Weber, Max. 1918. Politics as a Vocation. In *From Max Weber,* ed. H. H. Gerth and C. Wright Mills. New York: Oxford University Press, 1946.

Webster, Paul. 1989. Environmental Armies Take Up Position for Three-Day Battle. *The Guardian* (28 April).

Weingart, John. 2001. *Waste Is a Terrible Thing to Mind: Risk, Radiation, and Distrust of Government.* Princeton: Center for Analysis of Public Issues.

Weingast, Barry, Kenneth Shepsle, and Christopher Johnsen. 1981. The Political Economy of Benefits and Costs: A Neoclassical Approach to Distributive Politics. *Journal of Political Economy* 89 (41): 642–664.

Wellock, Thomas. 1978. *Critical Masses: Opposition to Nuclear Power in California, 1958–1978.* Madison: University of Wisconsin Press.

Westney, D. Eleanor. 1987. *Imitation and Innovation: The Transfer of Western Organization Patterns to Meiji Japan.* Cambridge: Harvard University Press.

Wheeler, William Bruce, and Michael McDonald. 1986. *TVA and the Tellico Dam, 1936–1979: A Bureaucratic Crisis in Post-Industrial America.* Knoxville: University of Tennessee Press.

Wildavsky, Aaron. 1964. *The Politics of the Budgetary Process.* Boston: Little, Brown.

Wilkinson, Jens. 1999. Betrayal at Narita. *New Observer* (October).

Wilson, James Q., ed. 1980. *The Politics of Regulation.* New York: Basic Books.

——. 1974. *Political Organizations.* New York: Basic Books.

WISE-Paris (World Information Service on Energy). 2000. Plutonium Investigation, no. 19 (November).

Wittner, Lawrence. 2003. *Toward Nuclear Abolition: A History of the World Nuclear Disarmament Movement, 1971 to the Present.* Stanford: Stanford University Press.

Wolverton, Ann. 2002. Does Race Matter? An Examination of a Polluting Plant's Location Decision. Paper prepared for NBER Summer Institute, Cambridge, Massachusetts.

Wood, Dan B., and Richard W. Waterman. 1994. *Bureaucratic Dynamics: The Role of Bureaucracy in a Democracy.* Boulde, Colo.: Westview Press.

Woodall, Brian. 1996. *Japan under Construction.* Berkeley: University. of California Press.

Xie, Yu, and Charles Manski. 1989. The Logit Model and Response-Based Samples. *Sociological Methods and Research* 17:283–302.

Yagi, Kenzo. 1995. *Kita no Shizen wo Mamoru* (Defending nature up north). Sapporo: Hokkaido University Press.

Yamagishi, Toshiyuki. 1988. Damu Suigenchi Ryūiki Keiei ni Tuite (About the management of dam water resource basins). In *Damu Nenkan,* 13–23.

Yamanaka, Yoshirō. 1996. Dengen chiiki shinkō no kadai to hōsaku (Policies and problems with the promotion of electricity-producing areas). Ph.D. dissertation, University of Tokyo.

Yasuda, Takeomi. 1975. Shūyō Hō tekiyō no saikin no jirei ni tuite (About some actual recent cases of applications of the Land Expropriation Law). In *Hoshō Jitsumu kōshūkai tekisuto* (The text of a practical course on the problems of compensation), 97–105. Tokyo: Nihon Damu Kyōkai.

Yasuda, Yoshiya, Shinobu Yonaha, and Satoru Aragaki: 1997. Eco damu senden ni tuite (About the ecological dam declaration). *Gekkan Damu Nihon* 5 (631): 5–12.

Yoshimoto, Kenichi. 2000. Damu wo Habanda Kitōmura (Kitō village, which thwarted the dam). *Chiri* 45 (3): 28–37.

Yoshioka, Hitoshi. 1999. *Genshiryoku no Shakaishi* (The social history of nuclear power). Tokyo: Asahi Shinbun sha.

Zeiss, Christopher. 1996. Directions for Engineering Contributions to Successfully Siting Hazardous Waste Facilities. In *Hazardous Waste Siting and Democratic Choice,* ed. Don Munton, 358–394. Washington, D.C.: Georgetown University Press.

Zengakuren Sanrizuka Genchi Tōsō Honbu (National Federation of Students, Sanrizuka Local struggle headquarters). 1971. *Tatakai wa Daichi to Tomoni: Sanrizuka 1967–1971* (Fighting with the land: Sanrizuka 1967–1971). Tokyo: Shakai hyōronsha.

Zysman, John. 1983. *Governments, Markets, and Growth.* Ithaca: Cornell University Press.